# Praise for *Thrive*

It is well cited that teachers need to survive their first year in teac.... .... . ed
to guide them through their formative stages once qualified.

This book provides that extra support which we have all needed, and shares efficient solutions to help new teachers get ahead of the rest and thrive.

Ross Morrison McGill @TeacherToolkit – the UK's most followed educator on Twitter, who writes at TeacherToolkit.co.uk

Written with wisdom beyond the authors' years, and presented in a practical and positive way, *Thrive* provides aspiring teachers with a one-stop guide to the initial stages of their teaching journey.

What's clever about the book is that you can either read it cover to cover or dip into it for specific guidance and inspiration in relation to a particular area of your teaching practice. The references to wider reading and reflection are also really useful, as they allow you to uncover and explore a wide range of other engaging and positive texts.

*Thrive* is a really welcome antidote to the media's negative portrayal of teaching and holds true to what I am often told by visiting teachers from overseas, who proclaim that 'education is Britain's best export'! I would encourage every teacher embarking upon the first steps of their teaching career to read it.

Rob Carter, Head Teacher, St Paul's Catholic College

What sets *Thrive* apart from other books is the combination of the authors' experience that shines through on every page and the authority that comes from their many references to research and wider reading.

Many teaching manuals talk about surviving in teaching as though it will be an ordeal, but this book will give the reader a sense that more is possible than just getting through another day. It is refreshing to see such a resource for those starting out in teaching that is so positive and optimistic, and what also impresses me is the way in which the authors manage to explain the basics clearly and carefully without talking down to their audience. The clear tips, tasks and case studies mean that this book will provide important continuing professional development for teachers who want to maintain the reflective practice they developed as a trainee.

*Thrive* is an absolute must for anyone who is starting out in their teaching career and wondering what the future holds, whether during their study, on their placement or in those vital first few years in the classroom. This book will, I'm sure, be a constant and much-referred-to guide and a huge help to those entering this at times overwhelming profession. It's the book I wish I'd had when I started out in teaching.

Mark Enser, Head of Geography, Heathfield Community College and education writer

In writing *Thrive* Martha, Emily and Ben have produced a valuable resource that points beyond survival to help new teachers embrace the real joy of being a teacher.

This is not a textbook issuing a prescribed toolkit approach – rather it presents a significant framework that provides both training and qualified teachers with strategies and reflective ways of thinking that can be applied in all contexts as they navigate through the initial stages of their careers. Each section is carefully thought out and considers those issues that are real concerns for educators at each stage of their early development.

I highly recommend *Thrive*, which will now become required reading for my initial teacher training students.

Dr Brian Marsh, Principal Lecturer in Science Education,
School of Education, University of Brighton

The teaching profession is safe in the hands of teachers like Martha, Emily and Ben. In *Thrive* they acknowledge the challenges that teachers face at the start of their careers, but present them with a coherent and realistic path to success.

It is so refreshing to read of young teachers who relish attending to their own professional development – it is clear the authors are committed both to their pupils' learning and to their own careers. Indeed it is the fusing of these two core motivations that keep them happy and fulfilled as teachers.

An innovative feature of *Thrive* is the melding of the training year into the first couple of years of teaching. Beginning teachers view this as one combined phase, but most training courses view these two periods in isolation – it is very helpful here to have the overview of the entire period, with each mini-phase attended to in its own section. The book also contests dour media narratives of teaching as a 'profession in crisis', and asserts the enduring value of engaging in research by presenting a compelling notion of evidence-based practice.

Teaching is a stimulating, exciting and rewarding career, but it can be tough at the start. This very welcome book reassures both the newly qualified and the recently qualified teacher that they have made the right career choice and that – especially in this early period of their career – they should aim to 'thrive', not just survive.

Dr Keith Perera, Assistant Head Teacher, St Paul's Catholic College,
Associate Fellow, University of Sussex

Refreshingly, *Thrive* is not a book on how to be 'outstanding', nor on how to 'survive' as a beginning teacher. Instead it gives us something we all need, and will benefit from – inspiration and practical advice from teachers who are just ahead of us in their careers, who can recall the challenges we face and who are willing to share their recent experiences and successful strategies.

Indeed, the book not only shows us how to get better at teaching but, just as importantly, illustrates how we can enjoy and thrive during the journey too. The authors take the first three years of developing as a teacher and emphasise the different, complex and fundamental ways in which professional learning happens – from initial teacher training, through the NQT year, to emergence as a recently qualified professional. There are useful sections covering: making the most of professional relationships with mentors, school leaders and other colleagues; practical strategies for planning, assessment, differentiation and managing time; researching teaching and learning; and navigating pathways in professional development and early leadership.

Throughout *Thrive*, Martha, Emily and Ben ensure that readers benefit from the perspectives of established school-based and university professionals alongside their own authentic, evidence-informed and practice-enriched voices. If I were a new teacher at the beginning of my career I'd welcome the opportunity to listen to them, learn from their experiences and, hopefully, thrive.

Dr Simon Thompson, Head of Education, University of Sussex,
Higher Education Academy 2016 National Teaching Fellow

In *Thrive* Martha, Emily and Ben have written a realistic, optimistic and valuable guide to the first three years in teaching. The book is logically mapped out and can be read chronologically to give those new to the profession a comprehensive walk-through of what to expect, while it can also help more experienced teachers to pursue further avenues in their career.

Full of fantastic insights from successful current teachers and those directly involved in initial teacher training, it offers an excellent resource of practical tips and advice in clearly delineated sections – I just wish I'd had it available to me during my own teacher training!

A must-read for anyone embarking on, or already in, their first few years of teaching.

Matthew Donald, history and politics teacher, St Paul's Catholic College

*Thrive* is a no-nonsense, practical guide to all aspects of teaching and being a teacher.

The first few years of teaching can feel daunting, but with this book's support any new teacher can thrive. Underpinned by educational research, the book is like a pocket mentor and provides a good first stop for professional advice as Martha, Emily and Ben draw from their own first-hand experiences – as well as on the perspectives of experienced educators – to offer helpful guidance for aspiring teachers.

An ideal resource for potential teachers, trainee teachers and, above all, newly qualified teachers navigating their formative years in the profession.

Dr Andy Chandler-Grevatt, Teaching Fellow in Education, University of Sussex
and author of *How to Assess Your Students*

Accessible, inspiring and easily digestible, *Thrive* is also a wonderful read!

The structure of each chapter, complete with to-do lists, tips, stories and signposts to further reading, is useful in allowing the reader to dip into each section as appropriate, and, as a training teacher myself, I consider the guidance included to be very valuable – with need-to-know content appealingly and practically presented for those starting their teaching journey. I feel well prepared for the NQT and RQT years having read this book.

**Elisha Hocking, trainee teacher**

Fantastically practical and written in a friendly tone, *Thrive* offers an honest and supportive perspective of the highs and lows of teaching and breaks down the possibly daunting and overwhelming prospect of embarking on a career in education into simple, achievable chunks.

Martha, Emily and Ben are clearly passionate about the profession and want everyone to share in this – while reading the book I got a genuine sense that they want me to succeed. By sharing their own trials and tribulations they make you feel like you are not the only trainee struggling to find a way through with *that* class. Indeed, the book offers a wealth of strategies which would aid even the most experienced teacher.

Its user-friendly layout allows the reader to dip in and out of chapters when looking for answers to specific questions in times of need and lays out handy to-do lists and up-to-date academic research in an accessible format – allowing the lessons learned to be easily transferred to the classroom using the authors' practical advice. The inclusion of a range of professional perspectives and expertise – from RQTs, deputy heads and PGCE tutors among others – is also a big plus which ultimately makes the book a readily available, round-the-clock team of mentors that celebrates the sharing of ideas and concerns and alleviates any sense of struggling on your own. The authors also actively combat the negative stigma surrounding teaching in the media and recognise the vital role the teacher plays in learners' educational journeys.

Armed with *Thrive*, teachers will be emboldened to take on any class and will feel empowered to not only survive their first few years in teaching but also become valued members of a department, able to inspire students and colleagues alike. It is an all-encompassing guide to teaching that will remain an essential resource for years into your practice.

**Nathan Goodby, PE teacher, St Paul's Catholic College**

# Thrive

in your

# First 3 Years

in

# Teaching

'Don't just survive, thrive'

Martha Boyne, Emily Clements and Ben Wright

Crown House Publishing Limited
www.crownhouse.co.uk

First published by
Crown House Publishing Ltd
Crown Buildings, Bancyfelin, Carmarthen, Wales, SA33 5ND, UK
www.crownhouse.co.uk

and

Crown House Publishing Company LLC
PO Box 2223, Williston, VT 05495, USA
www.crownhousepublishing.com

First published 2018. Reprinted 2019.

Crown House Publishing has no responsibility for the persistence or accuracy of URLs for external or third-party websites referred to in this publication, and does not guarantee that any content on such websites is, or will remain, accurate or appropriate.

British Library Cataloguing-in-Publication Data

A catalogue entry for this book is available from the British Library.

Print ISBN 978-178583304-5
Mobi ISBN 978-178583325-0
ePub ISBN 978-178583326-7
ePDF ISBN 978-178583327-4
LCCN 2018939264

Printed and bound in the UK by
TJ International, Padstow, Cornwall

# Foreword

So, you have picked up a copy of *Thrive: In Your First Three Years in Teaching* and you are holding it in your hands right now. Maybe you are still deciding whether teaching will be the career for you. Perhaps you are preparing to start your training year and are trying to imagine how it will feel to stand, exposed, at the front of a real classroom with real children. Maybe you have already tried on the role for size and only this morning you taught, rather nervously, your first lesson. Perhaps you have successfully completed your training year and are soon to be a full-blown teacher, complete with your own classes and your own tutor group.

Whoever you are – and however new you are to the profession – there is something we need you to know. Teaching is a joy. It is as exhilarating, as wondrous and, at times, as devilishly complicated as anything you have ever experienced before. Sadly, the media in Britain has a lot to answer for when it comes to the portrayal of our profession. Apparently, teaching is at crisis point. 'Teachers are overworked and beset by punishing accountability systems,' they proclaim. 'Teachers are leaving the profession in their droves,' they cry. 'Teachers are being set upon by unruly packs of bloodthirsty children,' they scream. Thankfully, these hackneyed sound bites are galaxies away from the truth. We suggest you ignore them.

While the first few years in teaching are undeniably tough, a sizeable majority of teachers *do* stay on and thoroughly enjoy the achievable challenges of their early careers. The majority of new teachers do learn how to balance their work and home lives. More and more new teachers are taking their professional development into their own hands by combining the shared practical expertise of their colleagues with evidence and theory from the wider education world. Now is an exciting time to become a teacher. Positive change is afoot and the profession is genuinely starting to learn from the mistakes of the past.

That is not to say that there won't be challenges on your path to expertise! You will never forget the throat-parching experience of standing in front of a class and realising – halfway through your circuitous explanation – that you do not understand the topic you are teaching any more than your students do! Nor will you forget *that* class who still, years later, seem to haunt your dreams like an army of chillingly dark phantoms. And – let's face it – after the luxury of the holidays the first day of the new term will always feel like a wrench – even for the most dedicated teacher.

The book you are holding is authentic, sensible and very practical. Martha Boyne, Emily Clements and Ben Wright have pooled together their collective knowledge and have proven, once and for all, that it is possible to become a tremendous teacher even in the first few months and years of your career. This book is both friendly and user-friendly – it can be read from cover to cover or dipped into as required. From behaviour management to being a tutor, from working with students on the autism spectrum to engaging in rigorous reflective practice, this book is packed full of sharp and useful advice on a range of issues that you will encounter sooner or later. It should certainly have pride of place on your first teacher's desk.

Perhaps the book's greatest strength is the way that it promotes a can-do attitude. Martha, Emily and Ben assert that teaching need not be an arduous battle against the odds. You too can thrive in the classroom. There are many ways to master the art and science of teaching – we would recommend you take every opportunity to learn from the wisdom of your colleagues and from the best research evidence available.

Your first step, however, should be to read this book – from cover to cover. We hope you enjoy *Thrive* as much as we have and we wish you every success in your classroom career, as you do just what the title suggests.

**Andy Tharby and Shaun Allison**

# Acknowledgements

There are many people we would like to thank for inspiring and supporting us in the writing of this book. First and foremost, we must thank the amazing Lianne Allison who encouraged us to actually put pen to paper when we first started dreaming of writing this book. We would also like to thank Dr Simon Thompson for steadfastly supporting us throughout the writing process. We must further thank both Lianne and Simon as they also gave up their valuable time to offer the profound and eminently useful insights found throughout the book.

We also want to thank Shaun Allison for his encouragement and for giving us the confidence to find a publisher and to turn our dream into a reality. Shaun and his *Making Every Lesson Count* co-author, Andy Tharby, also kindly agreed to write the foreword to this book, for which we are very grateful. We want to thank everyone at Crown House Publishing for giving us the opportunity to share our vision for thriving in teaching.

We have all worked with some incredible teachers at The Angmering School and St Paul's Catholic College and want to thank the teaching community of which we have been fortunate enough to be a part, especially the heads of department who have pushed us to be the very best we can be. Furthermore, we would like to acknowledge the many influential educators, trainers and authors of books on teaching who have passed on their insights, strategies and advice.

We can't forget to thank all of the students we have taught; thank you for being the energy that keeps us going. We must also thank the many cafes of Brighton for providing the coffees and hot chocolates that were absolutely necessary in the writing of this book. Finally, we want to offer our deepest thanks to our ever so patient partners – Philip, Rich and Emily – as well as our friends and family who have supported us throughout.

# Contents

# List of Figures

# List of Acronyms

| | | | |
|---|---|---|---|
| AfL | assessment for learning | PP | pupil premium |
| AoL | assessment of learning | PPA | planning, preparation and assessment |
| CAT | cognitive ability test | RQT | recently qualified teacher |
| CPD | continuing professional development | SENCO | special educational needs coordinator |
| DIRT | Dedicated improvement and reflection time | SEND | special educational needs and disabilities |
| DfE | Department for Education | SKE | subject knowledge enhancement |
| EAL | English as an additional language | SLT | senior leadership team |
| INSET | in-service training | SoW | scheme of work |
| KS | key stage | SPaG | spelling, punctuation and grammar |
| LSA | learning support assistant | TA | teaching assistant |
| MFL | modern foreign languages | TLR | teaching and learning responsibility |
| NQT | newly qualified teacher | | |

# Icon Key

 to-do

 expert advice from the school perspective

 expert advice from the university perspective

 Martha's story

 Emily's story

 Ben's story

# Introduction

This is not just a survival guide for your first three years in the teaching profession. Nor is it an academic text designed to be heavy on theory but light on practical ideas. It hasn't been written by someone who has only a distant memory of what standing in front of a class of teenagers for the first time involves. We believe that this book is something very different. It is about giving you the support and guidance to become a thriving secondary school teacher. It is supported by current evidence regarding best practice, but is rooted in practical strategies and ideas. It has been created by three full-time teachers who, at the time of writing, are each about to enter their fourth year in the profession. It has been written by teachers who are fortunate to have so far been successful in the jobs they love and written for teachers who want long, enjoyable and rewarding careers. We hope that you will find this book a useful guide and a source of inspiration; a platform from which to excel during your beginning years in teaching and beyond.

We came about writing this book through our shared passion for excellent teaching. Our story is an example of the power that finding like-minded, passionate colleagues can have. We met through the NQT training sessions during our first year in our first school. It was at a TeachMeet that we decided to set up our school's first ever journal club – a place to discuss academic research and consider how we could use this to improve our teaching. We were soon delivering our own continuing professional development (CPD), presenting at TeachMeets and, two years later, have now written this book. Our passion for enriching the lives of the students we teach and being the very best we can be has driven us to write this book and share our beliefs, ideas and approaches to thriving in teaching. We hope that you too will share our passion for teaching.

We quickly realised that we were not the kinds of teachers who were happy to just survive our early years in teaching; we wanted to excel, to be the very best we could be, to thrive. Our vision of a teacher who thrives is of one who is confident in their abilities. They go above and beyond, demonstrating an excellent understanding of what great teaching looks like and they have the skills to successfully and consistently implement this within the classroom. We want you to become this thriving teacher. So many teachers leave the profession prematurely, citing stresses from the high workload, long hours and tough working conditions as determining factors.[1] It is impossible to ignore these pressures, but we believe that having the right attitude and approach – alongside strategies which will support you to thrive – will enable you to see how the positives of a career in teaching can far outweigh the downsides.

---

1   Richard Adams, 'Demanding workload driving young teachers out of profession', *The Guardian* (15 April 2017). Available at: https://www.theguardian.com/education/2017/apr/15/demanding-workload-driving-young-teachers-out-of-profession.

We hope this book will provide you with clear strategies to equip you to thrive, but also give you a range of insights into the teaching profession that bring what we are advising to life. Each chapter begins with a checklist of what a 'developing' teacher would be expected to do; these are the basics and, with thought and focus, are achievable for all beginning teachers. These expectations are a prerequisite for thriving as a teacher, so ensure you read these carefully and that you are embedding these behaviours into your practice. Each chapter contains our thoughts, personal experiences and advice about becoming a *thriving* teacher. At the end of each chapter, we have included a to-do list so you can use these both to structure the strategies you implement and also as a quick reference guide to return to later. In each chapter this is followed by a to-read list so you can delve deeper into topics that you find particularly interesting or relevant, as space doesn't always permit us to go into the level of detail we could. The book is divided into three parts: detailing what you can expect in the training year, NQT year and RQT year respectively. Before we begin, Chapter 1 offers some advice about choosing your training route, in case you have not already committed to this.

We have included a number of our own personal stories, which demonstrate how we have put some of the ideas and strategies we discuss successfully into practice. We hope that these examples show the substantial, tangible difference that can be made by taking a thriving approach to teaching.

We have also been fortunate enough to have been given the opportunity to include expert advice from two people who are at the very top of their profession. Lianne Allison is deputy head teacher at Durrington High School in West Sussex and director of the South Downs School Centred Initial Teacher Training (SCITT) programme. She has also been a professional tutor. Lianne gives insights from the perspective of a professional tutor and deputy head teacher and she shares her personal wealth of teaching experience through her advice. Dr Simon Thompson is head of education at the University of Sussex, having overall responsibility for the PGCE, School Direct, NQT and further education programmes run by the university. He has directly been involved in training hundreds of PGCE students, supporting NQTs and being a tutor for students completing their master's in education, therefore he offers a wide spectrum of advice throughout the book. We hope that the insights given through our stories, alongside the counsel offered by Lianne and Simon, will add depth to the guidance we seek to provide.

We are passionate about building a community of thriving teachers, so please share your own experiences, ideas, strategies and stories with us on Twitter (@thrive_teach) or by email (thriveinteaching@gmail.com). You are entering into what truly is the best profession – full of meaningful experiences, laughter and deep satisfaction. We wish you a long, successful and thriving career.

# 1. Getting Ahead of the Game

A prospective trainee will:

✓ Carefully consider the different types of courses available as initial teacher training (ITT).

✓ Read a couple of books or articles from the recommended reading list.

✓ Gain work experience in a school prior to starting ITT in September.

If you have not already decided on your route into teaching, there are several different routes available to you, which are generally split into two camps: university-led training and school-led training.[1] To find the best option for you, try to discuss the possible routes with current trainees. Before you complete your application for either route you could ask the university, training provider or local school if you could be put in contact with some of their current students. Speaking to them directly about their experiences and the positives and negatives that they have encountered will enable you to make a more informed decision. Have a list of questions ready, for example:

■ Why did you choose to undertake the particular training route that you are on?

■ When did you start your first placement? Some start in September, others later, so have you seen any benefits in the timing you encountered?

■ What support was in place to prepare you for writing at master's level?

You will have hopefully completed some work experience in a school setting prior to starting your ITT. Securing a place on an ITT programme should not prevent you from continuing to gain further work experience. Gaining insights from a wider variety of classes – for example, from across Key Stages 3, 4 and 5 – will give you an idea of the subject knowledge you will need to develop during your ITT year, as well as the different skills required to teach various age ranges.

You should also try to observe lessons from outside your subject area. You could do this by asking to follow a student around for the day, which will give you an insight into a range of different lessons as well as the student's experience of them. Check with the school though, as you may be limited in terms of what you are allowed to do if you do not have a current Disclosure and Barring Service (DBS, formerly CRB) check.

---

1   For more information, see https://getintoteaching.education.gov.uk/explore-my-options/teacher-training-routes.

One of the things that most training providers would expect is for any trainee teacher to have gone into a school for at least five days. I think that's important for two reasons: firstly because it gives that person a clear understanding that this is something they actually want to do, so it reinforces their commitment to teaching and, secondly, just from those five days, the trainee teacher reorients themselves to what it's like being in a school. It allows them to begin to see the similarities to and differences from their own education. Otherwise the only model they go in with is their own teachers, for good or for ill.

I would also hope that they would already have a working understanding of what's going on in education now. They would be up to date with some of the debates and arguments that are taking place among teachers and policy makers, and aware of some of the Government policy that's coming in and start to form their own informed opinions.

Trainee teachers should take advantage of any subject knowledge enhancement (SKE) course offered. You may think that you know your subject because you've just done your degree, but what you're not thinking about is how that knowledge might need to be translated into something accessible for pupils. Even if you have a PhD in a subject a short SKE course can really help.

Finally, one thing you mustn't be misled by is the idea that a thriving trainee is the one who always answers questions and appears incredibly confident. My experience is that this does not always reflect reality and some trainees can be overconfident. You shouldn't be intimidated by those peers on your course. Everyone has a range of prior experiences which can be drawn upon and everyone on the course has been selected because the admissions tutors could identify their potential. As such, make sure you have your own voice and don't feel you have to demonstrate you know as much as someone else who may just have a lot to say.

Dr Simon Thompson, Head of Education, University of Sussex

You should also try to gain work experience in more than one school in order to have a more rounded experience. Only working in one school narrows your understanding of how schools work and your sense of what to expect when you are on placement. The more schools you gain experience in, the better prepared you will be for your ITT year. You will be more aware of the variations between schools and better understand what to expect if you are placed in a school which requires particularly strong behaviour management or one where you will need to stretch the most able as a priority. You will also develop a more rounded idea of the type of school that you might eventually want to work in when you are looking for your first teaching post.

While you are observing lessons, ask teachers to talk to you about the planning behind them. This will give you a better idea of what will be expected of you when you start planning your own lessons. Focus your observations on lesson structure and behaviour management. An awareness of these aspects will enable you to progress successfully during your ITT year. Look at the advice in Chapter 15: Observing Others for more ways to get the most out of these experiences.

Teaching is a profession which has a love of acronyms. Being familiar with these before you start your course will help you to understand conversations between teachers without feeling like you are listening to a foreign language. These acronyms will become part of your vocabulary but it can feel daunting when you're not aware of what half of these even stand for! We will refer to various acronyms throughout the book, so we have included a list of some common ones in the front of the book.

When I was completing my PGCE at the University of Chichester I was asked to speak to some applicants while they were being interviewed for places on the next year's course. The potential students were able to ask questions not just about teaching, but about my experience of completing the PGCE. Their questions were often based around how I had found meeting the university's expectations for assignments on top of a trainee teacher's workload. They found it helpful and I found myself wishing I had been able to speak to current trainees before I started the course. Take up any opportunity to speak to current trainee teachers on the course you have applied to and ask all the questions you would like to, however big or small. It could help you to make the decision about which course or institution is best suited to you.

☐ Contact local schools to arrange work experience and to speak to current trainees or take advantage of local or national schemes that help you to do so.

☐ Contact your local university to see if you can arrange to attend a session to talk to current trainees.

To-do

## To read:

Steve Bartlett and Diana Burton, *Introduction to Education Studies,* 4th edn (London: Sage, 2016).

Tracey Lawrence, 'Five ways to ensure a successful ITT year', *UCAS* [blog] (11 August 2017). Available at: https://www.ucas.com/connect/blogs/five-ways-ensure-successful-itt-year-tracey-lawrence.

Part One:

# The Training Year

So you've decided to take the plunge into a career in teaching – congratulations! We're so excited to be able to share the journey with you through this book.

Teaching is a career which is incredibly rewarding, right from the very first time you set foot in a classroom; something you will soon find out. Your training year is, however, undeniably hard, no matter which route you decide to undertake. We strongly believe that you will reap huge benefits by committing to thrive in your training year, rather than simply aiming to survive it. We will support you to be that thriving teacher you aspire to become.

The chapters in Part One are here to support you through the training year: from starting your course, through to applying for jobs and up until your very last day as a trainee. Whether you are enrolling on a university-led PGCE, School Direct course or SCITT route, everything we mention is relevant and should help you. This is your how-to-thrive guide to this challenging profession, which aims to make your first three years of teaching ones in which you flourish.

# 2. Making the Most of University Time or Theory Sessions

A developing trainee will:

✓ Value the importance of completing the pre-course reading.

✓ Consider how the lectures and seminars can impact on their teaching practice.

✓ Take time to discuss placements and essay ideas with other trainee teachers.

✓ Surround themselves with trainees who are positive, hardworking and fully engaged in the process.

✓ Ask questions regularly to ensure they understand how theory feeds into practice.

Starting your ITT may feel daunting and somewhat scary, especially if you have been out of education yourself for a number of years. Indeed, this may well be one of the hardest yet most rewarding years of your life. But if you are well prepared and have an idea of what to expect from your training, it will take the stress off during those first few (very important) weeks. Start your ITT year as you intend to go on by embedding the habits of a thriving trainee.

University time or sessions on theory can sometimes be underappreciated. You are probably eager to get into the classroom and get stuck in, which is understandable, but this time should be highly valued. Whether you're on a PGCE, School Direct or SCITT route, or another ITT programme, the theory researched, discussed and learned will underpin your practice. A thriving trainee will recognise the importance of theory and will ensure that they engage with the academic material in order to build their own practice. Being present during these sessions and taking an active role in discussions will ensure that you get the most out of them.

Start the taught component of your training by networking with trainees from outside your subject area or specialism. This will be invaluable for your experience throughout the course. You may find it interesting to share and reflect on the different experiences and paths that have led you all to ITT. Trainees from other subjects may also have different views on theory, content and practice. This will give you the opportunity to hear philosophical positions on teaching and the education system from a wider range of perspectives. Different subjects will involve different sets of skills and knowledge; some may be far more practical or hands-on than yours, for example, thus working closely with someone from another specialism is an opportunity to pick up ideas which could expand your own teaching repertoire.

One idea could be to try to sit with someone different each day when you attend these sessions. If you are asked to deliver group presentations, working in a group with people from numerous different subject specialisms will also enhance your work. Don't shy away from these experiences, see them as a platform for you to increase your profile within your cohort. Use these discussions as a way to broaden your understanding of teaching.

A thriving trainee will start to critically reflect on the content covered within these sessions from day one. An easy way to do this is to complete a short daily reflection log for each lecture, seminar or session, focusing on a topic discussed which you have found interesting. For example, your topic could be growth mindset or assessment and you could start by writing about your thoughts on the topic, and then reflecting upon how this relates to the classroom and your own teaching practice. Finally, you could spend a brief fifteen minutes reading some current literature about the topic, adding your thoughts to your log. By including references, you will also be able to revisit these in the future – perhaps as a starting point should you need to complete an assignment on that topic. This process also prepares you for becoming a reflective teacher. Reflecting after each lesson is a crucial skill all thriving teachers practice, so why not begin this process right away?

Don't treat the taught sessions and the school placement as two separate entities. Share your experiences across the two with your subject tutor and mentor. Bounce ideas off other teachers and use this as a way to further reflect on your own successes and areas to focus on for improvement. When in school, your mentor can help you to consider the implications of the theory and pedagogy you have encountered in their specific context. You never know, your discussions could lead to you starting a new initiative within the department, so keep talking!

One important thing to ensure during your weekly mentor meeting at school is that you don't just focus on planning your next lesson or on any behaviour management challenges you are having. You need to reserve some time to talk about the issues you have encountered during your taught component so that the mentor can scaffold the difference between the general ideas that you've been presented with and what's specific to that particular school.

Quite often a tutor might say 'Can you find out what your school is doing about x, y or z?', 'What does differentiation look like in your department?'

or 'What's the assessment policy in your school?' Ensure you then carry out that research and bring your findings back to the tutor. This is a very effective way of making links between theory and practice and you often get to contrast your experience of your placement school with those of trainee teachers in other schools.

Dr Simon Thompson, Head of Education, University of Sussex

**To-do**

☐ Create a critical reflection log, either on paper or digitally, to record your thoughts on taught sessions. If it is easily accessible, you are more likely to actually complete it.

☐ Use your log when preparing for mentor meetings to help you create links between pedagogy and school practice.

**To read:**

Alex Moore, *Teaching and Learning: Pedagogy, Curriculum and Culture,* 2nd edn (Abingdon: Routledge, 2012).

Michael Waring and Carol Evans, *Understanding Pedagogy: Developing a Critical Approach to Teaching and Learning* (Abingdon: Routledge, 2014).

# 3. Professionalism

A developing trainee will:

✓ Always be on time.

✓ Ask for help if needed to ensure that school or departmental policies are adhered to.

✓ Attend all required CPD sessions and engage with them.

Teaching is a profession and therefore demands a high level of professionalism. Being professional is not just a requisite of the job, it is something that can have a tangible impact upon your reputation with students and staff. Being professional is not to be underestimated!

The way you dress has a profound impact upon the impression you make. It is essential that each and every day you turn up to school dressed appropriately and professionally rather than casually. Business dress is usually advisable, but assess the level of formality required during your first few days in a new placement school. Some schools have higher expectations than others.

How you dress is a visual reflection of who you are and therefore of the type of teacher you wish to be. A thriving trainee will dress with care, ensuring that the image presented is one of a teacher who is in control and has high expectations; attributes which are no doubt shared with their approach to teaching more broadly, thus demonstrating a consistency of approach running throughout all that they do and are.

Of course, professionalism runs more deeply than just how you dress. It will be most clearly highlighted through your interactions with staff and students. The level of professionalism you show in these contexts can be hard to balance, but a teacher who is thriving will manage this well. Seeming human and building strong rapport with your students is really, really important, as developing genuine relationships built on trust and mutual respect is vital in order to get the best out of them. However, this must be balanced carefully.

A typical error during the training year can be to lose your professional approach and become too familiar or casual as the placement progresses. It is essential that your students respect you as being not just another adult in their lives, but as an adult who is qualified to guide them through their education. Therefore, you need to consistently demonstrate that your primary focus is on their educational development, rather than a desire to get on with them or be liked. Yes, you need to build relationships, get to know your students, laugh and joke with them and allow a human relationship to develop. Yet you must always maintain a 'barrier' between yourself and them so that they recognise there is a line which should not be crossed.

Even after you have gained the students' respect and feel that you can let your defences drop a little, you must always maintain your professional conduct and remember your role as their teacher. Getting too friendly, or relaxing too much, will – even if you don't believe it will happen with 'such a lovely class' – lead to a drop in standards of behaviour and effort, and therefore progress. Avoiding this means remembering that professionalism requires a consistency of approach within each and every lesson throughout the school year. Keep this in mind and you can still develop strong relationships with your students, while also ensuring that they work hard and achieve their maximum potential.

Your interactions with your new colleagues also need to demonstrate a high degree of professionalism at all times. One important way to achieve this is to show the courtesy of spending time within your department. While you will be tempted to spend all of your free periods, breaks and lunches with fellow trainees – and indeed the opportunity to share experiences, ideas, successes and challenges will be vital – it is important to also spend time with your departmental colleagues. Part of being professional is immersing yourself in the department who are looking after you by being available to share your thoughts and ideas and making time for discussion with others. Furthermore, this will give you a valuable insight into the challenges of cultivating a positive working atmosphere in what is often a busy and stressful environment inhabited by a diverse range of personalities. You will begin to see that for a department to be successful it is vital for all staff to maintain the highest degree of professional conduct when discussing other members of staff or students.

When you start training as a teacher you need to audit your social media accounts.[1] Students will make a point of typing your name into the likes of Twitter, Facebook and Instagram, for example, to see what 'dirt' they can dig up. You must spend time checking the restrictions on your social media accounts, ensuring that students would not be able to access any photos or information which would give them knowledge of your personal life. We suggest changing your name to a pseudonym (for example, using your middle name) so students are unable to search for you and setting all content on your accounts so only your friends can view it. Those photos of you and your friends on nights out at university are not something you'd want students to gain access to. It is never okay to befriend a student on any social media site and any requests or messages from a student should be reported to your school immediately. Check what profile pictures you are displaying and whether these are appropriate as well. It will take time to go through your accounts but is vitally important to do this before your first placement.

Another important aspect to consider when embarking on your training year is joining a teaching union. Not only do unions protect teachers but they provide vital support throughout your career. They also run workshops, conferences and publications covering everything from teaching pedagogy to work–life balance. At some point during your training year you will have the opportunity to join one of the unions, either at university or online, at a discounted price. We strongly urge you to join a union and become a member of a professional body.

---

1    See Childnet International's resource 'Social Networking: A Guide for Trainee Teachers and NQTs', available at: http://www.childnet.com/ufiles/Social-networking.pdf.

Perhaps the greatest challenge with regards to professionalism is that of professional consistency. Whether it is maintaining the same high expectations and standards for effort and respect from your favourite class or arriving at school with shoes polished and shirt ironed each and every day, professionalism should be at the forefront of your thoughts.

**To-do**

☐ Check workwear is suitable for the professional environment.

☐ Maintain professional relationships with both staff and students.

☐ Make a concerted effort to engage with colleagues and spend time with your adopted department.

☐ Take time to audit *all* of your social media accounts.

☐ Become a member of a teaching union.

**To read:**

Betty Jo Simmons, 'Teachers should dress for success', *The Clearing House: A Journal of Educational Strategies, Issues and Ideas*, 69(5) (1996): 297–298.

Association of Teachers and Lecturers, 'Social networking sites: how to protect yourself on the internet' [fact sheet], Ref: ADV42 (2016). Available at: https://www.atl.org.uk/advice-and-resources/publications/social-networking-sites-how-protect-yourself-internet.

# 4. Safeguarding

A developing trainee will:

✓ Know who the designated safeguarding lead in each placement school is.

✓ Attend the new staff meeting with the designated safeguarding lead in each placement school.

✓ Prioritise the safety of students at all times, including as part of lesson planning and in their interactions with the class.

✓ Inform the class teacher of anything they notice that they consider concerning or unusual.

During your training year, you should receive guidance about how to respond if a student comes to you about something which would be a safeguarding concern. In brief, don't promise confidentiality, don't ask leading questions and write down everything that was said in a statement as soon after the event as possible to ensure accuracy. Follow the current advice given by your training provider and school, which in turn will have come from the most recent government guidelines, to ensure you have up-to-date knowledge within this ever-changing area of teaching.[2] It is important to be aware that child protection issues are not always obvious, and may not arise as a result of a student seeking you out. Concerns worthy of further investigation could stem from an overheard conversation, a significant look or even a student's body language when discussing something completely benign. To this end, safeguarding should be an ever-present thought in all aspects of your teaching practice.[3]

Don't forget, as teachers we are never truly 'off duty', so if you have suspicions about something you see after school involving a student – at the train station, for example – it is still valuable information that should be passed on to the appropriate person. As mentioned in the opening checklist, you should go to the class teacher with any concerns in the first instance as they will most likely have more information about the student's situation and will know about any issues that may have been flagged up previously.

Every school is different, and has different student profiles. To gain a better understanding of the students you are teaching, arrange a meeting with the designated safeguarding lead. They will be able to take you through the most prevalent issues facing students in that school, and also any particular circumstances that are problematic for different individuals or groups.

Take a critical approach to safeguarding in your school. Does the environment feel safe? Do students know who to turn to? It may seem as if information is not being shared effectively but you should not assume this is the case. A lot of personal information about students is sensitive and is therefore only shared on a need-to-know basis. Still, this is an

---

2   See Department for Education, *Keeping Children Safe in Education: Statutory Guidance for Schools and Colleges*. Ref: DfE-00140-2016 (London: Department for Education, 2016). Available at: https://www. gov.uk/government/uploads/system/uploads/attachment_data/file/550511/Keeping_children_ safe_in_education.pdf.
3   For additional safeguarding guidance, see https://www.nspcc.org.uk/preventing-abuse/ safeguarding/schools-protecting-children-abuse-neglect/.

important question to ask the designated safeguarding lead, so that you can develop an understanding of what 'need to know' looks like in the school and the channels used to share information.

☐ Ensure safeguarding is an ever-present thought in your mind.

☐ Stay up to date with current safeguarding regulations and best practice.

☐ Always be 'on duty'.

☐ Speak to the designated safeguarding lead during every placement to get school and student specific advice.

**To read:**

Ann Marie Christian, *A Practical Guide to Safeguarding for Schools: Advice and Strategies for Primary and Secondary Schools* (London: Jessica Kingsley Publishers, 2018).

Matt Dryden, 'Radicalisation: the last taboo in safeguarding and child protection? Assessing practitioner preparedness in preventing the radicalisation of looked-after children', *Journal for Deradicalization*, 13 (2017): 101–136.

Jennie Lindon and Janet Webb, *Safeguarding and Child Protection: Linking Theory and Practice*, 5th edn (London: Hodder Education, 2016).

# 5. Subject Knowledge

A developing trainee will:

✓ Be aware of some of the subject knowledge needed for the relevant key stages.

✓ Skim read the national curriculum, and the course specifications used at their placement schools.

✓ Read up on the required subject knowledge while planning each lesson.

✓ Use textbooks to check the depth of knowledge needed for each lesson.

✓ Ask other teachers in the department for support with subject knowledge if needed.

Subject knowledge can be daunting when starting your training year. Though you may have a degree level understanding of your specialism, most trainees will often find that subject knowledge (of the content specific to each key stage) will need brushing up on. Each subject has lots of content which you will need to know, understand and be able to convey in a way that will allow your students to progress with their learning. Showing your students that you have a strong understanding of your subject is one of the quickest ways to inspire their confidence in you. Conversely, students who believe they cannot rely on your subject knowledge will quickly lose trust.

You may remember lots of subject content from your own schooldays, but with the changes to the curriculum and the requirements of the specific exam board that your school is using, you will need to ensure that your subject knowledge is up to date. After a couple of years of teaching your knowledge of the curriculum at each key stage will be secure and the subject knowledge 'worry' will ease.

Prior to starting your training year we recommend you attempt some past exam papers in your subject specialism. This self-assessment process is vital in highlighting any key gaps in your knowledge. The quicker you highlight these gaps, the quicker you can fill them. This will enable you to start your first placement feeling secure in your subject knowledge, so you won't need to worry about this on top of the other worries that come with training.

When you reach the second placement stage, you may find yourself moving to a school which follows a different exam board specification or curriculum. You will need to be able to adapt to this quickly. There could be small nuances that are different in the content covered and terminology used, and subtle differences in mark schemes, with different aspects being given greater emphasis. Therefore, it is essential that you refer to the exam specifications or curriculum early so you can reduce your stress during this placement.

A good way to keep track of the content needed is to create a subject knowledge audit document at the start of your training year (many training organisations provide one). You can then re-audit your understanding of subject content throughout the course, for example at the end of teaching specific topics or after a mentor meeting in which you have discussed particular ways to teach a topic to the appropriate level. Many training organisations will ask for this document to be used to evidence that you are working towards the requirement to demonstrate good subject and curriculum knowledge, as outlined in the *Teachers' Standards*.[4]

---

4   Department for Education, *Teachers' Standards: Guidance for School Leaders, School Staff and Governing Bodies*. Ref: DFE-00066-2011 (London: Department for Education, 2011). Available at: https://www.gov.uk/government/uploads/system/uploads/attachment_data/file/665520/ Teachers__Standards.pdf.

A thriving teacher will ensure that their topic-specific subject knowledge is at least one key stage above the class they are teaching. For example, by having an A level understanding of a topic you will be extending your knowledge base for your GCSE lessons. This will prepare you to answer your students' questions and to stretch your most able students. Use sources such as textbooks and revision websites to extend your knowledge.

Be prepared for students wanting to unpick your explanations and ask about any holes in them. They are (mostly) doing it to check their own understanding!

Subject knowledge is critical and must be developed. Subject knowledge CPD is the best form of CPD. There is debate among teachers about whether you can teach anything if you have the skills of teaching. However, pupils will miss out on the richness of your explanations if you only have a surface knowledge. Teachers with weak subject knowledge often set independent learning tasks that can have a high cost in time and a low impact on pupil progress. Attend courses, learn from experts in your school, read widely and, most importantly, continue to do so throughout your career.

Lianne Allison, Deputy Head Teacher, Durrington High School

Subject knowledge takes time to develop, but with perseverance and a bit of effort put towards learning the content prior to starting your training, you will be better prepared for your first teaching placement. Find out which exam board your placement school uses and ensure you have looked up the specific content requirements; the specifications can usually be found online. Subject knowledge is vital; you need to know the material well enough to be confident when planning and teaching your lessons. Feeling nervous about the topic of a lesson should be an indicator that you're not comfortable with the content, so addressing this is a first step towards being ready to teach excellent lessons with any class. Finally, extending the depth of your subject knowledge can make your lessons more engaging. It provides you with those interesting stories and facts that can bring your subject to life and pique students' interest.

Subject knowledge is not just something that requires focus in your training year, but a core element of your practice throughout your career. I moved to a new school at the start of my third year of teaching and found myself in a situation where I had to teach two different A level topics which I had never studied before, as well as a new GCSE specification. When visiting the school at the end of my second year, I picked up all of the core textbooks for these new topics and read them thoroughly over the summer. I highlighted and annotated key passages and created my own flashcards to help me understand these complex topics. I also read a couple of undergraduate level books, watched documentaries and listened to podcasts to give me a range of knowledge that went beyond the specification. Being a huge history geek, this wasn't such hard work for me! This gave me the confidence to then plan and deliver strong lessons for my students from the very start of the year. I knew that I wouldn't be able to thrive without that knowledge, so was happy to invest the time in it. I think I'll read another book on each topic this summer to further increase my understanding. Developing subject knowledge is essential, from the training year onwards.

**To-do**

☐ Make a concerted effort to gain subject-specific knowledge for what you are going to teach.

☐ Download and complete past papers from any exam board website. Use these to self-assess your subject knowledge.

☐ Once you are given the names of your placement schools, research which specification they each use and download it. Either look on the school website or email your mentor (a nice way to impress early!).

**To read:**

Philip M. Sadler, Gerhard Sonnert, Harold P. Coyle, Nancy Cook-Smith and Jaimie L. Miller, 'The influence of teachers' knowledge on student learning in middle school physical science classrooms', *American Educational Research Journal,* 50(5) (2013): 1020–1049.

# 6. Planning: Part I

A developing trainee will:

✓ Be organised and submit lesson plans in advance. (This point is essential!)

✓ Attempt to include a range of tasks and strategies which evidence a number of the Teachers' Standards.

✓ Complete a detailed plan for every lesson.

Planning is going to be a big part of your training year. At times it will feel like a *very* big part. Developing your ability to plan effectively is going to be essential to ensure that you thrive.

The first thing you will need to focus on is getting organised. Whether you are teaching a handful of lessons at the start of the year, or a fuller timetable towards the end, one thing never changes: your need to manage your time with great thought and care.

Most mentors or training providers will insist that lessons are planned and shared with them at least one working day prior to being taught (or two working days if your subject requires health and safety considerations or practical equipment). To be clear, if your lesson is on Monday, the plan should be in by Friday morning at the latest (or Thursday morning if following the two day rule). Although this is good practice, a thriving trainee will need to be even more ahead of the game than this. During the start of your first week in a placement, you will need to discuss with your mentor the sequence of lessons you will be teaching over the next half term. Check what the students will be assessed on for that unit and get to know the specification – depth and breadth – for the topics that will need to be covered to prepare them. Then work out how many lessons you have until the assessment and begin to plan out what you will teach in each. This will, and should, inevitably change as you reflect upon student understanding – you may wish to revisit areas that students struggled with or held misconceptions about – but having this general outline is essential to ensure you manage your time effectively.

Having a clear outline enables you to not just plan lessons one day ahead, but two, three, four or more in advance. Our tip is to buy a specifically designed teacher's planner. This will enable you to map out your lessons and to have your short-, medium- and long-term plans available at a quick glance. Your workload will feel more manageable and, importantly, listing out your objectives will give you the immense satisfaction of crossing things off once you have completed them!

Getting into the habit of planning more than one day in advance will:

■ Reduce the stress of desperately finishing a lesson plan immediately prior to the deadline.

■ Give you time to not only share this lesson with your mentor, but actually get some feedback on it so you can reflect on and improve it before you deliver the lesson!

One of the most frustrating things for a typical trainee teacher is when you think you've taught a lesson well – the students behaved well, you managed to fit in your plenary – but you are then told it was a poor lesson because students didn't show progress/it wasn't differentiated/it failed to check student understanding. As a trainee teacher it is normal to overlook these key things, or to think you've covered them when in actual fact your tasks or delivery haven't met your objectives. Reflecting on plans, alongside getting valuable feedback from your mentor, means that you can avoid these pitfalls, allowing you to focus on developing excellent practice and more advanced skills and strategies.

Furthermore, a thriving trainee will make sure that each and every lesson they teach aims to include the 'essentials' for a good lesson:

■ A starter that engages or 'hooks' the class.

■ Clearly laid out objectives, also citing why they are learning about this and how it fits into the 'big picture'. Make sure you know what you want your students to achieve in the lesson; your tasks and resources will then facilitate this.

■ Tasks that clearly progress student understanding of the topic or focus of the lesson.

■ Differentiated resources and tasks based on the needs of individual students in the class.

■ Tasks and activities that check student understanding, more commonly known as assessment for learning (AfL).

■ A plenary that consolidates learning and shows clearly that progress has been made.

An outstanding lesson plan is not necessarily determined by how it's written or by what format is used but by being absolutely clear about what students should have learned by the end of the lesson. Start with that and make sure that your planning gets them on a journey that helps them to arrive at those lesson outcomes and assesses whether they got there at the end of it. Often trainees focus too much on a really good activity without thinking about what the students actually need to know by the end of the lesson. Rather than just using a really great YouTube clip you've seen because it might be engaging, you should think about how a resource fits into the aims of your curriculum and how it will help students secure progress in their learning. Something as simple as having and sharing a very clear question – that is tackled at the start, reviewed mid lesson and answered at the end – is often the foundation of an effective lesson.

Dr Simon Thompson, Head of Education, University of Sussex

In particular, you should take extra care when planning tasks that require students to use their literacy and numeracy skills as students' competencies in these areas may not match their achievement in your subject. Thriving teachers will look for moments in the lessons to develop literacy and numeracy explicitly.[5]

**Thriving literacy tips:**

- Correct students' mistakes, both verbally and in their books. Be conscious of the importance of not only refining their spelling, punctuation and grammar (SPaG), but also developing the style of writing they will need to master for exams in your subject.

- Get students to improve their work before you mark it. Insist that they check it for SPaG, as well as to ensure that it makes sense. Getting students to self-assess will develop their ability to write fluently and improve their literacy moving forwards.

---

5   See, for example, Julia Strong, *Talk for Writing in Secondary Schools: How to Achieve Effective Reading, Writing and Communication across the Curriculum* (Maidenhead: Open University Press, 2013). David Didau, 'Back to school part 3: literacy', *The Learning Spy* [blog] (21 August 2014). Available at: http://www.learningspy.co.uk/literacy/back-school-part-3-literacy/. David Didau, 'The secret of numeracy (across the curriculum)', *The Learning Spy* [blog] (10 December 2014). Available at: http://www.learningspy.co.uk/featured/secret-numeracy/.

■ Develop students' vocabulary by including key words in every lesson and getting students to define and use these throughout. In assessments, make the use and inclusion of these words part of the success criteria.

■ Don't shy away from literacy practice even though it takes time and may not allow you to move through the content as quickly.

**Thriving numeracy tips:**

■ Find out what students have or have not covered in maths before integrating specific skills into your lesson. Their background knowledge and skills will severely affect the time and support required to complete numeracy tasks.

■ Always complete a worked example of any mathematical activity before the students start the work themselves.

■ Ensure the numeracy content in your lesson has purpose and is not merely an addition for the sake of 'ticking the box'.

Additionally, consider writing out questions to explore, behaviour management strategies and possible student misconceptions on your lesson plans. The key is to make sure that you don't get criticised for not at least planning to include these essential elements. You will, of course, have varying degrees of success in delivering all of the above – and will do throughout your career – but ensuring that you consistently include these elements on paper is a sign of a thriving trainee.

As the training year progresses and the amount of lessons increases, you will need to consider how to get quicker and more efficient at planning. Experience counts for a lot and planning will speed up. However, there are strategies that you can put in place to support this process.

The first involves being a reflective teacher (see Chapter 17: Acting on Feedback) and considering which tasks and activities were successful. From this, you can create a bank of ideas and activities that you wish to use again. We recommend having files on your computer for generic adaptable components – for example, starters, mains, plenaries, differentiation and AfL – so you can build up a repertoire of successful tasks. This will become your ideas bank which will both increase in size and also become more streamlined with regards to the quality of the tasks as you reflect on, adapt and improve them. Then when it comes to planning lessons you can dip into this ever-increasing bank of ideas to help you plan a successful lesson very quickly. Of course, you will have to change the content and adapt different elements in response to your students' needs, but the core idea and outline is there already.

Finally, once in the swing of planning and teaching lessons, there are a number of things that a trainee should do to progress their planning. One idea is to plan a lesson jointly with a mentor. This is really useful as it gives you an insight into how a more experienced teacher plans and can be especially helpful in demonstrating how to plan more quickly (experienced teachers have a great knack of planning lessons rapidly). It will also help you to see which areas of your planning might be going awry and to allow your mentor to quickly spot things you may be getting wrong or where you may benefit from more support.

Another way to develop your planning is to observe your mentor teaching a lesson that you have planned and then to sit down together to reflect on the successes and areas for improvement. A thriving trainee would then adapt the lesson based upon this before teaching the improved version, again reflecting on how effective the improvements were and what lessons can be learned for planning in the future.

**To-do**

☐ Buy a teacher's planner and use it!

☐ Make a mini-checklist of things to include in every lesson plan – for example, starter, main, plenary, questioning, etc.

☐ Have every lesson plan in on time.

☐ Plan more than two lessons in advance for each class.

☐ Trial joint planning with your mentor at each placement.

**To read:**

Shaun Allison, 'Planning to be great', *Class Teaching* [blog] (13 September 2015). Available at: https://classteaching.wordpress.com/2015/09/13/planning-to-be-great/.

Chapter 4 in Phil Beadle, *How to Teach* (Carmarthen: Crown House Publishing, 2010).

David Didau, *The Secret of Literacy: Making the Implicit Explicit* (Carmarthen: Independent Thinking Press, 2014).

Peps Mccrea, 'The 7 habits of highly effective lesson plans', *Medium* (22 June 2015). Available at: https://medium.com/@pepsmccrea/the-7-habits-of-highly-effective-lesson-plans-f785f1f8974e.

Ryan Shaw, 'I can hardly wait to see what I am going to do today: lesson planning perspectives of experienced band teachers', *Contributions to Music Education*, 42 (2017): 129–151.

Chapters 3 and 4 in Jim Smith, *The Lazy Teacher's Handbook: How Your Students Learn More When You Teach Less* (Carmarthen: Independent Thinking Press, 2017).

# 7. Giving Students Instructions

A developing trainee will:

✓ Plan their instructions to ensure they are clear and detailed.

✓ Give instructions both in writing and verbally.

✓ Practise tasks first, then model the work in front of students.

Picture this. You have designed a purposeful and engaging task, which is effectively differentiated to support and stretch. Yet the class don't understand what it is they have to do and so make limited progress with it, therefore wasting the time you have invested in planning. Often the primary reason for this frustrating outcome is that the instructions given were unclear. If instructions are poor, then the rest of your hard work will be wasted.

Think discretely about the instructions that will be given to the class alongside each and every task. One of the most useful things you can do is to actually complete the tasks yourself – especially if you feel that something is complex or open to misinterpretation – before the lesson. This will allow you to spot the potential misconceptions your students may have and then plan your instruction giving with these in mind. You can then warn your students with something like: 'Be careful on Question 2, because there is a danger you may …' or 'One thing that may confuse you is … so …' This will help to avoid potential misunderstandings and facilitate the task being completed effectively.

Ensure that the instructions you give are clear and concise. Give them verbally and also have them written on the board, so that students have two opportunities to take them in. Number your written instructions, so that they are a clear step-by-step guide to allow students to complete the task. Finally, once the task is up and running, periodically remind them that the instructions are on the board; it's amazing how quickly students forget about the support that is in place for them!

A thriving trainee should model example answers for their students, showing – preferably on the board, so all students can clearly see, or by giving a practical demonstration – what they need to do for each task. Get the students to note down or work through the example answer at the same time as you model the work, ensuring that each and every student has an accurate, worked example of the task which they then use to complete further examples. This is especially useful to support the less able students in your class. For later tasks in the lesson, you may wish to utilise the more able students in the class as models. If you have access to a visualiser or a camera which can be projected on the board (there are a number of applications which facilitate this, such as EduCam or iDocCam) then you could even show a live piece of work in progress from a student in the class and use this to frame a discussion about next steps. Perhaps you could even get that student to explain what they have done, therefore demonstrating your belief in their ability to deliver a high-quality explanation and displaying truly student-centred learning.

Once you have given your instructions, the final step is to check understanding. One of the most common, but least effective, ways to do this is to simply ask the whole class, 'Do you understand what you need to do?' What happens then is that those who do not understand will still respond with a yes to comply with the general consensus. If you want a quick way to break the consensus with honest answers, then asking 'Have I explained this clearly?' is better because it places the emphasis on the teacher. If a student hasn't understood then the fault isn't with them, but instead is in your explanation – you may find this approach gives students the confidence to speak up if they haven't understood.

Better still, is to actually check understanding. After giving instructions, ask one of the students in your class at random what they need to do and get them to explain it back to the whole class. This gives everyone another opportunity to listen to the instructions, this time given in guaranteed student-friendly language.

Lastly, a really subtle but effective change you can make to your instruction giving is in the language choices that you make.[6] For example, avoid phrases such as 'when I put you into pairs …' or 'what I'm going to get you to do now is …' Instead try to put the emphasis on the students and use positive language to encourage their engagement. Try saying 'once we're in pairs we will …' or 'what you are going to do now is …' and see if this improves student willingness to get going.

---

6    Emily Clements, 'What about our language? How we can use words to give our classrooms the nudge', *Thrive in Teaching* [blog] (27 May 2017). Available at: https://thriveteach.wordpress. com/2017/05/27/what-about-our-language-how-we-can-use-words-to-give-our-classrooms-the-nudge/.

☐ Trial tasks before the lesson.

☐ Build in time specifically for instruction giving and modelling when planning lessons.

☐ Practise the language you use for checking student understanding of instructions.

**To read:**

Richard Clark, Paul Kirschner and John Sweller, 'Putting students on the path to learning: the case for fully guided instruction', *American Educator*, 36(1) (2012): 6–11.

# 8. Behaviour Management: Part I

A developing trainee will:

✓ Be aware of good behaviour management techniques before taking over their first class.

✓ Know individual students in the classes that they will be taking over.

✓ Be keen to develop strong behaviour management techniques.

✓ Always ring parents when there is a concern.

During your training year behaviour management is often one of the most worrying aspects of teaching. How will I control an entire roomful of teenagers? How will I stop them talking when I need them to listen? What do I do if I encounter poor behaviour? These important questions will most probably be running through your mind frequently as the placement nears. A developing trainee will have some idea of behaviour management techniques from observations, mentor meeting discussions or pre-reading.[7] Experience of taking your own classes and observing others will be key in dispelling any

---

7    See, for example, Tom Bennett, *The Behaviour Guru: Behaviour Management Solutions for Teachers* (London: Continuum, 2010).

lingering fears and ensuring that you have developed a strong behaviour management style prior to embarking on your NQT year.

When you start your first placement, observe your mentor and class teachers closely for behaviour management techniques. It is a good idea to start by modelling your behaviour management on someone who knows the classes that are going to be in front of you.

From your very first lesson you should be using the school's behaviour policy. In doing so, you will become familiar with the policy more quickly and gauge how to implement it in your classroom. Eventually, it will start to become part of your teaching routine and the quicker you get used to consistently implementing your behaviour management the quicker you can focus on your teaching practice.

It may feel out of character, or even strange at first, but try to start strong, demonstrating the high expectations you hold to the students. You may not feel it inside yet, but don't let your students see you as anything but the strong, confident, thriving teacher you want to be. Go in with a clear plan of 'if this scenario happens, this is what I will do'. Have the behaviour plan written down as part of your lesson plan and have this out in front of you when you are teaching those first lessons. This will mean you do not need to memorise the behaviour plan, but should you need the information it is to hand. This will prevent you from nervously looking over at the class teacher when you need to make a behaviour decision, which would be noticed by students and seen as a sign of weakness to be exploited. Keep a record of the behaviour management techniques that you have used at the end of each lesson. This will not only build upon your evidence for managing behaviour effectively to ensure a good and safe learning environment (Teachers' Standard 7) but you can also analyse and reflect upon how effective that technique was. This record can form the basis for conversations with your mentor.

By attempting to manage behaviour from your first lesson you are well on your way to becoming a thriving trainee. Showing your mentor and the students that you're confident at making decisions – even if initially this is just a facade – will propel you through your training journey quickly. Mentors often focus on behaviour management because once you have this relatively under control it allows you to start playing around with other aspects of your teaching and developing across all other standards. It also gives you the confidence to take the sorts of risks in your planning that will ensure you are developing your practice fully.

All teachers have students they dread to teach because of their consistently challenging behaviour. You may come across one in your training year. Develop a backup plan should a technique go wrong or be ineffective with a particular student. Speak to their class teacher to seek out other behaviour strategies which have previously been successful. Refer to advice and pedagogy guidance from colleagues and educational literature to get new behaviour management ideas. This will give you the confidence of having a range of options to hand and enable you to concentrate on teaching. Finally, realise that behaviour doesn't always change overnight; it takes time to embed good behaviour. Consistency has to be key with behaviour management. You will gain students' respect if they see you manage each individual in the class with the same expectations and discipline.

> The secret to strong behaviour management is positive relationships. Learn those names quickly. Use positive language and show children that you respect and value them. Never use collective nouns. It is important not to label a class or year group as difficult as there will be lots of great children in that class or year group. We can lose our perspective and focus on the one difficult child if we aren't careful. Have firm boundaries and remember it is part of being a child to test them. When they get it wrong then hold them to account and forgive and move on quickly. Each lesson is a fresh start.
>
> Lianne Allison, Deputy Head Teacher, Durrington High School

Engage with parents on a regular basis. Set a target to ring a certain number of parents a week or send home a certain number of emails. If it makes it easier, agree with yourself that for every negative contact home, you will also make a positive one. Not only will this improve the positivity of your day – as well as making a parent's day – but the evidence suggests it will have a positive impact on the effort and behaviour of those students, while also benefiting your relationship with that student.[8]

However, when moving onto your second placement, and beyond, don't become complacent. Every teacher will have their behaviour management tested throughout their career. Equally, if you felt that during your first placement you were not strong enough on behaviour, take this as a fresh start. You will also need to take the time to become familiar with your new school's behaviour policy.

**Thriving behaviour management tips:**

- Learn names as quickly as possible. This will help you to build positive relationships and also hold challenging students to account.

---

8    Ruth Payne, 'Using rewards and sanctions in the classroom: pupils' perceptions of their own responses to current behaviour management strategies', *Educational Review*, 67(4) (2015): 483–504.

■ Have the students line up outside the classroom in silence *before* entering your classroom each lesson to remind them that you are in charge.

■ When the students come in, welcome them into your classroom, 'Morning, hello, afternoon, how are you today?' Being extra cheerful always helps!

■ Always ensure students sit in your seating plan. Do not allow them to move about.

■ Wait for silence before you talk. This will feel uncomfortable at first but is a good form of non-verbal communication. Waiting is key so be patient!

■ Count down from three to one to get quiet. Be consistent with this and always expect complete silence.

■ Don't turn your back to the class when working with one individual. Position yourself so you can see all students.

■ Insist on silence when taking the register.

■ When disciplining students, use names, but criticise the behaviour rather than the individual.

■ Give praise and rewards to any student whenever appropriate.

■ Following advice from behaviour management expert Bill Rogers, when giving students instructions, end your sentence with 'thank you' rather than 'please' to show your expectations of compliance.[9]

■ Use regular positive language with all students.

■ Don't hold grudges, each lesson is a clean slate.

■ Try subtly walking towards students who are talking while you're talking. This normally gets them to stop.

■ Catch the difficult ones being good and let them know how proud you are of them.

---

9   See Bill Rogers, 'Ensuring a settled and focused class' [video] (26 September 2012). Available at: https://www.youtube.com/watch?v=PLFcaovsriA&t=0s&list=PLF1FBp_bi4gbXAvyDu1oO5o_ LaJ6PufZm&index=6. See also Bill Rogers, *Classroom Behaviour: A Practical Guide to Effective Teaching, Behaviour Management and Colleague Support* (London: Sage, 2015).

■ Stand at the door and say goodbye when students are leaving so they are left with a positive lasting impression of you and your lesson.

■ Most importantly, make the two C's your mantra: confidence and consistency!

During my first placement I often focused too heavily on getting started on the activities or getting through that exciting quiz I had prepared. However, after one Year 7 lesson, the feedback didn't focus on any of my resources. Instead the class teacher concentrated on how I had let the students talk over me so that we could move on quickly. I still remember her saying, 'These are Year 7 students and by now you really should be getting them to be silent.' I recognised that it was not a question of my ability to do this, but that I hadn't seen the true value in doing so. From that lesson on, my understanding of behaviour management changed as I realised that we are actually doing a disservice to the students if we don't provide them with a positive working environment.

To-do

☐ Ensure you fully understand the placement school's behaviour management policy and escalation structure.

☐ Build your behaviour management strategy into your lesson plans.

☐ Create a reflective record of behaviour management techniques to trial and discuss with your mentor.

## To read:

Chapter 4 in Phil Beadle, *How to Teach* (Carmarthen: Crown House Publishing, 2010).

Tom Bennett, *The Behaviour Guru: Behaviour Management Solutions for Teachers* (London: Continuum, 2010).

Sue Cowley, *Getting the Buggers to Behave*, 5th edn (London: Bloomsbury Education, 2014).

Bill Rogers, 'Bill Rogers on behaviour' [video] (27 January 2017). Available at: https://www.youtube.com/watch?v=KTxGXiuLgb4.

Bill Rogers, *Classroom Behaviour: A Practical Guide to Effective Teaching, Behaviour Management and Colleague Support* (London: Sage, 2015).

# 9. Questioning

A developing trainee will:

✓ Include some key questions in every lesson plan.

✓ Use a mixture of open and closed questions to test students' recall and develop their thinking.

✓ Use Bloom's Taxonomy to design questions with a variety of command words to vary the level of challenge.

✓ Use a mixture of hands-up questioning and targeted questioning.

We all know how to ask questions, but knowing how to ask excellent questions is different. At first, questioning will take practice, so get into the habit of noting some questions down on the plan for each lesson – do not underestimate the importance of this! Your questions, with their various command words, can be a really effective tool for differentiation if you carefully consider which question stems to use for your students. This structure of questioning is modelled upon the work of Dr Benjamin Bloom, more commonly known as Bloom's Taxonomy, which you have most likely been introduced to already.[10]

We found it really useful to identify particular students on the lesson plan that we intended to ask each question to. In this way, a student of middle ability – a group often neglected in lesson planning – will get a question that has been designed and pitched for them rather than just the lower and higher ability students receiving this tailoring.

---

10  For a summary, see http://www.fctl.ucf.edu/teachingandlearningresources/coursedesign/bloomstaxonomy/. Also see Mike Gershon, *How to Use Bloom's Taxonomy in the Classroom: The Complete Guide* (CreateSpace, 2015).

| Low ability | Middle ability | High ability |
|---|---|---|
| State<br><br>Identify<br><br>Name | Describe<br><br>Rank<br><br>Simplify | Justify<br><br>Prove<br><br>Invent |
| What is ...?<br><br>Can you select ...?<br><br>What facts or ideas show ...? | How would you use ...?<br><br>Can you predict ...?<br><br>What would result if ...? | How would you adapt this to create a new ...?<br><br>What data was used to make this conclusion ...? |

There are several strategies that will make the questions you ask more meaningful. Firstly, reflect on the way you ask the questions. Simple changes like not naming the student you want to answer the question until after you have asked it and given everyone a chance to think stops all of the others switching off their attention.[11] If no one knows who is going to be selected to answer, then more students will engage with the question and try to work out an answer in case they are called upon.

It is natural for us as teachers to want to fill awkward silences in our lessons but this can be disastrous for our questioning. One of the best questioning strategies if you want to encourage deep thinking and high levels of engagement is called 'wait time' or 'take up time'.[12] This involves waiting for up to eight seconds – you may find it easier to actually count these in your head – after you have asked the question before saying anything, including selecting the student to answer the question. It sounds easy, but when you are standing up there in front of the class, it seems like an awfully long time. However, this is essential to give your students a chance to formulate their ideas so they have a good answer to share. You can delay further if you are using hands-up questioning by saying that you want to see at least half the students with their hands in the air before you will select someone to answer.

It is easy to prevent students from needing to think by interjecting too quickly with support – an easy mistake to make to fill an uncomfortable silence. By doing this you can end up leading their answers rather than leaving them to struggle and think more deeply. It is

---

11  Doug Lemov, 'Engaged cerebral classroom culture: Aidan Thomas' master class on wait time', *Teach Like a Champion* [blog] (4 January 2017). Available at: http://teachlikeachampion.com/blog/engaged-cerebral-classroom-culture-aidan-thomas-master-class-wait-time/.

12  Kenneth Tobin, 'The role of wait time in higher cognitive level learning', *Review of Educational Research*, 57(1) (1987): 69–95.

okay to let an individual student, or the whole class, ponder over an answer for a while before offering hints and suggestions. That being said, if you have offered wait time and the answer is still a simple 'don't know', an excellent way to turn this around is to scaffold students' thinking with further questions that lead them back to the original question.[13]

---

TEACHER:  Why do we have day and night on earth?

STUDENT:  I don't know.

TEACHER:  Do students in Australia experience day at the same time as we do?

STUDENT:  No.

TEACHER:  Why is that?

STUDENT:  Because they are on the other side of the earth?

TEACHER:  Okay, so when Australia has day, they are facing *what*?

STUDENT:  The sun. So when it's night we are facing away from the sun.

TEACHER:  So what causes that to change? Why do we have day and night?

STUDENT:  Because the earth spins on its axis and if we face the sun it is day, and if we face away it is night.

---

Not only does this teach your students that there is no easy way out of answering questions, it can also act as a confidence booster for those who genuinely do think it's 'too hard' for them.

Alternatively, if a student is able to provide an insightful or suitable answer to a question straight away, then you can build challenge on top of this by using follow-up questions. Ramp up the Bloom's verbs and get them thinking about the same thing but at a deeper level. Perhaps they could try to apply the content to an abstract concept, make a judgement or compare or evaluate importance. This is a good way to differentiate for the more able students in your class, so be sure to plan these extension questions into your lessons.

---

13  Shaun Allison and Andy Tharby, *Making Every Lesson Count: Six Principles to Support Great Teaching and Learning* (Carmarthen: Crown House Publishing, 2015), pp. 218–219.

To-do

☐ Plan the questions you are going to ask before the lesson; ensure these develop or check understanding.

☐ Differentiate your questioning to both support and stretch students.

☐ Use specific questioning techniques to keep the whole class on their toes.

☐ Be mindful of 'wait time' and don't be scared of silence while students consider their answers.

**To read:**

Chapter 6 in Shaun Allison and Andy Tharby, *Making Every Lesson Count: Six Principles to Support Great Teaching and Learning* (Carmarthen: Crown House Publishing, 2015).

Linda Elder and Richard Paul, 'The role of Socratic questioning in thinking, teaching and learning', *The Clearing House: A Journal of Educational Strategies, Issues and Ideas*, 71(5) (1998): 297–301.

Chapter 6 in Doug Lemov, *Teach Like a Champion 2.0: 62 Techniques That Put Students on the Path to College* (San Francisco, CA: Jossey-Bass, 2015).

Alex Quigley, 'Questioning – top ten strategies', *The Confident Teacher* [blog] (10 November 2012). Available at: https://www.theconfidentteacher.com/2012/11/questioning-top-ten-strategies/.

# 10. Differentiation

A developing trainee will:

✓ Have extension tasks ready on the board but not always refer to them or ensure completion.

✓ Not give students tasks which are too easy or hard for them, but attempt to ensure work is pitched at the correct level.

✓ Attempt different types of differentiation to match student abilities.

Differentiating effectively for your students is one of the most important aspects of being a thriving trainee. Ensuring that each and every student makes the most progress possible should be the mantra of everyone in our profession. Yet without carefully considered differentiation, the less able students in the class will fall behind and the most able won't be stretched.[14] So what do we mean by effective differentiation?

Differentiation doesn't mean just making the work easier or harder. This is a common misconception, and one fraught with difficulties. Effective differentiation makes the content accessible. See the learning outcomes of a lesson as achievable for everyone, but be aware that some students will need extra intermediate steps to help get them there.

It's essential to realise that all learners are different and although there are a range of strategies which can help to provide the intermediate steps in building understanding or accessing the content, these won't work all of the time for all students. You must cater for the individual. A thriving trainee will recognise this, and ensure that they also consider how effective their differentiation has been. Some reflective questions to consider are: Has that student now understood the task? Have they made good progress? What are they still struggling with? How could I differentiate more effectively for that student in the future?

A further point to consider is when to differentiate. It can be tempting to 'blanket differentiate' for all students who are targeted a low level, or who have SEND or EAL. The data has flagged up that these students may struggle, so therefore you should differentiate for them, right? Well, not quite. These students can find themselves receiving differentiated work in every lesson of every day, which is problematic for two reasons.

Firstly, we have no way of knowing whether they need that differentiated work in the first place if we never give them anything else. If they don't – and they could in fact complete the undifferentiated tasks – then we have made the work too easy for them, therefore limiting their potential progress. Secondly, blanket differentiation – especially if the work is too easy – prevents students from struggling with challenging work and making mistakes. It is often these cognitive struggles and these mistakes which allow learning to happen most effectively; getting something wrong – but then being given clear feedback on how to improve – embeds knowledge more deeply than when something is learned very easily.[15] Furthermore, surely we want our students to grow into adults who are used to having to work hard, struggle and make mistakes before getting it right? These are important life skills which can be lost through giving differentiated work out to certain students as a matter of course.

---

14  Richard J. Harris, 'Does differentiation have to mean different?', *Teaching History*, 118 (2005): 5–12.
15  Matthew Hays, Nate Kornell and Robert Bjork, 'When and why a failed test potentiates the effectiveness of subsequent study', *Journal of Experimental Psychology*, 39(1) (2013): 290–296.

A better approach is to drop in differentiated work as and when it is needed. Give all students in the class a chance to complete tasks without differentiation and then, if they are clearly struggling, use the differentiated work to support them. This ensures that you aren't dumbing down the content, yet that support is on hand should a struggling student require it.

There is a huge array of ways to differentiate. Every task should be differentiated to ensure the work is appropriate to student abilities, so a range of approaches will be necessary to support each individual. Here are some that we have found to be particularly effective:

- Verbal differentiation. It sounds simple, but one of the most effective forms of differentiation comes through speaking with your students. When circulating as students complete a task, offering verbal support to struggling students by explaining a task or pointing them in the right direction can make a huge difference. When used in combination with differentiated resources, this can really support those students who are struggling with a particular task. Also consider how questioning can be used to support less able students by utilising Bloom's Taxonomy to get them to recall facts or information or to explain ideas – this can be a way to ensure that all students have a solid understanding of the content. You can then use questioning to encourage students to begin analysing and evaluating, thus pushing them to move beyond basic understanding and ensuring that they realise the equally high expectations you hold for them all.

- Reduce the text. Reducing the amount of text students have to read can really help the less able. This doesn't mean removing key information, but removing the less essential information. Additionally, highlighting key information in a question or text – using bold, underlining or a different colour – can help struggling students to focus in on what they need to know to complete the task.

- Use images. Making a task visual can really support students. Think about placing images (hand-drawn or found on the internet) next to concepts or ideas to help explain or illustrate them in a different way. This could even be done as a storyboard to deliver your instructions visually. Another effective use of images can be to get students to depict key information or an idea as an image before answering questions about it. The process of translating written text into an image can also really encourage students to understand what they have read.

- Sentence starters. Have the first few words of each answer or the opening to each paragraph already written out – it is these first few words which students often find the hardest to write. You could put these onto a worksheet or have them on the board.

■ Key word glossaries. This is especially useful if the students need to read an extract, source or any other extended piece of writing. Think about the vocabulary students may struggle with or have not encountered before and create a glossary of these words. Either print this out ready to drop in for those who would benefit, or put on the board for all to refer to.

■ Modelling. You can't expect students to successfully complete a task, either practical or written, without having shown them how to do it. This is even truer for less able students. Always make sure to model an answer or a task before expecting students to complete it. For the less able, having a printed model answer in front of them, or watching your demonstration, can offer additional support during tasks.

● Live modelling. Model how to complete a task or answer a question 'live', either as a practical demonstration or on the board. Actually completing a question in front of your class – but with them guiding and advising you as you work through it – is a powerful way to support learners. Getting them to share the essential thought processes required to write an answer will support their cognitive ability to then write the answer or complete the task themselves. Ensure you talk through your struggles, pauses and changes. Encourage the class to reflect on what you've written and to encourage you to go back and add to or edit your answer to make it better.

● Creating a scaffolded writing frame for shorter and extended written work can make a huge difference. Your writing frame should be an adapted page of lined paper, with support throughout. This should include sentence starters, glossaries, 'helpful hints' boxes and images, alongside spaces for students to write their answers. This can also be effective for students with EAL, who can spend a lot of time considering how to begin the sentence correctly rather than on utilising the content from the lesson – which is the main focus (see Chapter 30: Supporting Students with EAL for more tips and advice). You can also use this technique for numeracy activities by creating a step-by-step scaffold that takes students through the calculations you are asking them to do. Then gradually reduce the steps in your support throughout the worksheet until finally they are able to work unguided.

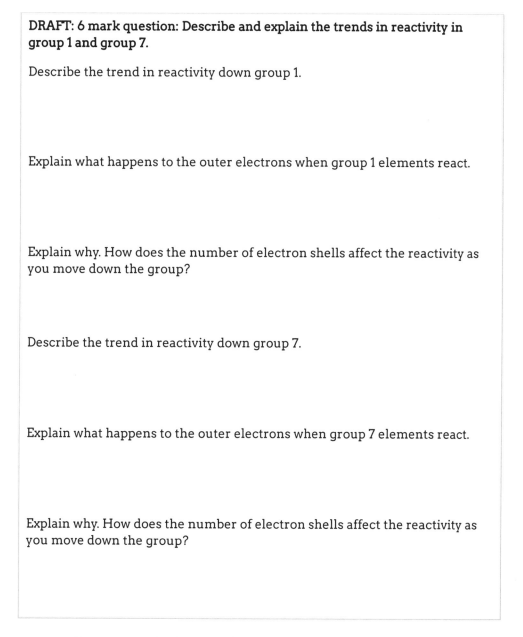

**DRAFT: 6 mark question: Describe and explain the trends in reactivity in group 1 and group 7.**

Describe the trend in reactivity down group 1.

Explain what happens to the outer electrons when group 1 elements react.

Explain why. How does the number of electron shells affect the reactivity as you move down the group?

Describe the trend in reactivity down group 7.

Explain what happens to the outer electrons when group 7 elements react.

Explain why. How does the number of electron shells affect the reactivity as you move down the group?

*Figure 1. Example of a writing frame used to write a draft answer in GCSE chemistry.*

So far we have only considered the less able when discussing differentiation. However, a thriving trainee will pay equal attention to ensuring that all students can access the work and that they are sufficiently stretched and challenged. Each and every task you deliver should have a challenge or extension task to ensure that students are consistently stretched in your lessons. Much as a thriving trainee won't 'blanket differentiate', nor will they limit their extension tasks to those deemed more able, or gifted and talented (G&T). Push all of your students to get onto these extension tasks – while not neglecting the quality of the main tasks – and you may be surprised by how many of them meet your expectations. Here are some ideas to ensure that all students are stretched and challenged in your lessons:

■ Encourage higher order thinking through creative and evaluative tasks. This is the bedrock of all extension tasks – if you are not allowing students to engage in higher order thinking then you are not stretching them. For example, the initial task might be to 'put these events in the correct chronological order'. The challenge task could then be 'what connections or links can you find between these events?' or 'which event do you think was the most important to help England defeat Spain in the Spanish Armada?' You can encourage high order thinking through verbal questioning and through written questions on the board or on a worksheet. Include these as standard in each task you get students to complete.

■ Independent learning. Give students an opportunity to learn independently as this is a skill they will need post-school and it will allow them to get the greater breadth of knowledge that they crave. Setting students who are ready for the challenge up with a project every half term – to research something in more depth, to build or create something, or to produce a presentation – will allow them to be stretched outside, as well as inside, your lessons.

■ Extra information. Doing something as simple as dropping in some extra information about your chosen topic during the lesson can be a good way to stretch students. Make sure that it isn't just more straightforward facts, but something more complex or nuanced that goes beyond what they have already learned. It could be something from a reference book or website, or an opinion piece from a magazine. Ensure that they then use their wider knowledge in their answers and assessments to embed this learning.

There really is no need to make lots of different worksheets depending on the ability of your group. Instead, know them well. Have the same high challenge learning objectives for all and scaffold up. That might mean a sentence starter for some students as you circulate the room or simply asking higher ability students to pick their start point or design their own questions and answers. Take care over the difference between differentiation (adapting for abilities) and personalisation (adapting for SEND, EAL, etc.). You really must plan different resources if the students can't access what you have.

Lianne Allison, Deputy Head Teacher, Durrington High School

During my second placement at a school that had a lot of students with SEND, I taught one individual who was particularly struggling in my lessons. He was diagnosed with autism and had very low literacy abilities. Yet no matter how I differentiated for him, he wouldn't engage well with the tasks, barely completing them and evidently struggling throughout. I arranged a meeting with the SENCO to discuss my concerns and get advice. He told me that many teachers were struggling to find the best way to help, but that one teacher had tried to link all of the tasks to Lego characters – which the student in question absolutely loved – with some success. So I gave it a go. Each worksheet was made into a comic strip, with Lego characters offering the instructions and advice in speech bubbles. The difference this made was profound. This student became fully engaged in the activities and, once he was willing to try 100% to complete the tasks given, was able to make significant progress in lessons.

I learned two lessons through this. Firstly, it made me appreciate the importance of asking advice from those who are more experienced and knowledgeable; without meeting the SENCO I don't think the student would have made such good progress. Secondly, I learned the importance of getting to know my students and treating them as individuals. The teacher who trialled the Lego approach later told me that he only found out about this passion because he had invested the time to speak with the student before class one day and it had come up in conversation. There is real value in getting to know your students personally and using this knowledge to tailor your differentiated resources to their individual interests and needs.

☐ Differentiate by giving students a helping hand to complete tasks, not by making tasks easier or downgrading or removing learning outcomes.

☐ Remember that all students should have stretch and challenge in every lesson, regardless of their ability level.

To-do

**To read:**

Peter Anstee, *Differentiation Pocketbook* (Alresford: Teachers' Pocketbooks, 2011).

Jayne Bartlett, *Outstanding Differentiation for Learning in the Classroom* (Abingdon: Routledge, 2016).

Sue Cowley, *The Seven T's of Practical Differentiation* (Bristol: Sue Cowley Books Ltd, 2013).

Ruth Powley, 'Meaningful manageable differentiation', *Love Learning Ideas* [blog] (31 January 2015). Available at: http://www.lovelearningideas.com/blog-archive/2015/1/31/meaningful-manageable-differentiation.

Andy Tharby, 'The dangers of differentiation … and what to do about them', *Reflecting English* [blog] (5 October 2014). Available at: https://reflectingenglish.wordpress.com/2014/10/05/the-dangers-of-differentiation-and-what-to-do-about-them/.

# 11. Assessment for Learning (AfL)

A developing trainee will:

✓ Include AfL in the planning of the plenary for every lesson.

✓ Attempt some form of AfL after tasks in lessons.

✓ Be aware of the end of unit assessment and develop students' understanding with this in mind.

One of the primary roles of a teacher is to ensure that the students we teach develop their understanding of the subject, and that they are learning, growing and becoming better at the key skills involved. Yet no matter how well you plan your lessons, the only way to really *know* whether your students are making progress is to check or 'assess' it. This is where AfL comes into play. AfL is the teacher's mechanism for checking understanding throughout a lesson, to ensure that the objectives are being met and that students have understood the content taught.[16] This then enables the teacher to decide if there are concepts or skills that they need to go over again, if the students show weak understanding, or if they are able to continue progressing through the topic.

There are a number of ways to check progress, so choose the most appropriate option to check understanding – but be aware that some methods of AfL provide more information than others. The problem with AfL is that it is often done as a token gesture, and without the thought required to make it a worthwhile use of valuable lesson time. You will be told by your subject tutor, and school mentor, to include AfL in your lessons. This is a good thing. Yet the thriving trainee will take a more sceptical approach and consider whether their chosen AfL tasks are *really* demonstrating student understanding. So here are two common AfL strategies which while on the surface may appear to demonstrate understanding, in reality don't:

1   Thumbs up/down. This is where you get the students to give a thumbs up/sideways/ down to show how much they have understood. This is problematic firstly because it gives no indication of *what* they have misunderstood and secondly it's impossible to know if all of the students with their thumbs up have really understood or are just demonstrating confidence/following their friends/don't want to be embarrassed/just want to get to lunch.

2   Traffic lights. A variation on the above where students decide between red, amber and green to show their level of understanding. As above – and for the same reasons – a flawed method.[17]

So what *does* work then? One of the most important, but often overlooked, forms of AfL is questioning.[18] However, effective questioning is easier said than done, so take a look back at Chapter 9: Questioning for a thorough review of how to thrive using this key method of AfL.

---

16  See Dylan Wiliam, *Embedded Formative Assessment* (Bloomington, IN: Solution Tree Press, 2011).
17  Andy Griffith and Mark Burns, *Outstanding Teaching: Teaching Backwards* (Carmarthen: Crown House Publishing, 2014), p. 173.
18  For more on the importance of questioning, see Mike Gershon, 'Classroom questioning: how to ask good questions', *Mike Gershon* [blog] (n.d.). Available at: https://mikegershon.com/ classroom-questioning-ask-good-questions/. Also, Dylan Wiliam, 'The right questions, the right way', *Educational Leadership*, 71(6) (March 2014): 16–19. Available at: http://www.ascd.org/publications/ educational-leadership/mar14/vol71/num06/The-Right-Questions,-The-Right-Way.aspx.

Here are some other strategies to try:

■ Mini-whiteboards. These are a great tool to use to check understanding. You could get the students to hold up pieces of A4 paper as an alternative, but we like to look after the environment, so tend to deploy the reusable mini-whiteboards! At a basic level, you can get your students to write answers to questions on them and then hold them up; this allows you to have a quick scour of the classroom to see who has got the correct answer and who has not and may therefore need additional support. If it was a judgement question – for example, 'what was the most important cause of the First World War?' – students could first write down their answers and then group together with peers who have the same answer. Once students are grouped, you could then check understanding further through questioning or by setting up a discussion or debate. You could even get students to write questions they have about the topic on the mini-whiteboards to both gauge common gaps in knowledge and to inform future planning. All of these things will help you to better recognise how much your students understand, which is effective AfL in action.

■ Sticky notes. Sticky notes work similarly to mini-whiteboards, allowing students to write down ideas/answers/questions. Yet the 'sticky' element adds another dimension as they can be affixed and moved again. You could, for example, have a multiple-choice question on the board and get students to stick their note next to the 'correct' answer. Even better, get the students to write the reason why they have chosen that option on the sticky note, as well as their name. Spending five minutes during/after a lesson reading these will give you a great insight into levels of understanding.

■ Washing line. Hanging a piece of string across your classroom can be a great tool to check understanding. If you are having a debate, make each end of the line the extremes of agreement and disagreement. Then get students to write reasons/arguments/evidence in support of their views on pieces of paper and attach them to the line with clothes pegs. Get students to justify their decisions, thus gauging understanding.

■ Physical activities. Similar to using sticky notes to show agreement with an answer, you could get students to stand in different areas of the room which correspond to different possible answers. Again, they may follow their friends, but some efficient questioning once they have chosen will still allow you to gauge understanding.

■ Discussions and debates. Getting students to discuss what they have learned is a great way to assess understanding. Whether it is during a simple discussion – perhaps following the use of mini-whiteboards or sticky notes – or a debate, take the opportunity to really listen to your students to see what they know or may have misunderstood. Make the debate more interactive by creating a tug of war element: students are free to change their minds if convinced by the counterarguments and the different sides try to convince others to join them.

■ Quick quizzes. Including a short quiz in the lesson is a good way to check understanding. This could be just five quick questions, which students can answer in the back of their books. Students can then share their scores with you by giving a quick hands up to indicate how many they got right – quickly make a mental note of who got one, two, three and so on. Or, to prevent potential embarrassment at low scores, students could write their scores on a mini-whiteboard and hold them up briefly. You do not need to record these scores but try to notice how many got low marks or if anyone stands out. Technology can be really effective here as well – search for 'Kahoot' or 'Quizlet' on the internet and get students involved in interactive quizzing in class. Even better, get the students to make the quizzes themselves for homework! There is good evidence to suggest that regular, low-stakes quizzing is a great way to develop deep learning – whereby students commit information to their long-term memories – as well as being an effective way to check understanding.[19]

Learning does not take place in one lesson, it takes time to become embedded and so it is important to build AfL which explores previously covered ideas into your planning. Check student understanding of things covered a week ago, or a month ago, to see how their knowledge has grown or if any misconceptions have developed.

A common challenge is that trainees might think they are assessing learning because they use some questioning. However, this tends to be done with specific individuals rather than used effectively to assess the understanding of the whole class. So the activities that are being used tend to be individual conversations between the teacher and a single pupil. Instead, try to engage the whole class with questioning. If that's closed 'yes or no' questions then follow up with a more exploratory set of questions requiring more detailed answers. Questioning could involve the use of a mini-whiteboard or blank sheet of paper where everybody holds up their answer or students could stand on a physical continuum to indicate agreement or disagreement, with the teacher posing questions about their

19  Henry L. Roediger and Jeffrey D. Karpicke, 'Test-enhanced learning: taking memory tests improves long-term retention', *Psychological Science,* 17(3) (2006): 249–255.

position. It's about using strategies which give the whole class the opportunity to share their understanding rather than just a couple of individuals.

Dr Simon Thompson, Head of Education, University of Sussex

A lot of trainee teachers simply assume that students have understood the content of the lesson, so don't fall into this trap! Make sure to include a number of opportunities for AfL within each lesson to ensure that you know whether students are understanding the content and making progress. Every task that you include in the lesson should be followed by an AfL exercise – for example, a mini-plenary – as this is the only way to know whether what you have taught has been understood.

Furthermore, a thriving trainee will be prepared to adapt and use different AfL techniques in lessons for different students in order to overcome specific misconceptions. How are you going to ensure that all students have understood the core content of the lesson? Try using hinge questions during your lesson – quick, but carefully considered, questions to gauge understanding – to decide whether to review a topic again or move forward.[20] Furthermore, consider differentiating follow-up tasks to help facilitate understanding (see Chapter 10: Differentiation for more advice on this) and be prepared to adapt future lesson plans to review certain topics or tasks that students struggled with previously.

**To-do**

☐ Plan AfL tasks into every lesson.

☐ Start to use different AfL techniques and recognise which are more suited to your subject and to the abilities of your students.

**To read:**

Mike Gershon, *How to Use Assessment for Learning in the Classroom: The Complete Guide* (CreateSpace, 2013).

Dylan Wiliam, *Embedded Formative Assessment* (Bloomington, IN: Solution Tree Press, 2017).

---

20  Dylan Wiliam, 'Designing great hinge questions', *Educational Leadership*, 73(1) (2015): 40–44.

# 12. Homework

A developing trainee will:

✓ Set regular homework in line with the departmental or school policy.

✓ Check homework suitability with the class teacher.

✓ Check understanding of homework, just as with any other task.

✓ Always mark homework promptly.

Homework is an integral part of planning and delivering lessons in which the students and trainee can thrive. Homework is essential and has a positive impact on students' learning, but only if the task is appropriate and focused.[21] Quality of homework is more important than quantity and a good trainee will check all homework tasks have a clear, achievable objective. Never set homework without marking it promptly as students will lose motivation to complete the tasks. As much thought should be put into homework as into planning a lesson.

There can be a tendency to set unfinished tasks as homework, but this can inadvertently punish the less able in your class as they will have more to complete. Always consider how your homework is differentiated for your students, applying the principles covered in Chapter 10: Differentiation. This may seem like an obvious thought, but it is something that can often be forgotten and the balance is tricky to get right. Homework should aim to extend and stretch but not to the point where it is inaccessible and puts students off.

Consider when you are going to set the homework task during the lesson, as you may find in your first few lessons that this is something that can easily be forgotten or left to the last minute when you are running out of time. The beginning of the lesson is the best time to set homework as this ensures you won't forget, and allows sufficient time to explain the task to the students. This will also stop you falling into the trap of setting unfinished tasks as homework.

Takeaway homework is a fantastic way to ensure that homework tasks consolidate learning, but are also challenging. The unique element to this approach is that students can decide which tasks to complete on the topic you have set. You therefore set a range of tasks each half term, some more challenging than others, and get students to choose the

---

21 See the Education Endowment Foundation's Teaching and Learning Toolkit, available at: https://educationendowmentfoundation.org.uk/evidence-summaries/teaching-learning-toolkit/homework-secondary/

ones they wish to complete – for example, they might have to complete two tasks per half term from a longer list of options. You can even lay out your takeaway homework menu as a series of starters, mains, sides and desserts to ensure that a range of different tasks are included. This works especially well with Key Stage 3 classes and is great for developing student independence. Ross Morrison McGill has written an excellent blog post on his pioneering takeaway homework concept.[22]

Flipped learning is a teaching concept in which students learn the lesson content at home – often by reading information and completing fairly simple analysis questions – meaning that lesson time can then be spent applying this knowledge in answering more complex evaluation or exam questions.[23] This can be a really good way to save time – as students can cover a lot of content at home – and also to ensure that more of the lesson is devoted to discussing, evaluating and using the content, rather than learning the basics. There are limitations to this method of teaching, however. Students must have access to the necessary resources – the internet, textbooks, etc. – and one size definitely does not fit all. You will need to think about ability and independent learning skills when deciding whether a class is ready for a flipped learning lesson, as this approach requires a degree of independence and trust if it is to be successful.[24] However, this is a great technique which you can adapt and bring to life during your training year as you will have time to experiment with using different teaching styles. You may be in a school where all students have their own electronic devices and this will make flipped learning easier. As one of us learned, don't rely on a flipped learning approach for an observed lesson: it can make for a difficult observation if half the class have not completed the work!

To-do

☐ Set homework at the start of lessons.

☐ Differentiate homework tasks to consolidate learning and stretch students.

☐ Experiment with takeaway homework and flipped learning.

---

22  Ross Morrison McGill, '#TakeAwayHmk', *Teacher Toolkit* [blog] (28 January 2014). Available at: https://www.teachertoolkit.co.uk/2014/01/28/takeawayhmk/.

23  Kathleen Fulton, 'Upside down and inside out: flip your classroom to improve student learning', *Learning and Leading with Technology*, 39(8) (2012): 12–17. Available at: http://files.eric.ed.gov/fulltext/EJ982840.pdf.

24  Tianchong Wang, 'Overcoming barriers to "flip": building teacher's capacity for the adoption of flipped classroom in Hong Kong secondary schools', *Research and Practice in Technology Enhanced Learning*, 12(6) (2017): 1–11.

**To read:**

Mark Creasy, *Unhomework: How to Get the Most out of Homework, Without Really Setting It* (Carmarthen: Independent Thinking Press, 2014).

Gerry Czerniawski and Warren Kidd, *Homework for Learning: 300 Practical Strategies* (Maidenhead: Open University Press, 2013).

Julian Stern, *Getting the Buggers to Do their Homework* (London: Continuum, 2009).


# 13. Creativity

A developing trainee will:

✓ Use the school's scheme of work and search the internet to find resources and ideas, utilising websites such as tes.com.

✓ Engage students at the beginning of the lesson with exciting starters and learning hooks to capture their interest.

It is hard to tell you how to be creative without stifling the very thing we are talking about. However, what we do want to impress upon you is the importance of creativity! Being creative can make your lessons more engaging, more memorable and more challenging.

For creative approaches to be effective in the classroom, however, they must add value to the lesson and actually increase learning. A creative task that is lengthy and overcompli-cated is not a good use of your students' time. This balance will take time to fine-tune and there will inevitably be lessons in which you get it wrong. Do not scrap resources from these lessons. Instead, reflect on what did and didn't work and try again with another class – practice and experience often make perfect with creative activities.

Try to think outside the box. Are there other ways you can teach the content? Are there ways in which the students can gain the information without you just telling them? Are there approaches which will get the students moving or talking? Try altering the lesson structure so that the students are working on something before you talk them through it, rather than the classic lesson structure of 'teach then apply'. Take inspiration from other subjects and think about making the most of tangible or craft resources such as modelling clay or pipe cleaners. You don't have to come up with all the ideas yourself: join mailing lists on teaching websites, get involved on social media sites such as Twitter – loads of ideas are shared for free on Twitter – and read books on approaches to planning and delivering engaging lessons.[25]

Creativity is also vital when you are differentiating lessons for students with SEND or EAL. Students with EAL will need more visual cues and support than native speakers; it will be helpful if the abstract is made concrete. If you are not focusing on developing writing skills at the time, you may also want to think about providing alternative ways for them to respond to work if writing is hindering their progress. For example, is there another way they can provide answers so their attention is on the thinking rather than getting their ideas written down on paper? Think about getting them to create something – a drawing or model of the answer, perhaps – or give them supportive resources that allow them to access the thinking of the lesson.[26] Students with SEND need creative individual and personalised support too. For example, how would you teach picture source interpretation to a visually impaired student? Or how would you teach sound waves to a hearing impaired student?[27]

> One thing that I will always remember from my training year is my first mentor telling me that if the content is a little dull, I should make up for it with the activity. The lessons I love teaching are those that include a verging-on-cheesy context-based puzzle or mystery. The starter introduces the context, and then students have to use higher order skills to crack the case. For example, in a lesson on genetics, my starter introduced the students to some fictional guests from *The Jeremy Kyle Show* who wanted to settle a paternity dispute. The students had to acquire and apply new knowledge of dominant and recessive characteristics to find out who the father was. The show's DNA testing machine was broken on that day so unfortunately they had to use deductive logic and their understanding of variation and inheritance instead.

---

25   One such example is Paul Ginnis' *The Teacher's Toolkit: Raising Classroom Achievement with Strategies for Every Learner* (Carmarthen: Crown House Publishing, 2002).

26   There are lots of examples available at: https://eal.britishcouncil.org/teachers/effective-teaching-eal-learners.

27   For advice and ideas, see The Macular Society's resource series: https://www.macularsociety.org/form/resources-help-make-lessons-accessible-visually-impaired-students and Ron Doorn, 'Teaching hearing impaired children', *TEACH Magazine* (2008). Available at: http://www.teachmag.com/archives/130.

To-do

☐ Ensure your creativity adds value to the learning taking place.

☐ Think outside the box and take inspiration from a range of sources.

☐ Be creative when differentiating.

**To read:**

Brin Best and Will Thomas, *The Creative Teaching and Learning Toolkit* (London: Continuum, 2007).

*Teach Thought,* '101 Ways For Teachers To Be More Creative' (n. d.). Available at: https://www.teachthought.com/pedagogy/101-ways-for-teachers-to-be-more-creative/.

Roy Watson-Davis, *Creative Teaching Pocketbook*, 2nd edn (Alresford: Teachers' Pocketbooks, 2010).

# 14. Mentor–Trainee Relationships

A developing trainee will:

✓ Be organised and prepared for mentor meetings, with all necessary forms correctly filled in.

✓ Not be afraid to ask for help, both inside and outside the classroom.

✓ Make good use of mentor meetings by asking lots of questions and extending the professional dialogue to ensure they fully understand the advice.

The more you invest into the mentor–trainee relationship, the more you will get from it. We know that the training year is tiring, and we know that you are busy. However, by taking enough time to properly prepare for mentor meetings they will become less like the chore that you must get through once a week, and more like the valuable and personalised developmental sessions that they should be.

Before each mentor meeting, make sure that you take the time to reflect on your week of teaching: what went well, what could have gone better, where was the learning hindered and what new things did you try this week? Come up with a list of issues or questions that you have for your mentor based on these reflections.

Your mentor will often ask you to think about how you could have gone about things differently, and what impact this might have had. They may also offer you suggestions based on things that have worked for them. Ask lots of questions! To help you think like a thriving teacher, you need to understand the reasoning behind the decisions that thriving teachers make. Start by asking your mentor to explain when they would implement a certain idea or what signals they would look for from the students to know whether an approach is working, then consider how you will apply this to your own practice.

Your mentor meetings also act as a safe space in which to discuss things you have observed in other lessons. Ask your mentor to help you reflect on things you have seen, and about the reasoning or pedagogy behind them. They shouldn't go back to the teacher in question to tell them what you think of their lesson, but it is still advisable to speak and act with a certain amount of diplomacy.

> The best mentors are kind. Hopefully they won't expect you to be perfect. It's okay to get things wrong. In the early survival days, coaching conversations can be deeply unhelpful if not conducted well. Ask your mentor to tell you what you should do and try to listen to them. A good mentor will encourage you to have a go and try new things and you'll feel safe to ask questions until you get things. As you learn to be more in control then the relationship can shift to coaching whereby you can find solutions yourself by talking with your mentor. If you are unlucky and have a mentor that you don't get on with then remember to remain professional. They are still the expert teacher and there are things you can learn from them.
>
> Lianne Allison, Deputy Head Teacher, Durrington High School

Ask about the pedagogy behind the topics you are discussing, but do bear in mind that most mentors are not experts in every aspect of teaching. Therefore, some meetings will develop into detailed pedagogical discussion, while others may provide you with some printouts or search terms to take away and process yourself.

Together with your mentor you will also set targets to work towards in the following week, using an observation notebook to inform your thoughts. An observation notebook is simply an exercise book that teachers can write their feedback in during your lessons – and not just the formally observed ones. Make sure that you are involved in the setting of your targets. If you have something you particularly want to work on then make it a target, but also seek advice from your mentor. Make sure your targets are achievable, specific and will make a tangible difference to your teaching practice. Vague wording is unhelpful: it would be much better for a target to be 'Include two tasks which stretch and challenge the most able students per lesson' than merely 'Improve differentiation.' 'Develop a behaviour plan for Student A which will prevent them from talking over me' is a much better target than 'Improve behaviour management.' You should also ensure that you and your mentor have the same understanding of what these targets will look like in practice so that you are both expecting to see the same developments in your lesson planning.

Finally, don't forget that your mentor is also a full-time teacher who will have lots of planning and marking to do themselves. Therefore, be mindful of when to ask questions and of how much you can expect from them. Do ask pressing questions as they come up, but if you can wait for an answer, try to save them for your designated mentor meeting. Some mentors will be willing to give up more time than others but remember that everyone's school experience will be slightly different, so be prepared to use your common sense with regards to this relationship.

**To-do**

- ☐ Reflect on your week prior to your mentor meeting, considering progress you have made and areas to improve.

- ☐ Have pre-planned questions ready to ask your mentor about your lessons, experiences, pedagogy and observations. Use the answers and feedback to improve your practice.

- ☐ Set mutually agreed targets which are specific, achievable and will make a tangible difference to your teaching.

**To read:**

Trevor Wright, *Guide to Mentoring: Advice for the Mentor and Mentee* (London: ATL, 2012). Available at: https://www.atl.org.uk/Images/ATL%20Guide%20to%20 mentoring%20(Nov%2012).pdf.

# 15. Observing Others

A developing trainee will:

✓ Critically observe the class teacher before taking over new classes.

✓ Balance taking notes during lessons alongside engaging with the class while they are working.

✓ Have a target of observing at least one lesson outside of their placement timetable per week.

The training year is hard, it is busy and you will feel like you spend all of your time planning lessons. It is the same for most student teachers. It is therefore all too easy to spend all of your free time at school working on planning and on filling in your next set of mentor meeting forms. However, we implore you not to fall into this pattern of working. As a trainee, you have more free periods than you will ever have again, so please make the most of them! One way you can do this is by observing other teachers throughout the length of each placement. We recommend setting a target of at least one per week.

Have a particular focus for each observation.[28] For example, you may want to look specifically at behaviour management strategies or questioning techniques. This way you will be able to examine the nuances of the teacher's practice and gather ideas effectively.

When arranging observations, send the teacher in question a quick email asking to observe them, giving the specific date and time you would like to see them teach and letting them know your observation focus. This will allow them to check whether they are doing something that would be worth your while observing. There is little point in observing a summative assessment lesson when you want to focus on group discussion, for example. They may even deliberately adapt their lesson to match your focus.

Observe a range of teachers from your department – for example, those who are very experienced and those who are less experienced; those who have been at the school a long time and those who are new to the school. You can then gain the wisdom that comes with experience, along with the new ideas that come with being recently out of teacher education.

---

28 For advice on this see: Liverpool John Moores University, *The LJMU Guide to Observing Teaching and Learning for Postgraduate Secondary Initial Teacher Education*. Available at: http://www.itt-placement. com/downloads/section-e/secondary/LJMU_GuideToLessonObservingTeachingAndLearning.pdf.

Though your mentor will tell you to conduct observations, they will not arrange these for you. What they can provide you with, however, are names. Ask them for the names of teachers outside of your department who are well thought of with regard to your particular focus. Seeking out modellers of good practice will ensure you get the most out of your observations.

There are an awful lot of things to consider when observing other teachers and it can feel overwhelming. Remember that experienced teachers have put a lot of work and persistence into the finished article that you can't see during an observation. If you are fortunate enough to see how an experienced teacher sets up a new class then you will gain an understanding of the start of that journey and you also need to consider how you will set your expectations with any new class that you work with. To understand the success of expert teachers then you need to see all of the groundwork that has been put in for weeks, months and years before. It will all seem effortless but of course it isn't!

Focus on a few things during your observation and don't try to consider everything:

■ Break your observation notes up into elements of teaching such as questioning, modelling and explaining.

■ Consider the level of challenge and whether the students are being appropriately differentiated for.

■ Consider the engagement levels and the positive use of language and behaviour systems.

■ Consider the feedback that the students are receiving and whether this is supporting their progress.

Finally go and observe some of your trainees and some less experienced teachers. Sometimes it is important to see fellow teachers making the sorts of mistakes that come from inexperience in order to give you an understanding of your own developing practice.

Lianne Allison, Deputy Head Teacher, Durrington High School

You can get more from an observation by looking back through students' books. Learning is a process that occurs over time, so look for developments and changes in students' work. Compare the work to marking or feedback in the books and try to connect the two. How have teachers made a positive impact on their students' understanding? What has worked well? What has been less effective? Look at the presentation of the work, the style of the feedback comments and the challenge level of the work. Use this to further inform your own planning, marking and expectations.

Observing other teachers is only a useful tool if you use it to support your own practice. Make some notes either during or immediately after your observation and critically reflect on these. Think about the outcomes of different teaching strategies and the suitability of them for all classes. Things that worked well for a high ability Year 10 class may not work so well for a bottom set Year 8 group. Trial approaches and ideas in your own lessons, or adapt what you are already doing to explore the effects of different strategies. Reflect again on whether they improved your lesson, whether they suit your teaching style or whether they could be further tweaked for you to use again more effectively.

At the end of a lesson you have observed, remember to thank the teacher. We would also advise you to tell them something you liked about the lesson. Just like trainees, experienced teachers care about their lessons and may be feeling anxious about how you perceived their practice. By giving them some positive feedback you can easily alleviate any concerns, as well as opening the door for supportive professional dialogue.

If you feel comfortable doing so, speak to the teacher in more detail about the lesson. Ask them about the motivation behind the choices they made. For example, they may have made a behaviour management decision that seemed too harsh or too soft to you, which may be due to their expectations for behaviour or a result of wider issues affecting the student in question. For example, the teacher may know that the student has been refusing to attend school for the past month and not want to scare them off on the rare occasion they have attended. Asking these questions will help you model informed decision making when you are faced with similar issues in your own practice.

There are further ways to make use of observations that we would recommend. Discuss with your mentor the possibility of spending a whole day observing off timetable. A particularly informative thing to do is follow a student for a day. This will show you how their experiences can be affected by the teachers they have, and also demonstrate just how transient and disjointed the school day can feel. One minute they are being told to focus on their style of written prose, and later in another lesson, they are being provided with lists of facts to commit to memory. It is important for teachers to have an idea of how their subject fits into the wider education of students and their school day.

You could do several day-long student observations, with a focus on different types of issue. Following a student with behavioural issues and seeing how their attitude changes as the day goes by is perhaps an obvious suggestion. How about following a particularly quiet student to see how their manner changes in different lessons and the approaches different teachers use to try to draw them out of their shell? You could follow a student with SEND to see how provision for their needs varies across the school or if the tasks they are given are similar from one lesson to the next. Any student who takes your interest – particularly if they're in your class and you are finding it difficult to engage with them – is worth following.

Another day-long observation that is absolutely worthwhile pursuing is following a teaching assistant (TA) or learning support assistant (LSA) for a day. In order to most effectively work with learning support staff, we must understand what their role entails and what best practice for communication looks like. Some are specialised in a particular field of support – for example, offering help to students with a visual or hearing impairment – so do let your mentor know if there is one particular area of practice you would like to see, and they will be able to arrange this. Gaining insights into the reality of their role and just how tough it is will help you to best utilise their expertise in the future.

To-do

☐ Arrange observations with a specific focus point in mind for each.

☐ Look at students' books during your observations to gain an idea of progress over time.

☐ Observe a range of teachers across your school, not just in your department.

☐ Arrange to follow a student for a day and to shadow support staff.

☐ Reflect on your observations and implement new ideas into your own lessons.

**To read:**

Matt O'Leary, *Classroom Observation: A Guide to the Effective Observation of Teaching and Learning* (Abingdon: Routledge, 2014).

Ginger Weade and Carolyn Evertson, 'On what can be learned by observing teaching', *Theory into Practice*, 30(1) (1991): 37–45.

# 16. Being Observed

A developing trainee will:

✓ Plan their observation lesson several days before they are due to teach it.

✓ Run through the lesson with the class teacher.

✓ Prepare for the observation by making sure they know the students by name and are aware of any individuals with needs that will have to be differentiated for in their planning.

✓ Have the lesson plan, class data and seating plan printed for the observer.

The first thing that you should understand is that an observed lesson is not like a normal lesson. By this, we mean it is expected that you will put more time and effort into your observed lesson than your normal lessons. This is obvious to experienced teachers, but sometimes isn't so to trainees. Although it could be argued that, consequently, observations don't provide an honest representation of a teacher's day-to-day practice, observers do want to see the best that you can be in an isolated lesson, so this is what you must plan for. Most ITT courses involve two formal observations that are conducted by the course provider followed by weekly or fortnightly observations by teachers at the school to monitor progress throughout the placement.

When planning your observation lesson, be really clear about the learning objectives and what it will look like when students meet these. Think about the activities you plan to use and the assessment tools you will use throughout the lesson to check class progress towards the learning objectives. Though this sounds basic, it is often good to refocus before an observation and double check that you have a clear destination for the lesson, as well as the directions to get there.

We find it helps to give the students some context for the learning, so remind students briefly at the start of the lesson about topics covered previously. Or, even better, get them to remind you! Your activities and your plenary should show that learning has occurred – the students didn't know something but now they do. Although most educationalists accept that true learning occurs over a series of lessons, all teachers are under pressure to evidence progress in each and every lesson.[29]

---

29  Roy Blatchford, 'How teachers can show student progress during lesson observations', *SecEd* (28 February 2013). Available at: http://www.sec-ed.co.uk/best-practice/how-teachers-can-show-student-progress-during-lesson-observations/.

Once you have your basic outline, you should set about refining it. Think about differentiation first: how you plan to extend and support all learners during each episode of the lesson. Next, look through your class data: are there students who need personalised differentiation? Are there students with SEND or EAL? Which students will need additional challenge? Then, go through your lesson looking for points at which less able students may become stuck or may struggle with logistics, instructions or content. Help these students to access the lesson by planning strategies of support to drop in at these points.

You may be lucky enough to have had a chance to get to know the class, which will help you to identify the sort of support or adjustment that particular individuals will need – for example, the font size that is readable for a student with a visual impairment. If not, then make sure to interrogate the class teacher to find out this information. Finally, to further personalise the lesson, design the questions you intend to ask, and consider which ability level they are suited to. Ensure you decide who you are going to ask key questions to as well. This is a good technique to make a habit when lesson planning. See Chapter 9: Questioning for more advice.

If you have taught the class several times before, then reflect on your previous lessons with them before you begin to plan your observed lesson. How was learning restricted? Who was off task? You could include these observations on the lesson plan if you want to show an understanding of the class dynamic. Or more simply, you could make a note to yourself to ensure that you deliberately target certain students with your classroom management strategies early in the lesson.

A tip for observed lessons is to over-plan. It is important you make every moment count, so make sure you have plenty of activities for the class to undertake, and several extension tasks to make sure you are always stretching that one student who seems to fly through everything you give them. If your plenary is question based, try to devise more than you plan to use. This will allow you to ask the most pertinent questions to check understanding, while also ensuring you have enough content to avoid the awkward waiting around for the bell phase if you have an extra few minutes at the end of the lesson.

Once you have planned your lesson, ensure you have time for the class teachers to give you some feedback. It is often useful to have more than one person look over your lesson, so you could also ask your mentor, who may well be better versed in the grading descriptors than the class teacher, or your professional tutor to have a look at it. They may be able to identify things that will easily improve your lesson which you may have missed, particularly if you have already spent lots of time on it. You could also run your ideas past other trainees at the school as they will have different strengths and may be able to offer some useful insights.

You may also wish to further prepare for your observation by marking a piece of work done by the class. This will allow you to check their current understanding and refresh your knowledge of points to focus on with particular individuals – for example, poor spelling or slow writing. It will, of course, be noticed by the observer that you are providing the class with meaningful feedback and utilising marked work to inform your planning – an important aspect of the Teachers' Standards. Also make sure that you have established your routines and seating plan before the observation lesson so that you don't find students saying unhelpful things like 'you never normally make us do that'!

Set up the classroom in advance of the lesson. If someone is using the room right before your lesson then ask whether they mind you setting your things up at the side of the room either before school, at break or at lunch. This will give you a nice calm and organised start to the lesson so you can prioritise settling the class and getting the learning started rather than setting up that complicated demonstration or activity.

Focus your observer on areas you are trying to work on. If you are gathering evidence for the Teachers' Standards then observations provide an opportunity to fill gaps. They are also a time to demonstrate progress towards your mentor targets.

Have faith in the person who is observing you as they are not there to catch you out. It can feel stressful as you are under scrutiny but getting things wrong and getting feedback is how we learn.

Be prepared to reflect on mistakes and don't be defensive. The observer may have a different opinion to you and their opinion will be valid. They were in a position to study the whole room. Explore how you could have done things differently with the observer. Effective evaluation is the key to future improvements.

Lianne Allison, Deputy Head Teacher, Durrington High School

After the lesson, you will be given feedback by the observer. Before you have this meeting, spend some time reflecting on what you were pleased with, aspects that didn't go as well and things you would do differently if you were to teach the lesson again. When you receive the feedback, be honest with the observer about your reflections, as they will be looking to see whether what you think matches up with what they did. Also, in your NQT year and beyond you won't have an observer to give you this level of consistent feedback, so developing your own ability to reflect now is of great importance. It is perfectly acceptable to make mistakes during your training year – and beyond. However, it is vital that you recognise these mistakes and can reflect on how to improve. This makes for a truly reflective practitioner.

In the feedback session, you may find that the observer disagrees about something that you honestly feel you did well. Teaching involves a lot of subtleties which are easily missed, particularly by someone who does not know the class. Do not be afraid to disagree with their feedback if you feel that you have, for example, differentiated for the class in ways that have gone unnoticed. In this instance, you could discuss individuals in the class and how you personalised the lesson to best support their progress. It is important to see these feedback sessions as a discussion, so don't be afraid to put forward your opinions too.

During my first placement, I was once observed by both my mentor and university tutor. This felt like a big deal because it was the first time that someone from my university was observing me and I wanted to impress. I had been doing well from the start of the placement, regularly achieving a 'Good' grade in formal observations. In retrospect I was probably coasting, a cardinal sin for thriving trainees! I thought the observation went fairly well, but when given feedback I was told it was just 'Satisfactory' and, to be honest, I got a bit of a telling off. The key problem was that I hadn't really reflected on feedback from previous observations that would have pushed me from 'Good' to 'Outstanding' and in doing so had in fact regressed in my teaching skills. I remember telling my university tutor that this would be a turning point for me and that I wouldn't ever allow myself to coast or accept just doing 'well' again. From that moment on I always took reflecting on and implementing feedback seriously, always aiming to be the very best I could be. I even nailed that 'Outstanding' in a future observation by my university tutor. Sometimes you just need a wake-up call to push you to reach your potential, although taking feedback on board earlier would have avoided the plateau in the first place.

☐ Take more time to plan an observed lesson than you would a normal lesson.

☐ Ensure you have covered all of the basics – starter, activities that clearly demonstrate learning, differentiation, AfL and plenary.

☐ Get feedback on your lesson plan from your mentor and other members of staff before the observation.

☐ Prepare thoroughly – mark student work and ensure the classroom is set up beforehand.

☐ Reflect on the lesson prior to receiving feedback from your observer.

To-do

**To read:**

Chapter 8 in Ross Morrison McGill, *100 Ideas for Secondary Teachers: Outstanding Lessons* (London: Bloomsbury Education, 2013).

# 17. Acting on Feedback

A developing trainee will:

✓ Understand feedback from lesson observations and attempt to incorporate this into their future planning.

✓ Act upon feedback in the following lesson with the observed class.

✓ Ask their mentor to clarify if unsure about feedback or how to act upon it.

✓ Have a system of documenting feedback from observations.

Teaching isn't an act which you can ever 'perfect'. There, we've said it. A thriving trainee recognises this and instead focuses on developing the ability to reflect on their practice and strives to consistently improve, day on day and week on week. Reflection is a skill that successful teachers will draw upon regularly. The trajectory of developing and improving your practice will not be smooth, nor will it always feel like you are moving forwards. Don't ever let this get you down or allow it to lower your confidence. Every teacher has thrilling, genuine highs and challenging, painful lows. A job such as ours, working with hundreds of individuals in an expectant, charged, exciting environment, necessitates as much.

The key to developing a balanced, level view on these highs and lows is to develop your skills as a reflective teacher. Being reflective means considering, with honesty and thought, the successes and failures you have had. Analyse a lesson as a whole but also unpick particular areas such as planning, differentiation, behaviour and feedback. A great resource for scaffolding your reflections is the 5 Minute Lesson Review developed by Shaun Allison and Ross Morrison McGill.[30] During your training year, your ability to be reflective will be supported by observations of your practice by more experienced teachers. This is the only year in your teaching career during which you will receive such regular feedback on your strengths and weaknesses, so although this may feel like a persistent pressure, a thriving trainee will see it as an opportunity.

One challenge during your training year is managing the sheer volume of feedback you are likely to get lesson upon lesson. Therefore, one of the most important things you can do is to have a clear focus on certain areas for improvement each week. Based upon lesson observations from the previous week, and in conjunction with your mentor, aim to work on just three key targets each week. We recommend keeping a log of these targets so that you can begin to spot trends regarding areas in which you are weaker and thus need to invest more time developing. This can also be used as evidence towards the Teachers' Standards.

To ensure that you make progress, you do need to invest considerable time and thought in these three targets. You can approach these targets in a number of ways:

- Take advantage of the experience your mentor, and other teachers within your department, has to offer by asking them not only what the target is but, more importantly, what tangible actions you can take to try to address it.

- Make sure that you are really clear about what your focuses are and how you can meet them. Ask for clarification if you are unsure.

- Discuss your targets and ideas for meeting them with your university tutor and your ITT cohort.

- Utilise the experience and knowledge of those around you.

---

30  Ross Morrison McGill and Shaun Allison, 'The #5MinReview by @TeacherToolkit and @shaun_allison', *Class Teaching* [blog] (29 September 2013). Available at: https://classteaching.wordpress.com/2013/09/29/the-5minreview-by-teachertoolkit-and-shaun_allison/.

■ Use your target areas as a focus for your observations of experienced staff (see Chapter 15: Observing Others).

A thriving trainee won't leave it there; they will do their own research to develop their skills and understanding around the target area. So get online, visit blogs and teaching websites, delve into peer-reviewed research or pedagogical literature and gather some ideas about how you can improve. You can even find some great tips on YouTube!

Of course, there is one final – and essential – step, which is to incorporate the ideas you have discussed, approaches you have read about or strategies you have seen in action into your actual lessons. You should ensure that every lesson will try to clearly address the targets you have been given. This will help to develop consistency, while also creating a virtuous cycle of reflecting on your targets, researching ways to address them, trying new ideas, reflecting on how successful you have been, trying other ideas and so on.

For this cycle to work, you must make sure that you are always reflecting upon how far you have developed your targets within each lesson. What was a success? Why did it work? Would it work with another class? Or another year group? What didn't work? Why wasn't it successful? Should you drop the idea, or can it be adapted and improved? Would it work better with another class? Or at another time of day?

You won't get it right straight away, and this is fine. As we said before, even the most experienced teachers may still misjudge a task for a class. In fact, recognising this is a strength. The key is to aim for gradual, tangible progress. As the weeks go by, a successful trainee will have to become adept at spinning plates. In your first week you had three set targets, in your second you have to keep improving on those first three targets while also adding three more, in your third … well, you get the idea. This is challenging, and you shouldn't be surprised if some plates spin slower or fall down. Do be prepared to pick the plates up, focus on how to get them spinning again and then ready yourself to pick up the new ones to add to the act. In the long term, the work you do on these targets each week should become embedded into your practice and this is how thriving teachers are developed. Starting this process in your training year – with the support and guidance of your mentor and university – will set you up for the years ahead!

To-do

☐ Work on a maximum of three new targets per week.

☐ Get into the habit of addressing your targets in your weekly lessons.

☐ Observe those teachers with strengths that match your targets.

☐ Engage with evidence and research to further develop your thinking and progress towards your targets.

**To read:**

Chapter 8 in Shaun Allison, *Perfect Teacher-Led CPD* (Carmarthen: Independent Thinking Press, 2014).

# 18. The Second Placement

A developing trainee will:

✓ Have developed the skills to cope with the greater number of lessons which will be added to their timetable.

✓ Build upon skills gained in the first placement.

✓ Develop remaining areas of weakness that were identified at the end of the first placement.

✓ Become less dependent on their mentor.

The second placement can be as daunting a prospect as the first one. There will be heightened expectations from your new mentor – as well as your own expectations – an increased teaching load and a brand new school, colleagues and students to get to know. Yet the second placement is also a fantastic opportunity for a thriving trainee to really push on and improve their practice in preparation for the NQT year to come. You will have developed some real strengths during your first placement, but the very best teachers demonstrate consistent strengths across all of the Teachers' Standards. The second placement is your opportunity to consolidate your existing skills and become a well-rounded trainee teacher.

One of the things I notice with school placements is that there is a kind of myth that when you go into the second it's going to be easier because you've just progressed from your first. However, the second placement can be harder, not just because you're teaching more hours but often because you've built up a comfort zone, you've understood the class-room and school routines and you've built up a contextual professional knowledge. Then you're dragged out of it and put somewhere new. At the same time you're looking for a job, completing the academic assignments that are coming in and on top of that the pupils know that you're a trainee teacher. Whereas in the first placement you joined the school at the start of the academic year, meaning they just saw you as another teacher, now you're an 'alien' who has dropped in halfway through the year.

Dr Simon Thompson, Head of Education, University of Sussex

Before you begin your second placement, have a clear development plan to work towards. This should be written at the end of your first placement in agreement with your mentor. Ensure that you have carefully reflected upon your areas of strength and those which still require improvement. Perhaps more importantly, consider how you are going to address your remaining weaknesses throughout the second placement. This should be the focus of the initial meeting with your new mentor: to discuss your strengths and weaknesses and devise strategies which will address the latter while building upon the former. Ensure that you have both short-term goals – which may be to target specific weaknesses – but also long-term goals, focused upon developing skills and competencies pertaining to specific Teachers' Standards. You can also use your second placement as an opportunity to take part in a larger project to meet some of the standards you are yet to evidence. This could be achieved by getting involved with designing displays for your department, or by assisting in the running of a club. Another key area of thought as you begin the second placement should be the job application process. Again, it would be wise to discuss this topic with your mentor during your initial meeting.

The second placement is not only important in developing your teaching practice, it is a great opportunity for a fresh start! You have the chance to create and develop a new and improved teaching persona, learning from any fundamental mistakes you may have made in the first placement and embracing the opportunity to put these lessons into practice with new classes. While children are incredibly forgiving – and forgetful – memories of mistakes made and difficult classes can dent teachers' confidence and hold them back from really pushing themselves. This is why the second placement is so important. Begin your second placement with the mindset that you are now a competent teacher who is ready to really push on. No one in your second placement school will have any reason to believe differently. You have laid the foundations to become a thriving teacher and now have the opportunity to strive to achieve the very best that you can.

During your second placement, try to take responsibility for developing a short scheme of work (SoW), including an assessment. Discuss this with your mentor at the start of the placement and discuss which classes and topics would be most suitable. Plan the overall 'big picture' of the scheme with your mentor, confirming not only the overall topic, but also the assessment style and focus, as well as an outline of the lessons that will need to be taught in preparation for the assessment. Taking this opportunity to develop a top-down view of what a sequence of lessons will look like is an essential skill for a thriving trainee. Not only does this allow you to stretch yourself – to put into action all of the various teaching skills you developed during your first placement – but is also excellent preparation for your NQT year, in which you may well be expected to plan SoWs for your whole department to use. Finally, make sure you maintain your reflective approach throughout this process and consider which aspects of the SoW were a success, and which you would change or adapt next time. This won't be a perfect sequence of lessons, but it will give you fantastic experience to take into your NQT year and beyond.

As you already know, your contact hours will increase during your second placement. This will be a challenge at first, but at around two-thirds of the way into the placement you will hopefully find that, although you are still incredibly busy, your planning strategies are making the workload manageable! If you are *only just* coping with the increased hours at this stage then insist on continuing at these hours and don't take on any extra.

It is really important to be realistic about managing your workload and not push yourself to breaking point. However, if you want an additional challenge, you might wish to ask for additional lessons, perhaps for the final two weeks of the second placement, to begin to work towards – and gain experience of – an NQT timetable. The increased number of lessons at the start of your NQT year can be a real shock, so getting a taste of it now can really help you to strategically – and mentally – prepare to hit the ground running and focus on developing skills in planning and organisation, as well as resilience for the start of your NQT year.

Don't forget to observe outstanding teachers in your second placement too. Make the time at the beginning to speak with your professional tutor for pointers regarding who to observe. You will also need to begin to decide on your own preferred approaches, whether this is managing poor behaviour or differentiating for students with EAL. You are now starting to develop your own personal teaching style. You will, of course, have to consistently adapt your approach depending on the individuals you teach, but will also need to begin to separate out those strategies which work better for you from those other ideas

*Figure 2. Create your own teaching style tree.*

which are less effective. Treat your personal pedagogical approach like a tree that you are going to decorate.

You must decide which strategies, approaches and techniques you are going to hang from each branch – for example, your preferred strategies regarding EAL, differentiation, SEND, etc. You won't be able to hang every single idea and technique for each facet of teaching on your tree, so you will have to be selective and your choices will define your approach. Treat the second placement as an opportunity to decide which approaches best fit your style and begin to decorate your tree!

> I was fortunate enough to have an outstanding mentor and professional tutor on my second placement. I felt that I ended my first placement at a good level, solid across the Teachers' Standards and ready to push myself towards 'Outstanding' practice. My mentor recognised this and set expectations at the very highest level – any mistake in the planning or delivery of my lessons would be picked up on and, importantly, I'd be supported to negate it in the future. My professional tutor had a fantastic approach to teaching, with the positive wellbeing of the students at the centre of all advice given. The placement had many ups and downs, successes and failures, but in my mind I knew that if I utilised the experiences and approaches of my mentor and professional tutor, alongside my first-hand experiences gained on placement and at university, I would add a lot of new approaches and methods to my tree. My tree is still growing, like every teacher's, and through a combination of engaging in research, keeping an open mind to a range of opinions and letting my experiences shape me, I am having to add – and remove – decorations each and every week.

**To-do**

☐ Write a clear development plan with your mentor at the end of your first placement ready to take to your new school.

☐ Continue to observe outstanding teachers.

☐ Begin to develop your own teaching style and decorate your tree!

**To read:**

> Andrew Pollard (ed), *Readings for Reflective Teaching in Schools* (London: Bloomsbury Academic, 2014).

# 19. Stress and Time Management

A developing trainee will:

✓ Be aware of how increasing workload can impact on wellbeing.

✓ Be aware that certain times in a term can be more stressful than others.

✓ Make good use of their support network – family, friends, mentor and professional tutor – and be honest with them about how they are feeling throughout the course.

Stress is a side effect of many jobs and teaching is a profession which is renowned for being highly stressful. Your training year will be hard and there will be times when you may find yourself working late planning, but accepting and managing this will put you on track to becoming a thriving teacher.

You need to be aware that there will be busy periods within the academic year during which stress levels will be higher. The first term of any year for any teacher, experienced or new, is always the hardest and often the longest. Within each term there can be pinch points where marking volume can increase suddenly due to a spurt of end of term tests, or pressure can increase due to GCSE and A level exams. Being prepared for these periods will help to alleviate stress.

One effective strategy that we have found helps to reduce stress is the use of mindfulness exercises.[31] These can be used within school at stressful moments – for example, when feeling overwhelmed by that long email list or when you are faced with a difficult situation in the classroom. They will help you to keep your cool and remain focused in the moment. There are many exercises that you can use; you need to find the most appropriate for you.

Teachers must have a work–life balance. Achieving this is easier said than done and your first three years of teaching will be the hardest. However, the following strategies should help you to maintain a positive balance while still enabling you to excel.

---

31  Jennifer Baker-Jones, Liz Lord and Willem Kuyken, 'Mindfulness in schools: is it just another trend?', *Impact: Journal of the Chartered College of Teaching*, Issue 2 (February 2018). Available at: https://impact.chartered.college/article/baker-jones-mindfulness-schools-another-trend/.

Firstly, decide on certain times when you are not going to work. For example, decide that Friday evenings and Saturdays are your allotted days off. This might not sound a lot now, but once you're into your training year this time will be very welcome, although unfortunately might be hard to achieve. Even when the pressure is really on, organise your time to ensure that you always get your well-deserved breaks – it might just be the thing that keeps you from getting overstressed during this tough year.

Without regular downtime the job can take over and begin to have a negative impact on your life. If you are able to, it would be good to reserve one evening a week to attend that sports club or meet with your friends. Being out of the house means that you legitimately cannot work, and thus won't feel guilty. Having a plan of when to work and when not to, and sticking to the plan, will allow you to still go to running club on a Wednesday evening, though you may need to do some extra work on the Tuesday. The key is knowing when to stop. No one can function well in the classroom if they have worked continuously for seven days on very little sleep. You need to be on top form for your lessons, so taking a break is okay!

Secondly, you will need to accept that not everything will get done. The to-do list is never blank as a teacher, and things are constantly being added to it. Prioritising your to-do list is essential. Make sure you complete the absolutely necessary and then, if you have spare time, start on the less urgent tasks and know what can be parked for now. Our mantra on this is do, defer, drop! Creating physical lists can be very helpful to prioritise tasks and ensure nothing important gets overlooked.[32] We often use the Sticky Notes app to organise our to-do lists: one for essential tasks (do) and one for tasks that will need completing but aren't urgent (defer). If any tasks don't fall into these two categories then drop them! You could also go back through your lists numbering everything according to its priority and then work through the tasks in order. Your lists can change and tasks can move across the categories; they are always working lists, so be prepared to return to them frequently.

One final piece of advice with regards to these lists is that sometimes we are inclined to feel that we can only relax once everything is done, but switching off despite still having tasks on your to-do list is a feeling you will learn to sit comfortably with. Be aware of what is possible to achieve in any one day and then, when you have finished, mentally and physically put the lists down, ready to be picked up again tomorrow.

---

32  Bianca Amponsah, 'How to cope with stress as a teacher', *The Education Network* (20 April 2017). Available at: http://theeducationnetwork.co.uk/coping-with-stress/.

When I first started my PGCE I found myself working all hours of the day and night, including at weekends. I was constantly controlled by my to-do lists and not able to switch off until I had completed them. This soon proved unsustainable and I was starting to become extremely tired. I realised I had to compartmentalise the job. I started setting myself working time zones on specific days – outside of the teaching timetable. In order to complete my work within these specific time zones I had to create two to-do lists: one for the priority work I had to complete and one for non-essential tasks. It was hard to relax when I knew I had more I could be doing and this was a feeling I couldn't settle with for a long time. However, due to starting this process early on in my PGCE year I have refined the process of creating two to-do lists and am now more able to sit comfortably with the feeling that there is always more to do! In this profession you can never complete everything by the end of the day. The sooner I realised this the quicker I was able to adopt a healthy work–life balance. I cannot stress enough how important it is to get into this habit early on in your PGCE so you become accustomed to it for your even busier NQT year.

**To-do**

☐ Find your favoured method of list writing. It may be on your phone, using an app or in a physical book. Discover which works best for you and stick with it.

☐ Identify the hobbies or social occasions you value most and be explicit with yourself about the activities you are not willing to lose. Be strict with your downtime – you deserve it!

☐ For advice and support from the Education Support Partnership on managing workload and work–life balance, visit http://www.bewellteachwell.org.uk/.

**To read:**

Harry Fletcher-Wood, *Ticked Off: Checklists for Teachers, Students, School Leaders* (Carmarthen: Crown House Publishing, 2016).

NUT, *NUT NQT Guide: Workload* (2017). Available at: https://neu.org.uk/help-and-advice/publications-and-resources.

Mark Williams and Danny Penman, *Mindfulness: A Practical Guide to Finding Peace in a Frantic World* (London: Piatkus, 2011).

# 20. Applying for Jobs

A developing trainee will:

✓ Look for jobs regularly on platforms such as the tes.com and the local authority website.

✓ Be aware of the type of school that is best suited to them – for example, large or small, mixed or single-sex, state or private.

✓ Prepare for interviews by requesting class data, which will normally include target grades and any SEND, EAL or G&T requirements.

Our first tip when applying for jobs is to be picky! Teaching is quite a transient profession, with teachers often being promoted within or moving on to experience a new challenge elsewhere. One advantage of this is that many jobs appear throughout the second half of the academic year. Teachers in England and Wales have to give three months' notice to leave at the end of the year, meaning that most jobs will appear in the run-up to 31 May. After this date, further jobs will continue to appear. You are at an advantage here, as from this point on other teachers cannot quit their current roles, leaving jobs that arise open either to those about to start the NQT year or those returning to teaching.

Our point is that you can afford – and, for your own development, need – to be selective about the schools you apply to. The school should be an environment in which you feel you will be able to thrive and develop as a teacher. Choose somewhere you can see yourself working, that will support you through the tricky NQT year, but also somewhere that will allow you to develop specific aspects of your practice. For example, the school may have more behavioural issues or EAL needs than you encountered on your placements.

When you have found a position that you may want to apply for, the first thing you really should do is visit the school. As a trainee, the chances are that the classes you currently teach are borrowed from a class teacher. If so, don't be afraid to speak to your mentor about arranging a morning or afternoon off to make time for school visits. It should be easy enough for the regular class teachers to take the lessons that day. Alternatively, maybe your timetable has a few free periods blocked together that you could make use of? If you are unable to get to the school during the working day, then it is still worth trying to arrange a visit after hours.

The school visit is really important and should not be underestimated! The benefit of visiting during the day is that you get to meet the students, and get a feel for the atmosphere and teaching in the school. You will, of course, still get a feel for this after hours but there will be fewer students milling around.

Normally, you will be met by the head teacher or perhaps a member of the senior leadership team (SLT). They will often give you a tour and answer any questions you have. Make sure you scour the school website and mentally note a few questions you will ask, focusing in particular on things that are not spelled out online. For example, what is the reward system? What is the set-up for tutor groups or houses? What is the marking policy within the department? What CPD opportunities are there for NQTs?

Just as this is an important opportunity for you to find out about the school, the school will also use the occasion to make a judgement about you. Emily was once told by a head teacher at interview that he knew he was going to offer her a position based on the way she spoke about the school during her pre-visit. So be sure to make a good impression.

The next step is writing your application. Fill in the application form completely and follow the instructions given about the personal statement or covering letter. If you are asked for one side of A4 do not give two, and don't use a very small font just to fit more on the page!

Talk about your strengths, evidencing everything by linking each point to something you have done during your training year. For example, if you say that you have helped develop engagement in your subject, link this to extracurricular activities you have run, or even a lesson activity that has worked to engage students beyond the lesson objectives. It is really important to consistently back up statements about your strengths with evidence. You should also refer to the job description and person specification to see which key attributes or values the school is asking for. Shape your writing around these, again evidencing how you meet each point. It is unlikely that you will be able to fit everything in so prioritise what you consider important, especially things that show off your experience. Consider the order in which you give information about yourself, putting the most valuable or impressive evidence earlier on.[33]

Once you get a call to interview, you will most likely be given a topic focus to prepare and deliver as a lesson, which can range from twenty minutes to a full hour. When you accept the interview, you should request data for the class involved. The school may send you a comprehensive data set including a seating plan, current and target grades,

33  See the TES careers advice pages for more on this: https://www.tes.com/jobs/careers-advice.

pupil premium (PP) information and details of students with SEND or EAL. They may, however, just send you the general target grade for the class. Work with what you get.

The school might not ask for a lesson plan, but make sure you provide one anyway. It does not have to be long, and you could use the pro forma you are used to working with. Be sure to highlight any actions you are going to take to support students with SEND or EAL and to plan your differentiation. This can be subtle and possibly missed by observers, so the lesson plan allows you to ensure they notice! If you are only required to teach part of a lesson, then still provide a plan as if you were teaching the whole thing, as this will allow the observers to see what you would have done were you given more time. Providing a detailed lesson plan demonstrates your organisational skills and thoroughness, as well as showing what you would have done if the lesson didn't go to plan. Finally, go through the lesson – and the plan – in a mentor meeting to get a pair of experienced eyes on it.

In your interview lesson, aim to show progress with clear learning objectives and thorough use of AfL. Make sure you move around the room and interact with the students as this will help you relax into the lesson. Perhaps start by giving each student a label to write their name on to help build rapport quickly, especially if you have not been provided with a seating plan. Don't feel that you have to teach a 'bells and whistles' lesson. It is much better to plan a solid lesson that allows all students to make progress and carries minimal risk of going awry; schools want to see that you can teach consistently strong lessons, not just a one-off extravaganza.

If you successfully pass the teaching stage you will then reach the formal interview process. You will most likely be asked to reflect on your lesson, so use any waiting time you are given to think about this. Offer specific suggestions about how you would improve areas that you felt were not up to scratch rather than superficially listing them. This shows true reflective ability.

There are plenty of lists of regularly asked interview questions online.[34] Make sure you use these to practise your answers. As with the personal statement, where possible, evidence your points with examples from your training year. Important questions that reliably come up at interview include:

- What does a good lesson look like?

- How do we become outstanding teachers?

- What are your strengths and weaknesses?

---

34  See, for example, Rebecca Ratcliffe, 'Top 10 questions teachers are asked at job interviews', *The Guardian* (29 January 2014). Available at: https://www.theguardian.com/teacher-network/teacher-blog/2014/jan/29/teacher-job-interview-questions-top-ten.

■ What other skills can you offer the school?

■ How do we ensure progress for all?

If you are unlucky this time, don't worry. The interview practice is valuable. It is also an excellent idea to ask for feedback or about how you should improve. Do this when they inform you about the outcome. Be sure to keep all interactions positive, even if you are disappointed. You never know when you may meet your interviewers again in the teaching world!

My first interview during my training year was at a school I had never visited before. I planned a thorough lesson packed full of assessment, following most of the advice we've set out in this chapter. During the lesson however, I panicked and made several rookie errors – for example, I let some behaviour issues slide and forgot to hand out extension tasks. After the lesson, I was waiting with the other candidates, berating myself for such silly mistakes, fully expecting to be sent home and not progress to the interview stage. However, I was lucky enough to be invited to stay for the next stage of the day. One of the first questions I faced in the interview asked me to reflect on the lesson. I used this opportunity to show how aware I was of the mistakes I had made and made sure to suggest how I would improve next time. They agreed that it could have gone better and at that point I thought I had really had it. The feedback after the interview was that due to the reflective skills I'd shown in the interview, I was one of the strongest candidates for the position. The moral of the story? Don't panic or give up if things don't go to plan. As long as you can show that you are pushing to develop your practice, you are making yourself look like an excellent mouldable NQT!

**To-do**

☐ Be picky – choose a school that you think will develop you as a teacher.

☐ Visit the school and treat this as an important opportunity to get a feel for it and to sell your own strengths. Ensure you have a list of questions ready to ask.

☐ Evidence your strengths in your supporting letter and prioritise what you're going to include, thinking about the order in which to do it.

☐ Plan a solid lesson that demonstrates key teaching skills and check this with your mentor.

☐ Prepare thoroughly for the interview by practising commonly asked questions.

## To read:

Paul K. Ainsworth, *Get That Teaching Job!* (London: Continuum, 2012).

Gerald Haigh, *Good Ideas for Good Teachers Who Want Good Jobs* (Carmarthen: Crown House Publishing, 2015).

Part Two:

# The NQT Year

Having finished your training year, you will – hopefully – now feel that you have a good grasp of the basics of classroom practice. No matter how successful you were in your training, this next year is a huge leap forwards in terms of your teaching. Your NQT or induction year is, at the time of writing at least, a statutory period aiming to bridge the transition from trainee to full-time on-your-own teacher. Induction was brought in after many teachers were found to be struggling with the increased demands of the job following their training year, with many leaving the profession altogether. We hope, of course, that you aren't considering this. So stick with us and we'll help you through!

Try not to think in terms of passing the NQT year but instead about how you can utilise the time to become the best teacher you can be for the children who will sit in front of you this year and in all following years. In Part Two, we will introduce you to the new opportunities and challenges that you will face when learning to thrive as an NQT.

# 21. Planning: Part II

A developing NQT will:

✓ Plan most of their lessons the day before as a *minimum*, even if morning planning is appealing.

✓ Print and check worksheets and resources the day before.

✓ Ensure that challenge and extension work is planned and delivered for every lesson.

✓ Share resources within their department.

✓ Plan a starter, main and plenary.

✓ Have clear learning objectives for every lesson.

A thriving NQT will find all of the above second nature but will also be able to get more from their planning. Planning every lesson to ensure that each minute of students' time is spent learning is a skill developed and refined with practice. To achieve this, you should over-plan every lesson, adding in extra tasks or activities. You don't want to find yourself with ten minutes spare at the end of a lesson. This is time which should be used to help students achieve their full potential, so ensure you have a range of tasks ready to stretch them. However, don't just add more of the same, these tasks need to be challenging and progress your students' learning. In order to ensure you are reaching this standard it is essential to plan your lessons the night before as a minimum. Planning on the day is not good practice as an NQT. Your planning skills are not yet refined enough to ensure you are able to plan a lesson containing all the requirements at the last minute and under pressure – you need to structure in reflection time.

Don't be afraid to try new things and be creative! Keep reading about pedagogy and research to give you new ideas. And keep embracing social media – Twitter and Pinterest are sure-fire sources of fresh approaches – and utilising TES resources.[1] Try to use one new task or activity a week. This may not sound like much, but it really adds to your repertoire over the course of the year. Try completing the tasks yourself to check that they make sense and are pitched at an appropriate difficulty level.

Try using a 'take 10' policy in which you take ten minutes every lesson to work in silence to create an atmosphere of focus and ensure that students develop their ability to work independently. Use this time for interventions with individual students or to carry out

---

1   See https://www.tes.com/teaching-resources.

some live marking (see Chapter 24: Marking and Feedback for more on this). By being consistent with your classes and embedding this into your planning, students will become familiar with the process.

Finally, being on top of your planning on a daily and weekly basis is an organisational feat in itself. As a thriving NQT you should organise your medium- and long-term planning regularly. Doing this ensures that you have enough time within the term or year to complete your SoWs. Reviewing your medium- (five to six lessons) and long-term (half a term's lessons) plans regularly and being able to adapt them for your classes demonstrates thorough organisation and brilliant teaching.

> During my NQT year I often shared my medium- and long-term plans with my teaching partners. This enabled me to show my organisational skills early on in the year, which led to me being given different organisational responsibilities within my department. Keep organised and take an active role in team meetings to show that you are engaging with planning at a departmental level and with the decisions being made. This will get you noticed and will prompt leadership to offer you additional opportunities and responsibilities.

**To-do**

☐ Check each lesson encompasses the planning techniques used during your training year (refer back to Chapter 6: Planning: Part I).

☐ Try one new task or activity per week.

☐ Check each lesson is planned with suitable challenge and accessibility in mind.

☐ Reflect on each lesson systematically.

☐ Spend time checking your medium- and long-term planning every three weeks.

**To read:**

Melanie Aberson and Debbie Light, *Lesson Planning Tweaks for Teachers: Small Changes That Make a Big Difference* (London: Bloomsbury Education, 2015).

Peter C. Brown, Henry L. Roediger and Mark A. McDaniel, *Make It Stick: The Science of Successful Learning* (Cambridge, MA: Harvard University Press, 2014).

Peps Mccrea, *Lean Lesson Planning: A Practical Approach to Doing Less and Achieving More in the Classroom* (CreateSpace, 2015).

Daniel T. Willingham, *Why Don't Students Like School? A Cognitive Scientist Answers Questions About How the Mind Works and What It Means for the Classroom* (San Francisco, CA: Jossey-Bass, 2010).

# 22. Behaviour Management: Part II

A developing NQT will:

✓ Start the year with set routines, clear expectations and seating plans for all classes.

✓ Start the year with high expectations, but perhaps won't maintain these throughout the year.

✓ Allow students to get away with things 'just this once'.

✓ Have a few techniques that are used across all classes.

✓ Always ring parents when there is a cause for concern.

✓ Usually chase missing homework.

Cast your mind back to the beginning of your training year; managing behaviour was probably one of the biggest worries you faced. This can be the same in your NQT year, particularly as you are now in a classroom on your own. This in itself is scary, let alone when you start to think about managing the behaviour of your new classes without another teacher there to save you! But fear not, start your preparation by recapping and reflecting upon the techniques that proved successful in your training year. By remaining confident and consistent – the two C's again! – you will find success in managing your new classes. Starting in September, which you may not have experienced on placement, makes things a little easier as your students will be particularly quiet during those first few weeks, meaning you can build your confidence quickly.

To thrive as a teacher, you need to be prepared to put in the hours, especially in your NQT year. But doing so will reap big rewards for the rest of your time at the school. As you already know from your training year, starting with high expectations from lesson one is essential. As an NQT you cannot afford to let this slip. However, the hard part is keeping this up throughout the year. Having set routines for a wide range of classroom scenarios – for example, the start and end of lessons, handing out books or resources, assessments, dedicated improvement and reflection time (DIRT) – will enable the students to become familiar with your expectations and teaching style quickly.[2]

It is most important to practise and maintain consistency at the start and end of lessons. Ensuring the start of every lesson is clear, focused and has a routine – whether this is lining up outside of the classroom or something else – will remind students they are in your lesson to learn. Remember to greet your students at the door at the beginning of each lesson, ensuring a positive start. Clear routines reduce the need for students to ask what they should do if, for example, they have forgotten their book or pen, enabling you to focus on starting the lesson rather than dealing with distractions. Never let this drop. It is easy to soften, but very hard to toughen back up!

Some of these techniques will be familiar to you from your training year and they are just as important now as they were then. A thriving teacher won't be afraid to go back over their expectations at any point throughout the year if they have changed a seating plan, if a lesson has featured particularly poor behaviour, or even just as a refresher after a half-term break. Reinforcing your expectations regularly throughout the year demonstrates your consistency and highlights that you expect consistency back from your students.

Expectations related to exercise books and the presentation of work should also be thought about and modelled to students throughout the year. Ensure that you know the expectations of the school – for example, underlining dates and titles, or writing in blue or black ink. Book work can often be forgotten about and standards can slip if not checked. A thriving teacher will utilise time in lessons to ensure students have underlined dates and titles, are writing in pen, have glued in loose sheets and haven't doodled! Reinforcing these expectations ensures that your students will be proud of the work they produce, thus encouraging a focused working environment during your lessons. Think about using students' books from other classes as models and explain why you have chosen them as exemplars. Again, consistency is key here. Even with lower ability students with whom you might be tempted to give more leeway, don't. Everyone can underline a title and write the date! Don't let standards slip, as when standards slip, so do expectations.

---

2    See also Martin Henley, *Classroom Management: A Proactive Approach* (London: Pearson, 2009).

Finally, make it mutual. It is a good idea to agree expectations as a class, perhaps in the form of a learning contract. By doing so the students can take ownership of the expectations as well. You could even ask them to share their expectations of you!

Our recommended behavioural expectations:

- Be silent when the teacher is speaking.

- Be silent when another member of the class is speaking.

- Always put your hand up to answer a question, never shout out.

- Be prepared: have your equipment ready for every lesson.

- Complete homework in full and hand in on time.

- Be proud of your book: ensure your presentation is outstanding.

- Always try your very best.

- Don't be afraid to make mistakes.

- Only hand in work that you are proud of.

- Be curious: ask lots of questions.

Always find time in the lesson to check that homework has been completed. Doing so ensures that students cannot get away without handing it in. Sometimes with large classes a homework exit strategy can work. When dismissing the class, stand by the door and ask students to physically hand in their homework. When they do, they can leave your lesson. Then you are left with the students who have not completed it, so you can issue sanctions and reiterate that they must hand it in the next day. Keep a list of names in your mark book so that if they fail to hand it in the following day you know who to chase. Think about emailing form tutors, waiting outside of lessons or catching them in the corridor – whatever it takes to get that homework! Whatever happens, ensure you issue further sanctions if it isn't handed in. This does require a bit of organisation.

A key mantra is to never think 'I will just let this one go', especially in your NQT year. If you let things go once you are demonstrably lowering your expectations, which can cause problems in the future. Follow up on every issue, both inside and outside the classroom. This takes time but the persistence will pay off and earn you a reputation as a fastidious professional.

Seating plans can play a vital role in behaviour management. You should organise your classroom to create the best possible learning environment for the students. Remember, you can change this when needed for different tasks or classes if, for example, you have a small group and you want them to be able to work closely together. Your classroom layout does not have to be set in stone. Experiment with your layout if it is not working. This demonstrates your ability to be reflective and desire to improve learning conditions in your classroom. Additionally, you should avoid sitting your students in 'hard to see' areas; you want to see them clearly as much as they want to see the board. To get an idea of their perspective, sit in various seats around your classroom to see if any issues are thrown up. This is your NQT year, so it's time to take ownership over what you do in your classroom!

Something I started in my NQT year, and still follow through with, is chasing students for homework outside of my classroom. After they have been given a day's extension – and after the school's homework policy sanction has been issued – if work still hasn't been handed in and I have a free lesson that day, I will go to the student's class at the beginning or end of a lesson and ask them for it in person. I have found that this trick really works if you continue to implement it throughout the year. Students very quickly realise they cannot escape and that you will remember that they haven't handed in work. If the student still does not produce the work, I issue another sanction and phone home. This does require *a lot* of organisation, but when done consistently reduces these issues later in the year.

When you get your class list in September, take the time to ask other members of your department whether you will be teaching any infamous characters. If you can, take the time to meet them before your first lesson. Explain that you are looking forward to them being in your class. This starts the relationship positively and may prevent the need to issue sanctions later on. As teachers we rely heavily on our relationships with the students, so make sure these interactions build rapport and that you show your appreciation when they do as you have asked. Dr Bill Rogers, an expert in positive behaviour management, has made several inspiring YouTube videos on this subject.[3]

---

3   For further inspiration and ideas on positive behaviour management, see Bill Rogers, 'Establishing trust to enable classroom co-operation' [video] (21 September 2012). Available at: https://www.youtube.com/watch?v=r351z1MqL10. See also Bill Rogers, *Classroom Behaviour: A Practical Guide to Effective Teaching, Behaviour Management and Colleague Support* (London: Sage, 2015).

Behaviour management shouldn't stay within your classroom and you can start by making yourself visible around school. Stopping students in corridors to enforce school rules and policies – asking them to sort out their uniform by tucking shirts in, for example – will have a big impact on your influence in the classroom and the respect students have for you. You should also use your time on duty to make yourself visible to students across all year groups. Think of duty as an opportunity to speak with students rather than merely monitor them.

Although you may have read lots of behaviour management books (see the to-read list in Chapter 8: Behaviour Management: Part I) during your training year, re-read them, alongside others, during your extra 10% remission time (see Chapter 36: Taking Advantage of Your Reduced Timetable). You will be able to apply different techniques and ideas more quickly as you get to know your students.[4] Behaviour management is a continuous process of development that does not stop even if you're deemed to be exceptional. Each year, students will react differently to particular styles of behaviour management. Having a range of strategies up your sleeve and being able to evaluate what did and didn't work at the end of a lesson is a sure sign of a thriving NQT. Reflecting on practice is a skill which can be lost during the chaos of your NQT year, but it is something all teachers should be doing on a daily basis.

To-do

☐ Write a list of your classroom expectations and ensure these are embedded in every lesson.

☐ Take behaviour management outside of the classroom and be a visible presence around school.

☐ Design a system for tracking homework in your teacher's planner.

☐ Reflect on your classroom layout and seating plans. Don't be afraid to change them.

**To read:**

Paul Dix, *When the Adults Change, Everything Changes: Seismic Shifts in School Behaviour* (Carmarthen: Independent Thinking Press, 2017).

---

4    For a few ideas to get you started, see Paul Dix, '10 tips for NQTs', *Pivotal Education*. Available at: https://pivotaleducation.com/classroom-behaviour-management/resource-bank/pivotal-how-to-series/10-tips-for-nqts/.

Martin Henley, *Classroom Management: A Proactive Approach* (London: Pearson, 2009).

Ansie Lessing and Renee Wulfsohn, 'The potential of behaviour management strategies to support learners with Attention Deficit Hyperactivity Disorder in the classroom', *Education as Change*, 19(1) (2015): 54–77.

Rob Plevin, *Take Control of the Noisy Class: From Chaos to Calm in 15 Seconds* (Carmarthen: Crown House Publishing, 2016).

# 23. Parent–Teacher Relationships

A developing NQT will:

✓ Contact home when a student's behaviour has been poor.

✓ Make positive phone calls home.

✓ Be organised ahead of parents' evenings to gather data.

✓ Be organised when report writing to gather data and profiles for students.

There are many reasons you could give to avoid making contact with parents: you're too busy, it probably won't achieve anything or even that another teacher will deal with it or has probably already tried speaking to them. However, a thriving teacher will demonstrate to the students that they have a direct link with home. A positive relationship with home can be a profound tool in terms of encouraging good behaviour and an improved attitude towards your subject.

During the training year you will, hopefully, have been encouraged to make a phone call home when a student was disruptive or exhibited poor behaviour. However, much more can be achieved from contact with home by making a few changes to the when, what and how of these interactions.

The main piece of advice that we can offer is to make sure you balance your negative and positive contact. Start with a rule that for every negative phone call you make, you will also make a positive one regarding another student. In particular, if you see one of those 'naughty' students do something good or have a good lesson, then ring home. Parents really appreciate this, and the student normally comes into your next lesson beaming. It's a great relationship builder!

Of course, our most direct opportunity to speak to parents is at parents' evening. Most teachers will have class data – targets, assessment results, homework records – to hand. To develop your practice, you can up your game by taking students' books along with you. Take the books of those who need to improve their work ethic or presentation, and take some books to model good practice to the students and their parents. This can be a really useful piece of evidence to frame a discussion around effort. Often students surround themselves with similar peers, so they may not see the output of others in the class and may be surprised at what some are achieving, thus encouraging them to raise their game.

You can also make more of parents' evening by printing lists of upcoming deadlines and assessments, along with lists of websites and resources that parents can use to help their child complete homework or revise. Many parents would love to be more involved with their child's education but struggle to know what to say or suggest to them. You can help to bridge that gap and provide an important support structure outside of your classroom.[5]

We have already discussed maintaining high expectations in the classroom, and this can be extended into the contact you make with home. Don't wait for behaviour to decline significantly before ringing parents. A thriving teacher will notice when a student's behaviour starts to fall below their expectations and will call home early, rather than waiting for a more serious display of poor behaviour. Nip these behaviours in the bud quickly and get the student back on track before it's too late. Don't worry that parents will feel you are complaining over nothing; most want to be updated about what goes on in our classrooms and will appreciate the heads-up.

A few weeks later, you can increase the impact of your relationship with home by following up with parents. You might have good news to share if the behavioural situation has improved, or if the student's last bit of homework was not only on time but completed to a new higher standard. Positive calls home can have a huge impact on improving or reinforcing student motivation.[6] Not only will the positivity build a relationship with the parent, but for parents who get many negative phone calls it can be a massive relief to hear something good about their child.

However, we have one important caveat to place on ringing home: dealing with parents is not black and white. There may be instances in which ringing home would not be appropriate, or could negatively impact your relationship with the student. If you mention that you will be ringing home and see a more serious change in their attitude that seems

5   Gregory Marchant, Sharon Paulson and Barbara Rothlisberg, 'Relations of middle school students' perception of family and school contexts with academic achievement', *Psychology in the Schools*, 38(6) (2001): 505–519.

6   Weihua Fan and Cathy Williams, 'The effects of parental involvement on students' academic self-efficacy, engagement and intrinsic motivation', *Educational Psychology*, 30(1) (2010): 53–74.

disproportionate, then reconsider. Speak to their form tutor or head of year to ask about issues at home, as you may find that there are reasons why you shouldn't call. It may be that the parents have already had many negative phone calls and are struggling to manage the situation, or it may be that the home relationship is already very fraught. This doesn't mean that you should do nothing, however; you could email their form tutor outlining the problem so that they can deal with it alongside any other issues.

If you are genuinely too busy to make those phone calls then you could always use email to inform parents of news quickly. The advantage here is that you can send your message to many people at once, which might be easier if, for example, you want to reward a whole class for an excellent lesson. You should also make best use of the report system at your school. If you send home comment reports, be sure to take the time to personalise these and tell parents exactly how lessons are going and what their child can do to progress.

Thriving teachers will also put the ball in the parents' court. At the beginning of the year, send an email to your students' parents – you could limit this to just Key Stages 4 and 5 – encouraging them to contact you. You could outline your expectations about what students should be doing at home – revision, homework, etc. – and ask parents to look out for these tasks. You could also ask them to contact you if any other issues arise which would benefit your teaching to know about. Many won't contact you, but for those who do this builds a very strong relationship between school and home.

> In my NQT year, I had a really tricky Year 9 class, which included several students who had notorious reputations across the school. They were intimidating to say the least! However, after one really positive lesson, I made a phone call to the father of one of the boys. His initial reply when he heard I was from the school was, 'Oh god, what has he done now?' I quickly told him about all the brilliant work that his son had done that day. He was so grateful and relieved to have a positive phone call for a change. Next lesson, the boy came bounding in grinning and told everyone that I had actually bothered to ring home! From that lesson on, he knew that I was bothered about him, and so he reciprocated by upping his effort level. For the next two years we had a great relationship, which almost took on a mentoring role, and I would say this allowed him to get more out of school than he may have done before. This is why I love teaching!

☐ Make some positive phone calls home to build up parent–teacher relationships.

☐ Be proactive when contacting home to nip concerns in the bud.

☐ Bring books to parents' evening to demonstrate students' work to parents and to model exemplar book work.

☐ Send an email to all parents at the beginning of the year to outline your expectations and build initial relationships.

To-do

**To read:**

Janet Goodall, John Vorhaus, Jon Carpentieri, Greg Brooks, Rodie Akerman and Alma Harris, *Review of Best Practice in Parental Engagement*. Research Report DFE-RR156 (London: Department for Education, 2010). Available at: https://www.gov.uk/government/uploads/system/uploads/attachment_data/file/182508/DFE-RR156.pdf.

Beng Huat See and Stephen Gorard, *What Do Rigorous Evaluations Tell Us About the Most Promising Parental Involvement Interventions? A Critical Review of What Works for Disadvantaged Children in Different Age Groups* (London: Nuffield Foundation, 2013). Available at: https://www.nuffieldfoundation.org/sites/default/files/files/What_do_rigorous_evaluations_tell_us_about_the_most_promising_parental_involvement_interventions.pdf.

William H. Jeynes, 'The relationship between parental involvement and urban secondary school student academic achievement: a meta-analysis', *Urban Education*, 42(1) (2007): 82–110.

# 24. Marking and Feedback

A developing NQT will:

✓ Keep on top of their marking, in line with the departmental or school policy.

✓ Use marking techniques which speed up their marking but don't detract from the quality of the feedback students get.

✓ Use DIRT so that students can improve their work, thus completing the marking cycle.

Marking students' work and giving precise feedback is an essential part of teaching and a core element of ensuring consistent progress from your students. The key is to go above and beyond.

Before we look at the actual practice of marking, a word from us on when is best to mark. It is very, *very* easy to leave marking till last, to take a bag of books home with you – never to be marked – or to have a pile of essays sitting in your in-tray for days, maybe weeks, on end. The solution is simple; mark during the day in your PPA time and leave your planning until after school. A thriving teacher would never begin the school day without having all of their lessons planned. Planning will never be the thing that doesn't get done.

The key with marking is to recognise that it isn't about you or what you do; the focus must be on your students. It can be easy to see marking as a tick-box exercise in which you find some spelling mistakes, write some formative comments, ask a few questions and end with a what went well (WWW) and an even better if (EBI). Don't allow yourself to view marking through this narrow lens. Your marking must always be designed to have the greatest possible positive impact on the students you teach. Start by identifying recurring whole-class misconceptions and then come up with a plan to address these. The key question to ask is 'Is the class making the sort of progress I expect them to?'

During my NQT year I developed a whole-class marking crib sheet, having seen something similar on Twitter.[7] The idea was that I would flick through a set of books, spending around two minutes on each. This was to gauge the overall progress of the class, while also noting certain students who needed extra help. This would take me around one hour per class; far less time than if I had marked all the books individually.

---

7    See Amjad Ali, 'Marking crib sheet', *Try This Teaching* [blog] (24 October 2016). Available at: https://www.trythisteaching.com/2016/10/marking-crib-sheet/.

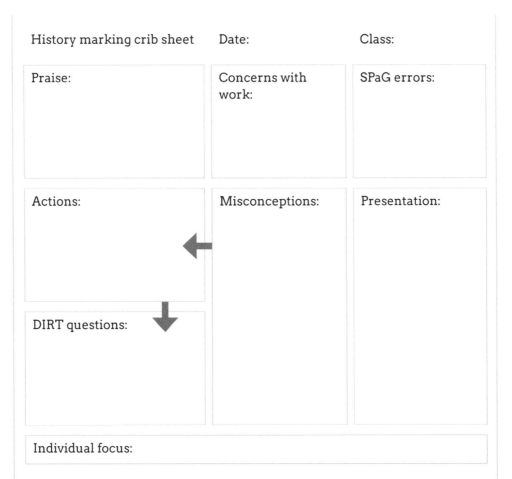

History marking crib sheet     Date:     Class:

Praise:

Concerns with work:

SPaG errors:

Actions:

Misconceptions:

Presentation:

DIRT questions:

Individual focus:

*Figure 3. Marking crib sheet.*

I gave a copy of the history marking crib sheet to each student in the class, highlighting whole-class achievements and common pitfalls. For those students who understood the content, this was as much feedback as they required, and a quiet word to those low effort students alongside the crib sheet often gave them the boost they needed. My DIRT lesson for students who'd demonstrated secure understanding would be all about stretching and pushing them through questions and tasks to encourage higher order thinking.

For those students who were demonstrating misconceptions I would 'target mark' their books in more detail to enable me to tailor a range of tasks focused on unravelling the misunderstanding. They spent the DIRT lesson working on these and ensuring that gaps in understanding were being tangibly closed. For example, in one class some students had struggled to write a comparative conclusion about the main reasons why William the Conqueror won the Battle of Hastings. The DIRT lesson asked them to think of some arguments to support what they had decided was the most important factor – skill, luck or Harold's mistakes – but also to think of reasons why the other factors were less important. They then had a mini-debate to express their views. Afterwards they utilised some of the arguments and comparisons explored in the debate to write a more comparative conclusion. I followed this with a short peer assessment task to encourage further support and guidance. When I next marked their books, I focused on this DIRT task to check progress and plan future tasks to develop this essential skill. I have found that structured debate and peer assessment are useful strategies to encourage argument building and deeper thinking.

Marking became much less about writing lots of comments in students' books and more about what misconceptions they had and how we could unravel them. Thus I spent less time marking in the traditional sense and more time plugging these gaps. For me, this is excellent marking, with a focus entirely on the students. I then shared this, not only with my department but with the school more widely, thus extending the positive impact beyond my own classroom.

Feedback given when marking should be specific and actionable. Think carefully about which targets you want to ask your students to focus on and ensure that they have clear advice about how to close the gaps in their knowledge or skills.

For the thriving NQT, marking should involve a consistent review of what is and isn't working in the classroom. School policy might be to mark once per half term, but flicking through books more frequently and marking homework regularly is essential. You must have a well-organised process for writing up marks and collating the data. Whether this is using an Excel spreadsheet, a mark book or an app like iDoceo, be sure to collate data accurately and to review it critically. Also, don't be afraid to mark students' work and not give a grade. There is evidence to suggest that a purely formative approach can have benefits, especially if you feel your students are becoming preoccupied with the grades they are getting rather than focusing on *why* they are getting them or how they can improve their work.[8]

However, collecting data is not enough; you must use this data to inform your marking, not the other way round. Developing teachers mark books, record the marks and then rarely give these another glance. For the NQT who aims to thrive, marking needs to begin with the data from the previous round. If your data suggests that a student is struggling, then you need to have this in mind when marking their work and seek to find out why. There may be a range of causes. Is behaviour an issue? Are you differentiating effectively? Is homework being completed to a high standard? Your marking must highlight any issues and seek to reduce their impact. If a specific question or topic has proved a problem, then your marking must discover why this is the case and your DIRT lesson must close this gap.[9]

**Thriving DIRT tips:**

■ Plan adequate time for the class to respond to your feedback. To make this a meaningful activity, the class must be allowed long enough to address targets and act on feedback fully.

■ Any task can be a suitable DIRT task. It could be a new worksheet that provides further practice in a different way, a redrafting of the original work or an activity that requires students to reapply the learning to a new context. The key is that it targets the weaknesses and learning gaps that you have identified in your marking.

■ Don't be afraid to get students, using feedback from you or their classmates to support them, to improve or redraft their work more than once. This process of frequent improvement can lead to some truly outstanding final products which then set a benchmark to aspire to in future pieces of work.[10]

■ However, maintain the pace as you would in a normal lesson. Don't give students the opportunity to take their feet off the gas or see this as an easy activity.

■ Provide students with access to any additional information or content that they didn't understand the first time round, which may also include reteaching something.

---

8    Tom Sherrington, 'Rethinking marking and feedback. It's all about the response', *teacherhead* [blog] (9 October 2016). Available at: https://teacherhead.com/2016/10/09/rethinking-marking-and-feedback-its-all-about-the-response/.
9    Andy Tharby, 'Strategic marking for the DIRTy-minded teacher', *Reflecting English* [blog] (13 December 2013). Available at: https://reflectingenglish.wordpress.com/2013/12/13/strategic-marking-for-the-dirty-minded-teacher/.
10   See Ron Berger, 'Critique and feedback – the story of Austin's butterfly' [video] for a great example of this in action. Available at: https://www.youtube.com/watch?v=hqh1MRWZjms.

■ To encourage students to use this as a reflective process, check that they have understood the improvements they need to make. Can they suggest how they will avoid making the same mistakes next time? What did they find difficult?

■ Create the right classroom climate by explaining why DIRT is valuable. Prove that it is a low-stakes task – with no element of judgement about weaknesses – and, most importantly, celebrate mistakes – theirs and yours!

■ Finally, trial different DIRT techniques that suit the dynamic of the class in question. For example, we find that strict silent conditions allow the students to focus a lot more but that group work can help low confidence learners. Use your judgement and adapt the approach as needed.

A word on DIRT lessons. It is standard practice in all good schools to ensure that students are given time after teachers mark their books to reflect on the marking and improve their understanding based upon it. Yet some DIRT lessons are not as productive as they could be.[11] Firstly, ensure that each student in your class will be completing tasks that are tailored to their needs, basing this upon your whole-class and targeted marking. It is better for each student to have two or three clear tasks – with convincing learning outcomes – than a whole list of things to do. Focus on what will make the most difference and then give your class time to do these tasks well. Always set high expectations in DIRT lessons. Make the students aware that these lessons are perhaps the most important in developing their understanding, so insist on quiet, or silent, work and expect all the targets you have set to be met within the lesson. Alternatively, work to address targets could be set as a homework, but be aware that as these are the areas that students struggled with in the first instance, tasks will need to be clear and structured.

**Thriving target setting tips:**

■ Ensure that students can see clearly what they have achieved successfully and provide a target or further question based on the gaps in their knowledge or understanding.

■ Ensure WWWs and EBIs are specific to the individual and not too general – for example, good detail.

■ Check previous targets to monitor students' progress; alarm bells should sound if they are getting the same targets repeated.

■ Consider intervention if targets are repeated. For example:

---

11   John Hattie and Helen Timperley, 'The power of feedback', *Review of Educational Research*, 77(1) (2007): 81–112.

- Invite a student to a specific lunchtime session to recap subject knowledge or skills.

- Write targeted feedback which the student can use to improve.

- Speak with parents.

- Speak with the student – discover where the challenges lie and consider ways to overcome them. Boost their confidence so that they recognise that they *can* improve!

■ Consider using specific language that supports, stretches and challenges students. For example:

- You have really improved upon …

- Have you thought about …?

- Can you expand upon …?

- Check your understanding of …

### Thriving peer and self-assessment tips:

Peer and self-assessment can be a very effective way to progress student understanding and metacognitive abilities – thinking about and understanding how we learn – and is also time-saving. If students are able to gauge what they have done well and what they need to improve with accuracy, then the opportunities for them to make progress are vast. This can be both within the classroom and, importantly, outside of lessons. However, time must be invested in preparing students to peer and self-assess effectively. Modelling is key, otherwise – as is often the case – this assessment won't really help them to progress at all.[12]

■ Model answers for students, going through mark schemes in detail and showing example answers at different levels – for example, to demonstrate describing vs explaining. Students must be able to recognise good work in order to assess it.

■ Challenge students to highlight different aspects of model answers and match them to the mark scheme to enhance their understanding of the exam requirements.

■ Allow students to mark other pieces of work, from peers, past papers or model answers, for practice.

---

12  See Allison and Tharby, *Making Every Lesson Count*, pp. 89–122.

■ Create the right culture and atmosphere within the classroom for peer assessment to work. All feedback must be constructive and students must feel that they are in a safe environment where they won't be ridiculed and they are able to express their opinions.

## Thriving verbal feedback tips:

■ Ensure verbal feedback is ongoing throughout lessons.

■ Exploit verbal feedback as an efficient use of time. It's a lot quicker than writing your feedback out and allows for instant responses, and improvements, from your students.

■ Allow students to ask questions to clarify understanding immediately.

■ Use it as an opportunity for personal feedback. Spending time feeding back one-to-one with your students is a great way to strengthen bonds with your class.

■ Ensure it is specific, modelled – for example, by giving an example of a perfect answer or sentence starters – and tangible; i.e. it must be readily achievable.

■ Consider when and where you offer verbal feedback as this is also important. Is it public or private? Firm or gentle? General or specific? You need to know your students really well to make verbal feedback as effective as possible.

■ Don't bother with a verbal feedback stamp – how does this add to your students' understanding?

Marking and feedback takes up a large amount of time, so make sure that it's worth it. We know that it has a big effect on progress but the pupils need to work as hard as teachers. If they aren't using your feedback to make better progress then you are wasting significant chunks of time. Experiment with time efficient methods such as live marking and marking checklists but stay within the parameters of your school feedback policies. Mark with others in your team so you can pick up strategies that more experienced teachers use.

Lianne Allison, Deputy Head Teacher, Durrington High School

**Thriving test feedback tips:**

■ Never give a test back without ensuring that the students complete further work to close the gaps in their knowledge or understanding.

■ Set targets while marking test papers. For example, if a student failed to explain what selective breeding was in an answer, their target could be to 'describe what selective breeding is and explain the processes involved'. Remember that this will need to be differentiated, if appropriate.

■ Always work through answers with the students. Students can use a mark scheme and a different coloured pen to improve their work, so their edits clearly stand out. Make sure you model the thought processes involved in understanding the question and developing an answer.

■ Model perfect answers with students in lesson time. Students can then compare their own work to these models.

■ Encourage students to list key words that they have avoided using. Their target is to learn and use these in future answers.

**Thriving live marking tips:**

■ Save time by live marking while students are getting on with another task.

■ Write a short comment or question in a student's book that aims to help them progress their thinking or correct their work and then move away to work with another student. Students can address this then and there and can even ask you for support with it.

■ Set the class an independent task with clear instructions so that everyone is busy while you are going around individual students.

■ Aim to mark four or five students' books in a lesson, using either your seating plan or register to select which. In the next lesson, move on to the next four or five students and so on. Don't try to get round the whole class in a single lesson as it will take too long.

A simple last tip: don't let marking slip! A thriving NQT should be an ambassador for consistent quality marking both within their department and across the school, with every class throughout the whole year.

In my lessons, I like to set longer answer questions in order to assess the depth of students' understanding and knowledge of a topic. To save time, I developed a marking grid specific to the question posed. I would tick points students had completed and highlight areas for improvement. This would then be stuck into their books so they could use DIRT to improve their work. This sped up marking but still gave students detailed and targeted feedback. After a year I had a whole bank of marking grids which I still refer back to and use. Here is one such example:

| | |
|---|---|
| Explain the reactivity series and why some metals can be extracted using carbon while others cannot. **(6 mark question)** | |
| Stated the reactivity series and listed metals in order of their reactivity. | |
| Explained where carbon is in the reactivity series. | |
| Described how displacement reactions are used to obtain metals from compounds. | |
| Explained why a more reactive metal or carbon can displace a less reactive metal from these compounds. | |
| Gave an example of when carbon can displace a metal from its compounds. | |
| Gave an example of when carbon cannot displace a metal. | |
| SPaG and paragraphs. | |
| Teacher's comments: | |

*Figure 4. Marking grid.*

To-do

☐ Mark during PPA time; don't leave it until the end of the day.

☐ Mark frequently and have a system in place to collect and collate data.

☐ Use data from previous marking to inform future targets and planning.

☐ Embed feedback into lessons to tackle misconceptions as they occur.

☐ Plan effective DIRT lessons to complete the feedback cycle.

☐ Try live marking in a lesson. Plan who you are going to focus on in that first session.

## To read:

Chapter 5 in Shaun Allison and Andy Tharby, *Making Every Lesson Count: Six Principles to Support Great Teaching and Learning* (Carmarthen: Crown House Publishing, 2015).

Victoria Elliott, Jo-Ann Baird, Therese N. Hopfenbeck, Jenni Ingram, Ian Thompson, Natalie Usher, Mae Zantout, James Richardson and Robbie Coleman, *A Marked Improvement? A Review of the Evidence on Written Marking* (London: Education Endowment Foundation, 2016). Available at: https://educationendowmentfoundation. org.uk/evidence-summaries/evidence-reviews/written-marking/.

Mike Gershon, *How to Use Feedback and Marking in the Classroom: The Complete Guide* (CreateSpace, 2017).

John Hattie and Helen Timperley, 'The power of feedback', *Review of Educational Research*, 77(1) (2007): 81–112.

Ross Morrison McGill, *Mark. Plan. Teach.: Save Time. Reduce Workload. Impact Learning.* (London: Bloomsbury Education, 2016).

# 25. Tracking and Progress

A developing NQT will:

✓ Complete all data inputs on time.

✓ Reflect on data, spot underperforming students and plan interventions accordingly.

✓ Discuss students' performance with their other teachers to share ideas that work, and those that don't!

✓ Use relevant school data platforms – like 4Matrix and FFT Aspire – when necessary.

Tracking and progress may be one of the things that you didn't really notice during your training year. You might have been expected to fill in the odd tracking spreadsheet or seat students according to their target grade but, in all likelihood, you won't get really involved with data until the NQT year when you have your own classes.

The first thing you need to do in order to thrive is to actually *use* the data. It is not enough to just input it into an intricate colour-coded spreadsheet – no matter how pretty it is – and not do anything with it! Start by identifying students who are under target, and then have a look over the work you assessed to work out why this is the case. Try to focus on subject knowledge or skills gaps. Once you have done this, use the information to plan interventions.

But how do you actually intervene effectively? There are several things you can do. Firstly, speak to others in your department and find out what resources are available and what has worked within your school context before. If you identify that the student in question holds a specific misconception or has misunderstood a learning point then you could deliberately plan a starter or homework that targets that area. Then, when going through the task, you need to make sure you target the student with your questioning and be sure to add detail and go over their misconception. If lots of students have a similar misconception, don't be afraid to reteach a topic in class.

If a student seems to be consistently working below target then you could consider changing your seating plan to see whether this makes a difference. You could try moving them to a seat – perhaps at the front of the room – that gives you better sight of them and more chances for interaction during lessons. Or you could move them so that they are near higher ability students who might be able to support them during work with more challenging conversation, often at a faster pace.

You may also find that you need to differentiate tasks to support individual students further. Make sure your learning objectives are really clear and then provide students with the tools they need to achieve these. We don't want to encourage you to plan separate lessons for each student in the class as this would take way too much of your time. It can also create social and emotional issues for your students if they are consistently receiving notably different treatment to their peers.

There are lots of strategies that you can have in your back pocket to apply in many situations. Here are some of our favourites (for more details return to Chapter 10: Differentiation):

■ Consider the extra literacy and numeracy support your students might need. You could, for example, recap key skills as part of your starter.

■ Make sure worksheets start off easier and then ramp up in terms of challenge. Your more able students will fly through the early questions, or you could suggest they skip a few, while you can spend your time with students who are stuck on question one.

■ Provide resources using a range of methods and media – for example, as simplified text, picture storyboards, videos or glossaries.

■ Give students defined roles in group work that suit their individual strengths, such as organiser, time manager, researcher, note taker, etc. This allows everyone to participate in the lesson.

■ Consider peer tutoring. Getting students to support and teach each other can be very powerful and research suggests it can have a large impact.[13]

■ Have a plan in your head regarding the students who you will talk to while the class are doing independent work and set up a routine of visiting particular students over a number of lessons.

■ Have optional writing frames and support scaffolds available for students to use during lessons – for example, lists of key words or connectives. These can help anyone who struggles with longer answer questions (once again, there is an example in Chapter 10: Differentiation).

■ If you find students are struggling to transcribe information or take notes from the board, make sure you only ask them to write things that are absolutely necessary or

---

13  Shona Macleod, Caroline Sharp, Daniele Bernardinelli, Amy Skipp and Steve Higgins, *Supporting the Attainment of Disadvantaged Pupils: Articulating Success and Good Practice*. Research report, Ref: DFE-RR411 (National Foundation for Educational Research, Ask Research and Durham University, 2015), pp. 50–51.

print off notes and leave blanks for key words. This means they are still working by reading, and will practise writing key words, but they will not have to write as much overall as you are focusing them on the really salient points.

> Knowing all the students and meeting all of their needs is the most complex thing that you will have to do. A good system for recording progress is key to this and is a valuable tool as it will be necessary to share progress with others such as school leaders and parents. If students aren't making expected progress then you need to be able to show what you have done to intervene both in the classroom and out of it, if needed – for example, revision sessions and meetings with parents. Become expert at finding students' gaps with your assessment methods, recording these gaps and then acting to address them.
>
> Lianne Allison, Deputy Head Teacher, Durrington High School

Once you have started using an intervention strategy, as with many of the other strategies we have discussed in this book, it is important to reflect on its effectiveness. Use AfL tasks and plenaries to assess the knowledge of the students you have identified as underachieving. Use assessments to further track their progress to see if they have improved. You should also consider how much time your interventions require. If they are very time-consuming, then is there a way you could streamline the process or perhaps another strategy could be just as good but quicker to implement?

So far, we have discussed how to support struggling students; however, you also need to make sure that you are differentiating for your higher achievers. If a student is consistently above target, try to keep them there. (Have a look at Chapter 32: Challenge for more information on this.)

In many schools, tracking and monitoring will also include a conversation about those students who are in receipt of PP. This is an important group in terms of school performance, with all schools looking to 'close the gap' between the attainment levels of students who are in receipt of PP and those who are not.[14] Try to actively include them in the lesson with your questioning and as part of your routine of visiting individual students during independent work. Perhaps consider marking their books first, as you will be the most fresh, and spend a few extra minutes ensuring your feedback is the best it can be.

---

14 Macleod et al., *Supporting the Attainment of Disadvantaged Pupils*, p. 15.

We also want to mention out-of-class interventions. In some schools these will be arranged centrally within a department and all teachers will be expected to do their fair share. In others, this will be seen as the responsibility of the individual teachers and in some this will not be an expectation at all. Strategies will include revision sessions and homework support clubs, both of which are normally held during lunch or after school, or small-group teaching which often takes place during normal lesson time with the support of a fellow teacher. If you do set up revision sessions for your classes, give them a timetable of topics to ensure they come to the sessions they will find most useful, or formalise the process by making attendance compulsory and inviting them by sending a letter home.

As a final thought, although we are encouraged to use success criteria and mark schemes as a way to gauge progress, a thriving teacher will also consider the work in front of them for what it is, regardless of whether it meets these criteria. Use your professional judgement to take a step back from the criteria you've been given and make the call on whether that student has understood what they have been taught and whether they have made progress in other ways. For example, a student may have achieved well below their target grade in a recent assessment, while demonstrating that their ability to analyse a source or use creative adjectives has actually improved, which is worth noting and celebrating. Use these small improvements as an additional source of praise for students who are progressing well, but also as a silver lining for those who may have performed less successfully against the formal criteria.[15]

---

To-do

☐ Ensure you use data tracking sheets to inform future planning and teaching.

☐ Set up a routine for students who are underachieving – for example, checking understanding in each lesson. Place extra emphasis on students with PP.

☐ Consider different intervention strategies both inside and outside the classroom and assess their effectiveness. Only keep doing things that are having an impact.

---

15  David Didau, 'Proof of progress – part 1', *The Learning Spy* [blog] (30 January 2016). Available at: http://www.learningspy.co.uk/assessment/comparative-judgement-trial-part-1/.

**To read:**

Daisy Christodoulou, *Making Good Progress? The Future of Assessment for Learning* (Oxford: Oxford University Press, 2017).

Department for Education, *Secondary Accountability Measures: Guide for Maintained Secondary Schools, Academies and Free Schools, January 2018*. Ref: DFE-00278-2017 (London: Department for Education, 2018). Available at: https://www.gov.uk/government/uploads/system/uploads/attachment_data/file/676184/Secondary_accountability_measures_January_2018.pdf.

Shona Macleod, Caroline Sharp, Daniele Bernardinelli, Amy Skipp and Steve Higgins, *Supporting the Attainment of Disadvantaged Pupils: Articulating Success and Good Practice*. Research report, Ref: DFE-RR411 (National Foundation for Educational Research, Ask Research and Durham University, 2015).

# 26. Exam Classes

A developing NQT will:

✓ Consider long-term planning to ensure content is covered ahead of the exams, allowing good time for revision.

✓ Send generic letters or emails home around exam time outlining the revision sessions that they or their department are running.

Exam classes, in both Key Stage 4 and 5, can naturally feel more important and high-stakes due to the nature of the tests that they need to prepare the students for. You may find you are not given a Year 11 or sixth form class in your NQT year. Do not worry if this is the case; it doesn't mean you're perceived as a bad teacher! Schools often try to alleviate the stress caused by an already hectic NQT year by giving exam classes to more senior members of staff. However, if you do have exam classes you must ensure that you are planning and teaching effectively; not only helping your students to understand the content of your subject, but also preparing them for the exams ahead.

A thriving NQT will build regular exam practice into their planning. Don't rely on the practice afforded during mock weeks in the school's academic calendar as this won't be enough. Try setting regular mock exams right up until the real thing, giving students more experience of the question style and timing. This stops them taking their feet off the gas and keeps them practising! This could also be in the form of starters or plenaries, or entire lessons based around exam questions. Practising exam questions in timed conditions will enable students to gain familiarity with how the real thing will be. Make sure you embed this practice from the beginning of the course: this should be symbiotic with content coverage.

To ensure you're fully prepared for teaching exam technique, read examiners' reports from previous years. You will be able to notice areas where students commonly drop marks or recurring misconceptions and can then share this knowledge with your students. At A level, model this reading with the students so that they can further develop their exam technique.

I think it's absolutely key to never say 'I know this is boring' or 'I know this is dull'; if you say that then you've lost already. It's important to maintain your enthusiasm for your subject, to find ways in which it is relevant or engaging or to come at it from a different angle.

Avoid, at all costs, going down the exam question after exam question route. The opportunity to explore and practise exam questions is key, but you also need to make sure that you maintain the range of engaging activities that you use in Key Stage 3. Otherwise students can soon decide they were tricked into their curriculum choices or become disengaged. The principles of engaging students are very similar whether they are 11 or 18. Most of us respond well to engaging challenges.

As a subject specialist, you should try to remain engaged through tailored CPD from subject associations. This will help you maintain your focus and enthusiasm for your discipline. In particular, try to get involved with any of the CPD run by the examination board. They demystify some of the exam questions and often have examples of students' work. Hearing explanations of why students have reached a particular grade can help you feel more assured in your own marking.

Although it sounds crazy to volunteer for more marking during the summer holidays, take advantage of any opportunity you may have to become an examiner within the subject. This will give you even more confidence in your own marking.

Dr Simon Thompson, Head of Education, University of Sussex

A good tool for exam practice is the 'walking talking mock', an idea formulated by PiXL.[16] Give students a copy of the paper, and then use a visualiser or interactive whiteboard to talk through the questions, underlining or highlighting command words and any other important information. Talk through the thinking you would undertake in order to form and structure an answer. Allowing students to share in your thought processes and reflect on strategies is an important metacognitive skill to be developed, especially early on in the course. Next, give them an appropriate length of time to answer the question, based on how many marks are on offer, and then take them through the mark scheme while they self-assess their answer. Through this technique students start to replicate how you, as an expert, interpret an exam question, as well as gain practice under exam conditions for maximum impact. This approach is demonstrated in more detail in several YouTube videos.[17]

You do not have to mark every exam question you set your students. Peer marking is a useful tool for both you and the students. By building time into lessons for students to peer mark, or even to self-assess, they will become more familiar with mark schemes. Students need to be aware of the exacting language that they should use when answering questions in your subject, so allow them to develop this through critical peer marking. A really good idea is to put the mark schemes into friendly and clear language. For example, if the mark scheme refers to 'your own knowledge', show students what this means. Are there clues which suggest the sorts of details they need to include in their answers? For example, should they be using facts, figures or dates?

To begin with, collect in the peer assessed work and quality check it. Ensure that students have interpreted the mark scheme correctly and allocated marks appropriately. This will allow them to peer mark with confidence in future.

A thriving NQT will take exam preparation further by getting to know their students' strengths and weaknesses in detail. Student A may struggle with structuring an exam answer, whereas student B may struggle with timing. Considered interventions will help to close the gap and improve the performance of these students (see Chapter 25: Tracking and Progress for more on interventions). Getting to know your students in this way takes time, but starting early gives them the best possible opportunity for success in your subject.

---

16  Shaun Allison, 'Walking talking exams', *Class Teaching* [blog] (27 November 2014). Available at: https://classteaching.wordpress.com/2014/11/27/walking-talking-exams/.

17  For a worked example, see Shoreham Academy's 'Maths walking talking mock calculator paper part 1' [video] (7 February 2014). Available at: https://www.youtube.com/watch?v=ATK76UyFYY0&feature =youtu.be.

☐ Build regular exam practice into your lessons.

☐ Set regular timed exam questions and mock papers.

☐ Read examiners' reports and share knowledge with your classes.

☐ Try a 'walking talking mock'.

☐ Introduce peer marking as a time-efficient way to mark practice questions.

**To read:**

Steve Oakes and Martin Griffin, *The A Level Mindset: 40 Activities for Transforming Student Commitment, Motivation and Productivity* (Carmarthen: Crown House Publishing, 2016).

Steve Oakes and Martin Griffin, *The GCSE Mindset: 40 Activities for Transforming Student Commitment, Motivation and Productivity* (Carmarthen: Crown House Publishing, 2017).

# 27. Revision Strategies

A developing NQT will:

✓ Encourage their students to create revision materials, but with little guidance.

✓ Encourage their students to use these materials to revise, but with little guidance.

Revision has always been an important aspect of exam success, but with the new specifications – being both linear and featuring reduced coursework – it has become more important than ever. Furthermore, exams have become increasingly content-oriented and support has been removed – for example, in science, equation sheets no longer feature on papers. Students have to remember more than ever, and it is our job to ensure that they are best placed to revise this content successfully. A thriving teacher will realise that there is not one 'best' approach to revision; rather, it depends upon what works best for your students. Let us go into some revision approaches and strategies that the research, our own experience and feedback from our students suggest are most effective.[18]

## Spacing/distributed practice

Ensure that your students are starting their revision for an assessment or exam in plenty of time. This will avoid cramming, which is proven to be a less effective way of remembering information. It is better for your students to revise a topic for twenty minutes every few days than to revise for two hours straight once a week.[19] You need to support your students to create a revision timetable that factors in spaced learning. Spending part of a lesson explaining the concept and then setting the task of creating the timetable as homework would be a good use of time.

## Interleaving

Interleaving is closely linked to spacing but, rather than focusing on how to structure the timing of revision sessions, the focus is on how best to utilise the time spent revising.[20] The idea is that instead of spending many hours in a row revising the same subject – referred to as 'blocking' – students should mix up their focus regularly and revise a range of subjects each day. Covering a range of subjects daily should be factored into any revision timetable. Interleaving doesn't only increase retention, but also means that students discover connections between subjects and utilise skills across different disciplines.[21] You can embed interleaving into your lessons by planning to revisit topics throughout the school year, regularly returning to them – if only briefly – to embed understanding and encourage students to recall and remember the information. A recent, although small scale, study

---

18  John Dunlosky, Katherine A. Rawson, Elizabeth J. Marsh, Mitchell J. Nathan and Daniel T. Willingham, 'Improving students' learning with effective learning techniques: promising directions from cognitive and educational psychology', *Psychological Science in the Public Interest*, 14(1) (2013): 4–58. Available at: http://elephantsdontforget.com/wp-content/uploads/2016/08/Learning-White-Paper.pdf.

19  See 'Robert Bjork – storage strength vs. retrieval strength' [video] (12 July 2012). Available at: https://www.youtube.com/watch?v=1FQoGUCgb5w; and 'Robert Bjork – spacing improves long-term retention' [video] (13 July 2012). Available at: https://www.youtube.com/watch?v=TTo35X2rqls.

20  Sean Kang, 'The benefits of interleaved practice for learning'. In Jared Cooney Horvath, Jason Lodge and John Hattie (eds), *From the Laboratory to the Classroom: Translating Science of Learning for Teachers* (Abingdon: Routledge, 2017), pp. 79–93.

21  See the research summary from UCLA Bjork Learning and Forgetting Lab, 'Applying cognitive psychology to enhance educational practice'. Available at: https://bjorklab.psych.ucla.edu/research/.

suggests that the best approach is to use both spaced learning and interleaving in combination to produce the best outcomes.[22]

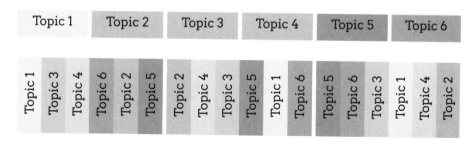

*Figure 5. Blocking of topics vs interleaving.*

*Source: adapted from Allison and Tharby,* Making Every Lesson Count, *pp. 132–133.*

## Low-stakes testing

One way to embed interleaving into your lessons is to include frequent low-stakes tests as a matter of routine. Frequently quizzing your students in lessons will not only allow you to interleave content, but also provide you with regular feedback on how well your students can remember key information.[23] One tip, especially for exam classes, is to start all, or at least most, lessons with a quick recap quiz of content from previous lessons. The quiz could focus on recent material, something learned much longer ago or a combination of both. You could have the questions on the board as students enter, or printed and placed on their desks. Using an app like Quizlet to produce flashcards can be really effective as these can be used for frequent testing and quizzes. If your students are producing flashcards by hand, then show them the Leitner system, which focuses on regular low-stakes testing, but also includes a clever method to ensure those flashcards that prove hardest to remember are looked at the most often.[24]

---

22  Jonathan Firth, 'The application of spacing and interleaving approaches in the classroom', *Impact: Journal of the Chartered College of Teaching*, Issue 2 (2018). Available at: https://impact.chartered.college/article/firth-spacing-interleaving-classroom/.

23  Megan Smith, 'Five benefits of quizzing according to cognitive science', *TES* (25 May 2016). Available at: https://www.tes.com/us/news/breaking-views/five-benefits-quizzing-according-cognitive-science.

24  For information on the Leitner system and how it can be used, see Parents24, 'How to study flashcards using the Leitner system' [video] (24 August 2016). Available at: https://www.youtube.com/watch?v=C20EvKtdJwQ.

## Collaborative revising

While revising with other people can be distracting – a warning worth sharing with your students – there is some evidence to suggest that it can be beneficial given the right conditions.[25] The main benefit is that when testing each other, if one person doesn't know the answer then another most likely will. Sharing learned information in this way can help embed the knowledge. Encourage your students to find suitable study partners and to spend some of their revision time utilising their shared knowledge to help them all work more effectively.

## Use of technology

Technology can really aid the effectiveness of revision. Here are some websites, apps and ideas which have helped our students:

**Quizlet:** An app which is great for creating flashcards. Also enables you to self-test using the flashcards. In class, students can work in groups to find answers to questions based upon their shared flashcards. You can also access flashcards created by other people, as well as share your own, which can further enhance the quality and breadth of your students' revision materials.

**Educake:** A brilliant app if you're a science teacher, as you can pick sections of the specification to set as homework, which marks itself. This is a great way of revising previous topics. You can tailor the questions to suit the ability of your students and get immediate and personalised feedback regarding their progress.

**Podcasts:** There are numerous websites providing revision podcasts; some require a subscription, such as Audiopi and GCSEPod, while others are user created and free. These can be useful as students can listen to them on the go, whether walking to school, on the bus or in the car. You could even get students to record their own!

**Revision Timetable Maker:** Many websites, such as getrevising.co.uk, offer a free revision timetable maker. These are great tools to support your students when creating revision timetables. Just remind them to incorporate the concepts of spacing and interleaving.

---

25 Helena M. Blumen and Yaakov Stern, 'Short-term and long-term collaboration benefits of individual recall in younger and older adults', *Memory and Cognition*, 39(1) (January 2011): 147–154. Available at: http://www.cumc.columbia.edu/dept/sergievsky/pdfs/shorttermandlongterm.pdf.

To-do

☐ Develop an understanding of spaced learning and interleaving. Use this knowledge to support your students when making revision timetables.

☐ Revisit topics regularly in lessons to embed understanding through regular low-stakes testing.

☐ Encourage collaborative practice and the use of technology to support revision.

**To read:**

Aaron S. Benjamin and Jonathan Tullis, 'What makes distributed practice effective?', *Cognitive Psychology*, 61(3) (2010): 228–247. Available at: https://www.ncbi.nlm.nih.gov/pmc/articles/PMC2930147/.

Robert Blakey, *I Hate Revision: Study Skills and Revision Techniques for GCSE, A-level and Undergraduate Exams* (lulu.com, 2014).

Richard E. Mayer and Richard B. Anderson, 'The instructive animation: helping students build connections between words and pictures in multimedia learning', *Journal of Educational Psychology*, 84(4) (1992): 444–452.

Henry L. Roediger, Adam L. Putnam and Megan A. Smith, 'Ten benefits of testing and their applications to educational practice'. In Jose P. Mestre and Brian H. Ross (eds), *The Psychology of Learning and Motivation: Cognition in Education*, 55 (Oxford: Elsevier, 2011), pp. 1–36.

# 28. Supporting Students with Pupil Premium (PP)

A developing NQT will:

✓ Know which of their students qualify for PP.

✓ Plan the seating position of those students carefully to give them easy access to learning and additional assistance, if needed.

It is important that you understand what PP status means for your students and the reasons why they may qualify for it. The PP indicator was introduced in 2011 as a way of helping teachers and schools to identify and assist disadvantaged students. Under the scheme, schools also receive extra funding for each student on roll who qualifies. The criteria cover students from low-income families, those who have been in care or looked after by the local authority for more than six months and those whose parents have been or are serving in the military.

Students from disadvantaged backgrounds generally do not make as much progress as their counterparts.[26] By this, we mean they do not make the expected progress from Key Stage 2 to GCSE, and often achieve below target in terminal assessments. Of course, we are talking statistically here, and we are sure you will be able to picture several of your students who do not fit this pattern!

Teachers can fall into the trap of confusing 'pupil premium' with 'low ability' and therefore may make many assumptions about the best way to support these students – all too often through support sheets and differentiated activities. As a thriving NQT, you need to move past any misconceptions, and see all students as individuals. The behind-target progress made by students with PP may be a result of one of many barriers to learning, from lack of access to necessary resources to the absence of a quiet working area at home. The important message is to never assume; get to know your students and find out how you can support them best. Positively discriminate to offer support and close the attainment gap that students with PP are statistically predicted to be subject to.

A really easy way of supporting students with PP is to be a good role model. When you are dealing with behaviour, model the language and the temperament that leads to positive resolution rather than further escalation and sanctions. As with all students, it is really important that you show them how to deal with issues when things don't go right in lessons, or when they are coping with potentially difficult emotions. You can do this by building relationships founded in mutual respect. Find the time to get to really know them, which might come from speaking to them outside of lessons, asking about their weekend or supporting them pastorally. It is essential you are aware of the specific background situation so that you can tailor your approach appropriately. For example, a student with a parent serving in the military may need more pastoral and emotional support, whereas a student who is in receipt of PP due to their family's financial situation may benefit more from tangible resources like books and revision guides that may otherwise be unaffordable.

26  Ofsted, *The Pupil Premium: How Schools Are Using the Pupil Premium Funding to Raise Achievement for Disadvantaged Pupils*. Ref: 120197 (September 2012). Available at: https://www.gov.uk/government/uploads/system/uploads/attachment_data/file/413222/The_Pupil_Premium.pdf, p. 7.

It is more valuable to teach the material well the first time round rather than relying on interventions later. We're confident that you will thrive as a good teacher. However, if you are looking for some specific guidance for supporting pupils with PP, here is our list of considerations:

■ **The individual:** Find out about their situation from a head of year, or perhaps the teachers of an older sibling at the school. Use this information to plan to support them. Also find out what their hobbies and passions are and take an interest in them. Could you link any of your lesson concepts to these to keep the student engaged? How can you best tailor your teaching and interventions to cater for and support their individual needs?

■ **Their position in the seating plan:** You could place students close to the front so that you have lots of opportunities to build strong relationships with them and keep an eye on their work. Equally, you may want to place them around the classroom, perhaps near to students who model a good work ethic or who are achieving high grades to encourage positive conversations. Give them the golden ticket to the best seat in your classroom!

■ **During the lesson:** Give them moments to shine! If you happen to overhear them insightfully discussing content, then 'randomly' pick on them when asking someone to feed back to the class. Actively engage disadvantaged students during the lesson and make sure they are always asked a question. If you are doing a demonstration with student volunteers, try to include them. On a slightly separate note, if they have not got a pen or pencil, go easy on them and lend them one for the lesson. There may be wider issues that have caused their seeming lack of preparedness.

■ **When marking books:** Ensure feedback is as valuable as you can make it. You could either mark their books first when you are fresh, or after a few other books when you are in the swing of it. Make sure you include specific positive praise to motivate students.

■ **When planning lessons:** Whether through marking, assessment activities or general classroom discussions, try to identify gaps in understanding and learning. You may want to keep a record in your planner. Build tasks to close specific learning gaps into lessons, perhaps through a starter or homework. Any gaps identified will most likely be something that others in the class need to work on as well!

■ **When setting homework:** If you are setting homework that requires internet access, check that this is achievable, as not all students will have this at home. Could students use the school's computer facilities – for example, at lunchtime or after school? If not, could you provide them with printed material to take home instead? Also, beware that some students on PP have hectic home lives, and trying to fit work in can sometimes be a challenge. Don't let them off when it comes to deadlines but have open discussions about these barriers and support them to complete work on time.

■ **If they miss a lesson:** Try to provide them with catch up work or resources to plug the gap if they are missing lesson time. If you have a student who is often not in class, then lots of worksheets may not be the best option as without the detailed instruction and support you'd offer in lessons this could be overwhelming. Try providing photocopies of the textbook or revision guide, which provide a more succinct and straightforward way to access the content, to highlight or summarise to get them engaging with the material they have missed.

If you are a form tutor, you also have a responsibility to pay particular attention to your students on PP. As a tutor, you are the pastoral link which that child has in school. Touch base with these students each day. Try to check whether students have the equipment they need in the morning and lend them things if necessary, so they can get through the day without having to explain the issue to several different teachers. Equally if there are issues with uniform, bear in mind that financial difficulties may be preventing parents from buying new things and be sensitive to this. Contact your head of year or the senior leader with responsibility for PP as it may be possible to cover these costs using the funding.

**To-do**

- ☐ Speak to heads of year to identify the reasons why students in your classes are in receipt of PP.

- ☐ Get to know the students on PP individually and build positive relationships with them.

- ☐ Revaluate your seating plans. Are students in the best place to receive support, either from you or from peers? Can you give them golden tickets to the best seats in class?

- ☐ Identify gaps in learning and deliberately integrate these into lessons.

**To read:**

John Andrews, David Robinson and Jo Hutchinson, *Closing the Gap? Trends in Educational Attainment and Disadvantage* (London: Education Policy Institute, 2017). Available at: https://epi.org.uk/wp-content/uploads/2017/07/closing-the-gap-web.pdf.

David Foster and Robert Long, *The Pupil Premium: Briefing Paper*. Number 6700 (House of Commons Library, 2017). Available at: http://www.researchbriefings.files.parliament.uk/documents/SN06700/SN06700.pdf.

# 29. Supporting Students with SEND

A developing NQT will:

✓ Be aware of students with SEND in their classroom.

✓ Consider appropriate differentiation techniques for students with SEND.

✓ Build a strong rapport with students with SEND.

✓ Consider which tasks are suitable for specific students while lesson planning.

✓ Attempt to adapt their teaching approach for students with SEND, but not always specifically for individuals.

The term SEND encompasses many different types of special educational needs and disabilities, some of which you will have probably encountered during your training year. However, you are now an NQT and, depending on your school, you may be coming into contact with a greater number of students with SEND, and a range of needs you have yet to experience differentiating for in your teaching.

A thriving NQT should make the effort to meet with the SENCO and the rest of their department at the beginning of the year to discuss any students with SEND who they will be teaching. Remember, many of these students will have been taught by your colleagues before and they will have some personalised top tips which you will find invaluable – for example, behaviour management strategies they have found particularly successful, or differentiated teaching and learning techniques. You must ensure that you read the individual action plans for all your students with SEND. Even if these are not readily available, you must take the time to ensure you locate them. It is a good idea to make a copy of the action plans and keep them somewhere you can access quickly when planning lessons throughout the year. Finally, students' form tutors are a great source of knowledge, so seek them out in school or send them an email as they may well be able to advise you further still.

You must ensure that you think about how you are going to best provide for the needs of your students with SEND. When lesson planning, don't forget the importance of differentiating for them, whether this is verbally, by providing them with different, more suitable equipment or through different types of worksheets. (See Chapter 10: Differentiation for further advice on supporting students to access your lessons.)

A thriving teacher will spend time while planning new lessons assessing what tasks or concepts could potentially be difficult for students with SEND. By seeking out potential areas of difficulty early on, rather than while hastily planning the night before, you are giving yourself time to research and request different materials which will be of benefit. Remember, if a student cannot access the work they are more likely to exhibit behavioural problems through frustration, or just copy off friends, thus limiting their own learning. The education of every child is equally important and it is our job to overcome any hurdles our students might encounter.

Do not underestimate the expertise of your TAs and LSAs. You may well find they have worked with students in previous years or in other lessons and therefore know a lot about how best they can be supported. Take the time to show them your lesson plans in advance and utilise their expertise to ensure maximum support is offered in class. (For further information, see Chapter 31: Working with Support Staff.)

## Students with a Visual Impairment

Visual impairments can range from colour blindness or partial vision to complete blindness, but all students with one will have specific individual needs. When considering your seating plan, position students so they are easily accessible to you as well as their TA or LSA, if they have one. It may specify in their individual action plan the optimum distance they should be from the board. If not, then speak to the student yourself and ask where they would find it best to sit. You should also consider background noise – for example, from open windows or doors – as this can distract from your voice.[27] Always address the student by name and introduce yourself using your name when trying to get their attention, as they may not recognise your voice or realise you are talking to them – for example, 'Hello Sarah, this is Miss X here. Could you …?' You should also be aware that raising your voice suddenly in the classroom can shock, so try to avoid this.

Always prepare adapted worksheets before the lesson. It is not good practice to rush out to the photocopier during the lesson to blow up some text to size 28 font when you real-

---

27  For more advice, see https://blindandvisuallyimpairedstudents.weebly.com/differentiated-instruction.html.

ise a student can't read what you've prepared. Remember that images will need enlarging too. Photocopying can make images faint, so be prepared to address this in advance of the lesson, perhaps by drawing over the outlines. Ensure you carefully consider text on the board as this also needs to be in a font which is accessible for students with visual needs. If you have an interactive whiteboard, we find that Comic Sans works well.

If one of your students reads Braille and your school is lucky enough to have a Brailling machine, then use it! This will take prior organisation as work for Brailling will often need to be sent more than a week in advance, but it is invaluable if it provides the student with something they can read independently. Providing a TA or LSA with the worksheet means they can work closely with the student. Embossing machines are also a brilliant tool for producing diagrams or maps. Again, ensure this is done in plenty of time.

A thriving teacher will acknowledge that students with a visual impairment will need more support with practical work. In science, for example, when you are demonstrating how to carry out an experiment, ensure you have a second batch of equipment which the student can handle while you are explaining how to use it. They will then get a feel for the shape and size of the equipment and will understand the task in more detail. Wikki Stix are a valuable tool when students are working with rulers, graphs or maps. By shaping and pressing them onto the textbook or worksheet students can feel the shape of a graph or the length of a measurement.

A thriving teacher will also be aware of colour blindness. Students can suffer blindness of any different combination of colours, or total colour blindness, so ask your students if there are any colours which work best for them. Take the time to ensure your presentations and worksheets have a suitable clear layout; pastel backgrounds and black writing often work best. Colour blindness may mean students are unable to identify different colours in a diagram, colour changes in science practical work, marking in a particular pen or even differentiate between different coloured pens in a pot. These are all things you may not have considered! We recommend downloading the app Chromatic Vision Simulator which will simulate colour vision deficiencies for you. Use this to check that the work, and even the displays on the wall, is suitable for students with colour blindness. If there is little awareness of colour blindness in your school, then there could be an opportunity for you, as a thriving teacher, to take an active role in developing this understanding among your colleagues.

# Students with a Hearing Impairment

The most obvious piece of advice to offer about supporting students with a hearing impairment would be 'speak clearly'! However, this is often overlooked when you're in the midst of a full day of teaching. There are a number of things to consider when teaching students with a hearing impairment. The pace at which you would naturally speak can often be far too fast, so regularly ask students if you're speaking at an appropriate speed. By putting the onus on you, rather than asking whether they understand, they are more likely to give you an honest answer! Don't cover your mouth when speaking and try to reduce the movement of your head as this can impact negatively on how well a student with a hearing impairment is able to understand you. Ensure your seating plan is appropriate and that the student has a clear view of your face, as they may rely on lip-reading. Having windows and doors open increases background noise, so always check with the student whether it's too distracting to open these and keep them closed if necessary.

Some students may benefit from a soundfield, which involves a device similar to a microphone that the teacher wears around their neck to amplify what they are saying across the room, making it easier for the student. If you are using one, then don't forget to take off your lanyard as this often knocks the device and reduces clarity. Raising your voice when using the microphone can be painful for the student, so remember to move it away from you if you do need to raise your voice, but remember to move it back after!

Group work can be a challenge for students with a hearing impairment if lots of people are speaking at the same time. Positioning them in a quieter area of the room with better acoustics and reminding the class that one voice at a time in groups is essential will dramatically improve the student's ability to follow and understand the discussion.

Consider using visual aids to support students with a hearing impairment, such as adding pictures to worksheets and presentations.[28] Use subtitles when playing video clips and consider repeating the clip more than once so your student can have several opportunities to follow what is going on.

---

28  For more tips and ideas see https://blindandvisuallyimpairedstudents.weebly.com/ differentiated-instruction.html.

# Students on the Autism Spectrum

A thriving teacher will make contact with parents of those students who are on the autism spectrum and ask them for advice. They will most likely appreciate that you are being active in seeking out the best ways to provide for their child. Remember that each student is unique, so what works for one may not benefit another.

At the beginning of the year, it can help to set out mutually agreed routines and stick to these when working with students on the autism spectrum. Any change in routine will be hard, so prepare them for any alteration well in advance. For example, if you are altering your seating plan then be sure to tell students about this at least one lesson ahead.

A thriving teacher will consider their use of language, keeping it simple and concrete to avoid any confusion with tasks or explanations. When giving instructions, try to use as few words as possible to keep them clear and limit the amount of active choices that students need to make about the task. Always allow students a good amount of time to process information. Avoid ambiguity, idioms, jokes and sarcasm, as this may be misinterpreted or misconstrued.[29] You may sometimes find that a student just stares back at you when asked a question. If so, rewording it can often help you to make yourself understood.

Make your lessons personal! As a thriving teacher you will be doing this anyway, but it is even more important if you working with a student who has autism and may have very specific and intense interests. This will quickly build up rapport and trust between you. It is highly stressful for the student to change subject teachers each year, so this personalisation can offer a degree of consistency and comfort.

Ensure students on the autism spectrum have a safe space to go to if they are getting stressed or anxious, and always let them leave if they need to. This space may be central in the school or somewhere in the department. Clarify this at the beginning of the year so you are prepared if the situation arises in which they need to seek a safe place.[30]

---

29  See http://www.autism.org.uk/professionals/teachers/classroom.aspx.
30  Pat Hensley, '22 tips for teaching students with autism spectrum disorders', *Teaching Community*. Available at: http://teaching.monster.com/benefits/articles/8761-22-tips-for-teaching-students-with-autism-spectrum-disorders.

# Students with a Physical Disability

In this context, a physical disability is any limitation on a student's physical functioning, mobility, dexterity or stamina. Firstly, assess your classroom for obstacles. All students should feel they can move freely around the space without assistance. This in turn will develop independence, which is something we would like to encourage from all of our students!

If a student uses a wheelchair, again ensure your seating plan and your classroom set-up allows for ease of mobility. If access is a challenge in each lesson it could cause the student to dread or dislike your lessons, which in turn could lead to a poor student–teacher relationship. When talking one-to-one with students who are wheelchair users, if possible place yourself at their eye level. Ensure you adapt activities and tasks so they are inclusive of all students; consider how students with a physical disability will be able to participate in all classwork when planning your lessons. Again, this comes down to differentiation. Use your creativity to ensure your classroom is an inclusive one!

# Students with Dyslexia

Dyslexia is the general term for disorders that involve difficulty with learning to read or interpreting words, letters and other symbols. Once again, it does not affect intelligence, so you don't specifically need to differentiate to support understanding. However, you will need to adapt your teaching approach to ensure that students with dyslexia can easily access your lessons.

Ensure all instructions contain only essential information and no other distracting or unnecessary wording.[31] Try to reduce visual stress by using a pale green or lilac background and black text for presentation slides and worksheets. Always check with students whether they would like to use coloured worksheets as sometimes there is a social stigma attached and they may not want to be seen as different from the rest of the class. However, you could always print *all* worksheets on that particular background colour so the whole class are using the same resources. Avoid asking students with dyslexia to read aloud, or at least be sure to run this past them beforehand. Some may be keen to contribute but for others this may be an embarrassing or daunting task.

---

31  David Imrie, 'Supporting students with dyslexia: tips, tricks and tech for teachers', *The Guardian* (9 September 2013). Available at: https://www.theguardian.com/teacher-network/teacher-blog/2013/sep/09/supporting-students-with-dyslexia-teachers-tips-pupils.

Source diagrams that help to explain written material and break up long pieces of text with these. This allows students to follow written text without necessarily understanding every word, something called 'reading for meaning'. Finally, avoid the expectation to copy from the board or a book; give printed resources or instructions to your students instead.[32]

To-do

☐ Discuss the students in your classes who require SEND support with other members of your department and the school SENCO.

☐ Speak to the students to discuss your current provision and how it could be improved.

☐ Take advantage of technology and other resources when planning lessons for students with SEND.

☐ Tailor your differentiation techniques to students' specific needs.

**To read:**

Veronica Birkett, *How to Support and Teach Children with Special Educational Needs* (Accrington: LDA, 2003).

Sarah Herbert, *The Inclusion Toolkit* (London: Sage, 2011).

Natalie Packer, *The Teacher's Guide to SEN* (Carmarthen: Crown House Publishing, 2017).

Wendy Spooner, *The SEN Handbook for Trainee Teachers, NQTs and Teaching Assistants* (Abingdon: Routledge, 2011).

32  See https://www.nessy.com/uk/teachers/essential-teaching-tips-dyslexia/.

# 30. Supporting Students with EAL

A developing NQT will:

✓ Be aware of students in their classes who speak English as an additional language.

✓ Attempt to differentiate for these students, but not always in an individually tailored way.

Students with EAL are those who don't speak English as their first language. Levels of linguistic ability can vary greatly, from those who are virtually fluent to those who have perhaps only just begun to learn the language. One regrettably common mistake that teachers make is blanket differentiating for students with EAL with easier work. Cognitively, of course, they will have the same spectrum of abilities as the rest of your students; it's just that they have a language barrier to overcome. Therefore, your role is to negate this barrier, allowing them to access your lessons and be suitably challenged. Your job as a thriving teacher is to ensure that students with EAL not only understand the content of your lessons and develop subject-specific abilities, but also develop their English language skills.

**Thriving EAL tips:**

■ Place students with EAL at the front of the class so that they can clearly hear your pronunciation of words and you can easily support them.

■ On the board, use specific colours as code for certain parts of the lesson – for example, purple for writing tasks, blue for reading tasks, etc.[33]

■ Don't 'um' and 'err' too much, and keep your instructions and explanations clear and simple.

■ Make sure you grade your language. This means try to use the most basic vocabulary possible to explain tasks and content, especially when speaking directly to a student with EAL. You could consider using language from Bloom's Taxonomy to support you in this.

■ Ensure all instructions for tasks are delivered orally, supported by hand gestures and also written on the board. Break tasks down into small, simple steps.

---

33  Mike Gershon, 'How to succeed with EAL students in the classroom', *The Guardian* (7 November 2011). Available at: https://www.theguardian.com/teacher-network/2011/nov/07/eal-students-classroom-teaching-resources.

■ Model all tasks. Include a written example on any worksheets and/or live model working through an example on the board.

■ Use pictures or other visuals to show key words. A visual glossary will support the development of new vocabulary.

■ Try to focus on language forms and structures, where appropriate. For example, consider explaining which tense is being used or offer synonyms and antonyms for key vocabulary.

■ Ensure that all reading tasks have a clear focus, whether this is finding specific answers or highlighting key information.

■ Ask your department to invest in bilingual dictionaries. Also consider the value of utilising translation software, such as Google Translate, for individual words or short extracts.

■ Wherever possible, include more drama and role play in your lessons as this models language use.[34]

---

**To-do**

☐ Search online for the best resources to support students with EAL.

☐ Speak to colleagues who may already have resources or strategies that work well in your subject and school.

☐ Tailor your differentiation techniques to the specific needs of students with EAL.

---

**To read:**

Mike Gershon, *How to Teach EAL Students in the Classroom: The Complete Guide* (CreateSpace, 2013).

Chris Pim and Catharine Driver, *100 Ideas for Secondary Teachers: Supporting EAL Learners* (London: Bloomsbury Education, 2018).

---

34  See https://eal.britishcouncil.org/teachers/great-ideas-pages.

# 31. Working with Support Staff

A developing NQT will:

✓ Have a clear understanding of the support students in their classes will need prior to their first lesson.

✓ Investigate any guidance and support offered by the SENCO.

✓ Ensure that students are supported appropriately within lessons.

✓ Always say thank you to support staff.

✓ Learn the names of support staff.

Support staff are an essential element of a successful lesson as it's their role to help you deliver excellent provision for the students in your classroom, especially those with particular learning needs. You should utilise support staff's expertise before, during and after your lessons.

A thriving teacher will share medium- to long-term plans with each of the support staff assigned to their students, approximately twice per half term. Planning should outline the topics and lessons that are coming up and any potential concerns or challenges relating to the students they support. This will allow support staff to prepare for specific lessons and also to potentially prepare the students they are supporting using some specific content. Furthermore, you should encourage support staff to give you feedback on any lessons or tasks which they feel may cause problems for the students they support. This will allow you to adapt, change or differentiate tasks accordingly. It is also good practice to give advance warning of any extended projects or assessments you are planning, so that you can discuss any additional preparation or support that may be needed.

Within the classroom, direct support staff to help where you best see fit. Support staff will likely have a role to play in helping specific students. However, you are best placed to advise them regarding support in your subject area and can also advise when to give students a chance to be more independent. One danger is that support staff can come to do too much for the students they are attached to, thus preventing them from developing independent learning skills. If you feel this is the case, or if you want to see what students can do with less scaffolding and support, then don't be afraid to direct support staff to take a step back. Furthermore, it is essential that *you* don't neglect those students who have support staff helping them. During every lesson, encourage support staff to circulate and work with other students in the class, either offering support and guidance or managing behaviour. This then gives you a chance to spend one-to-one time with the students they usually support and utilise your expertise to guide them. You are the class teacher and it is your responsibility to support every single student regardless of whether support staff are present to help particular individuals.

A thriving teacher will also use the expertise of support staff when considering the effectiveness of particular teaching strategies or interventions. Make sure you ask support staff on a regular basis how students are responding to your lessons, your differentiation strategies and even your style of teaching. Having an impartial appraisal from someone who is particularly aware of given students' needs is invaluable and will allow you to reflect on and improve the provision. Also discuss how you can improve the quality of learning for the students they support. They are experts, not only regarding specific learning needs, but also in the individual students who they probably spend a lot of time with. Try to keep a log of these conversations so that an ongoing dialogue can be created. Note the cycle of advice given by your support staff, your response to it, the changes you have made as a result and any impact this has had. A log like this will allow you to keep track of how your work with support staff is impacting on student progress, which is fantastic evidence against the Teachers' Standards, and will help shape future interventions and approaches.

To-do

☐ Share medium- to long-term plans with support staff.

☐ Direct support staff as needed, whether this is specifically targeted for particular students or across the whole class.

☐ Use the expertise of support staff to plan and teach effective lessons and develop strategies to benefit all students.

**To read:**

Trevor Kerry, *Working with Support Staff: Their Roles and Effective Management in Schools* (London: Pearson Education, 2001).

# 32. Challenge

A developing NQT will:

✓ Have extension tasks or questions prepared as a part of every lesson.

✓ Attempt to push the majority of students to reach their potential.

✓ Challenge more able students with tasks to develop higher order thinking skills.

We talked about tasks to stretch all students in Chapter 10: Differentiation, so please do have another look there for some initial ideas. This chapter focuses on creating a culture of challenge within your classroom, which is something any thriving NQT should look to embed.

To ensure your lessons, tasks and classroom environment challenge your students, you need to take them out of their comfort zone and push them to reach their maximum potential. Ensuring that students are stretched has been highlighted by Ofsted as being of particular importance, especially at Key Stage 3.[35]

Challenge is often seen as relevant only to the most able, or G&T, students. However, while part of your remit is certainly to push your most able students, all students in your class should be regularly challenged and removed from their comfort zones, including the least able. Furthermore, keep in mind that students will all have specific areas of strength and will find some topics easier than others. You may at times be surprised to find a student isn't as challenged by a particular topic as you had anticipated because it matches their skill set or interests, meaning they thrive in it. Remain reflective and prepared to vary your approach. Students can be challenged in a number of ways; through well-pitched tasks, differentiation, extension tasks and through developing a prevailing culture of challenge in the classroom.

A culture of challenge begins with setting high expectations for your class. Keep on top of these expectations, as this in turn will foster the classroom climate you are aiming for. Don't just have vague expectations which you could easily let slip; be sure to fully set them out, ensure the students are clear on them and have tangible goals in order to meet

---

35  Ofsted, *Key Stage 3: The Wasted Years?* Ref: 150106 (September 2015). Available at: https://www.gov. uk/government/publications/key-stage-3-the-wasted-years.

them.[36] Take a look at Chapter 22: Behaviour Management for further advice about expectations.

Challenge involves not accepting work from students until it is of an excellent standard, the very best that they can do. Therefore, encourage your students to embrace mistakes in class. If they get something wrong then they have a chance to improve it and make it better, which is what we are striving for. This is an element of a growth mindset culture – based on the work of Carol Dweck – in which students are encouraged to embrace challenge, make mistakes and learn from them.[37] Conversely, students are described as having a fixed mindset if they see their ability as predetermined and display an unwillingness to engage with their mistakes.

You may find that your more able students who display a tendency towards a fixed mindset are particularly reluctant to embrace the challenge culture. They might think that their work is 'good enough' already, especially if they typically get good grades, or they may be reluctant to risk pushing themselves further and to leave their comfort zone. Therefore, you have to challenge these students to go beyond what is typically good, to achieve their best instead. Get them to revisit their work and improve it. Ensure that you have given them clear criteria for excellence, so that they know what they should be aiming for. Show them the areas that they need to work on to achieve their very best. Develop a culture where all students are challenged to go 'above and beyond' what they initially think they are capable of. First drafts usually won't be at this high level, so creating a culture of redrafting and improvement is of great importance.

A key part of challenge is making sure that the students are actually engaged, because if they are uninterested it doesn't matter what differentiation strategies you have in place. They need to be interested, they need to understand the value of the lesson, they need to understand why they are doing a task and what benefit it's going to bring.

I think another key thing with differentiation is knowing when to introduce obstacles and when to take them away. When do you put in a limited time

---

36  See Mark Enser, 'A culture of excellence – excellent geography', *Teaching It Real* [blog] (1 July 2017). Available at: https://teachreal.wordpress.com/2017/07/01/a-culture-of-excellence-excellent-geography/.

37  Carol Dweck, *Mindset: Changing the Way You Think to Fulfil Your Potential* (London: Robinson, 2017), pp. 3–14.

frame to answer a question? When should you give students more time to do a task? Having an open-ended question that everyone can access can get everyone involved in the lesson while not dumbing down the learning outcomes. Having one worksheet for those who understand and another for those who don't is kind of reductive. That's not to say that it doesn't work, but if that's your diet throughout your whole school life you'll soon be switched off by it.

Dr Simon Thompson, Head of Education, University of Sussex

Don't be afraid to teach content at the very top end of what students are expected to know, or even a level above. Teaching 'to the top' embeds challenge in all aspects of your lessons and will ensure not only that the most able are stretched, but also that all are aiming high. You may be amazed how many students, with practice, can reach the very highest grades available. Utilise Bloom's Taxonomy to ensure your questioning pushes and challenges students.[38] The taxonomy allows you to pitch your questions to stretch all students in your class, across the spectrum of abilities. Of course, when teaching to the top, you will need to prepare differentiated resources that you can drop into the lesson to effectively support any students who require it (see Chapter 10: Differentiation for more on this). Encourage your GCSE classes to submit work at Grade 9 or even AS level standard. Furthermore, your A level students can submit work at undergraduate level! In order for this to be successful you will need to share the success criteria and model answers with your students first. Give them a chance to hit the very top end of what you are teaching them. Likewise, give your classes mixed-media reading lists containing a variety of books and articles to read, Twitter accounts to follow or documentaries to watch to give them a rich insight of the topic. This will allow your students to challenge themselves further and broaden their understanding of the subject.

Don't be afraid to get creative with challenge. Consider mixing up your seating plan to encourage students to push themselves. This could involve placing students of similar abilities together so that they work together to solve complex problems or pairing those of different abilities to stretch the less able and give the more able the role of 'teacher', thus developing their ability to explain complex material as something more easily understandable. You could even give your more able students the role of TA in some lessons, in which their extension task is to support – and challenge – other members of the class.

---

38   See Patricia Armstrong, 'Bloom's Taxonomy', *Vanderbilt University Center for Teaching*. Available at: https://cft.vanderbilt.edu/guides-sub-pages/blooms-taxonomy/.

You could get your class, as individuals or in groups, to plan starters or plenaries for your lessons. Give them an upcoming topic and encourage them to read ahead and plan a task. This sort of independence and ownership, as well as the opportunity to design an engaging task, will offer real challenge.

Consider giving your students a chance to stretch themselves both in class and as homework by setting additional challenging tasks, perhaps involving an element of research. Giving students a relatively open-ended research project is a great way to challenge them to go beyond what has been learned in class. This could culminate in a written essay. Don't shy away from asking younger students to complete extended writing tasks similar to those you'd usually set for older year groups. They may surprise you and rise to meet your challenge.

Finally, don't limit challenge to the academic. Consider ways to challenge other skill sets, abilities and character traits in your students. For example, give them a task that involves their resourcefulness and encourages them to think outside of the box, such as a puzzle – Tarzia is a great program for making these. Giving your class a difficult decision, or series of decisions, to make will develop their reasoning skills. Set your class a task which will inevitably involve many failed attempts and mistakes before getting it right to develop resilience. Include activities where teamwork is essential – for example, giving different clues to different people, all of which are necessary to finish the task. Challenge comes in many forms, so don't be afraid to develop it in directions beyond the merely academic.

During my NQT year I wanted to organise some events to stretch my most able scientists outside of the classroom. I decided to set up two 'Science Investigation Saturdays', focusing on scientific knowledge at a level higher than Year 7 and 8 usually cover in lessons. I planned, organised and invited students to attend these events, designed to inspire and push them. Although the planning and organisation took up lots of time, I can use and adapt the sessions again in the future. Lots of colleagues offered to help out and these events were both successful and enjoyable for the students and staff. Following this, I was then offered a minor G&T leadership role within my department.

☐ Plan to stretch all students, not just the most able.

☐ Insist on all final work being the students' best.

☐ Develop a culture of challenge in your classroom through high expectations.

☐ Remember the value of other skills: don't just challenge students academically.

To-do

**To read:**

Mike Gershon, *How to Use Bloom's Taxonomy in the Classroom: The Complete Guide* (CreateSpace, 2015).

Torsten Payne, *Stretch and Challenge for All: Practical Resources for Getting the Best Out of Every Student* (Carmarthen: Crown House Publishing, 2017).

John Senior, *100 Ideas for Secondary Teachers: Gifted and Talented* (London: Bloomsbury Education, 2014).

# 33. Sixth Form Teaching

A developing NQT will:

✓ Read the textbook to gain knowledge of the content required for the lesson.

✓ Use past papers to gain an understanding of exam board expectations and marking criteria.

✓ Have a medium-term plan, mapping the next few lessons, but not a long-term plan to map out the entire year of teaching.

✓ Use past paper questions in lessons to build exam technique from an early stage.

✓ Set students up with clear organisational expectations at the beginning of the year.

If you were lucky, you may have had the chance to teach a few sixth form lessons during your training year. If you did, then you will already appreciate that this is very different to teaching Key Stages 3 and 4 and can feel a lot more intimidating!

To thrive in a sixth form environment, the most important thing to do is gain the trust and confidence of your students. Their future depends on the outcome of the two years they will spend studying your subject, so the main thing they will look for from you is a secure understanding of the content and the exam requirements.

To help you meet the first of these expectations, we strongly suggest that once you have had a thorough look at the textbook content, you review some university level material. This could be your own notes, if you have recently graduated, or you may find it useful to invest in an undergraduate textbook. We are not saying that you need substantial amounts of knowledge above the demands of the course, but enough to extend and truly explain any of the topics you are covering. This will enable you to confidently answer many of the unexpected questions that will come up. Adding fascinating and niche details can help to bring your lessons to life and truly engage your students.

It is important to have that kind of confidence with your subject knowledge. When it comes to sixth form teaching you've really got to know your stuff, even more than the textbook you are using or exam paper you are teaching towards.

I think you've got more opportunity in sixth form to allow students to express their ideas and thoughts and to start to hypothesise for themselves without it being so much of a knowledge transmission.

Behaviour can be quite difficult to manage, as often there is not much of an age gap between you and the students, but you've still got to remember that you are the adult; you are the teacher. You can be friendly but you're not their friend, and that's an easy mistake to make. It's about maintaining that professional distance.

One of the challenges is to create a good system that allows you to assess regularly but also gives you some balance. Think about ways in which your students can self-assess or peer assess some of their work, otherwise you can become overloaded with all the assessment and marking.

Dr Simon Thompson, Head of Education, University of Sussex

To develop your knowledge of the exam requirements, start by reading the specification. We would suggest doing this well in advance as it will help you to identify the emphasis of the course and the synoptic links that you may want to point out from the beginning.

You should also refer to the specification as you teach to make sure you cover all of the requirements. Look out for added notes such as 'Students do not need to know ...' and make sure you highlight these points in your lessons. It may be that you give students an explanation to help them understand a particular process which they will not need to recall for the exam. It is important to provide additional details to help them make connections in their minds and develop true understanding. However, it is equally important that these same students do not spend crucial revision time going over unnecessary details.

Sixth form students can appear more mature than their GCSE counterparts; however, remember that Year 11 was not actually that long ago – only six to eight weeks! In Year 11, lessons offer structure through learning objectives, starters and plenaries. Suddenly, in the new academic year, many teachers fall into the trap of not using any of these techniques and switch to lecture style lessons, only exacerbating the jump from GCSE to A level. A level students often ask for more plenaries in particular, as these help them to consolidate the learning from the lesson and to start developing self-regulation skills, so make sure you keep to the same basic lesson structure.

That being said, sixth form teaching offers an amazing opportunity to use more challenging and creative lesson activities. In theory, students have chosen your subject because they want to be immersed in it, so they should be more resilient and hard-working in lessons. Involve students more frequently in cognitively challenging open tasks to really get them engaged with the content. You can also arrange tasks such as debates, seminar style discussions and peer teaching opportunities to give them a chance to add their voice to the subject. One fantastic challenge is producing a journal article or report in the academic writing style of your subject. Give students some examples to read first to get them engaging with real subject literature. A word of caution on presentations though: students do like their time to be used well in A level lessons, so make sure that each individual or group has a different topic so that they are not covering the same content multiple times.

You can also trial flipped learning (see Chapter 12: Homework for more on this). This will work better with some topics than others. The basic concept involves you providing the resources for students to review at home. This could be the textbook, an online resource – for example, a website or video – or even an academic journal article. In the following lesson, they then complete some questions or discuss the themes that emerged from the reading. The aim here is to do the 'easy bits' of knowledge acquisition at home and leave the more challenging application and analysis until the lesson, when you are there to support them. There are a few issues that can arise, such as students not actually doing the work at home or failing to understand the content. An easy way to overcome this could be to request proof of work, such as notes or a summary paragraph on the content, and to check learning in a starter.

Sixth form students ultimately need to be prepared for their A level examinations. This requires good understanding of the exam structure and grading criteria. To help students achieve this, spend lesson time deliberately unpicking mark schemes and modelling answers to longer questions. Explain your thinking, including how you unpick the question and structure the answer. Students need to develop the metacognitive processes required to answer exam questions; this is so important. Even better, try answering live as a group on the board – including all of the mistakes and corrections that come with formulating a strong answer – and then train the class to evaluate the work using the mark scheme. This will help them to see answers from the perspective of the examiner. Develop this further by getting students to peer mark work, moderating their marking to make sure they all truly understand the mark scheme. Another idea would be to go through model answers from previous years' exams, highlighting where and how marks were achieved – ask your department for more information about these.

As we mentioned previously, sixth form students will not have magically developed independent study skills over the post-GCSE summer.[39] You therefore need to help train them towards greater independence. This can include organisational strategies such as filing notes under topic dividers, storing completed work and exam practice in a structured manner so they can refer back to it easily as needed and completing large independent tasks without becoming overwhelmed. Start by showing the students all of the resources they have access to: the exam board website – look in particular for past papers, examiners' reports and the specification – YouTube for revision videos, and books, articles and any other resources available to them in the school library. They will also need support to structure their reading around the subject at the start of the course. You could give them suggestions about which pages and questions to address in the textbook or related web links that they can use to add to their notes.

Many will start the year trying to copy down every word on the board and every word you say. This prevents them from spending lesson time actually thinking and asking questions. These students will need explicit training in note taking. Ask them to take notes while you give a five minute lecture, and then to reflect on these – do they need everything they have written down? How will they add their deeper thinking and questions later? Show students strategies such as the Cornell method, in which the page is divided to help structure note taking.[40] Collect in students' notes on a particular topic every so often to check the quality and offer further advice. Doing so will also allow you to check for evidence of independent work outside of the classroom.

39   Joanne Philpott, *Captivating Your Class: Effective Teaching Skills* (London: Continuum, 2009).
40   See Cornell University, 'The Cornell note-taking system', adapted from Walter Pauk, *How to Study in College* (Belmont: Wadsworth, 2001). Available at: http://lsc.cornell.edu/study-skills/cornell-note-taking-system/.

Some students will struggle academically with the jump from GCSE to A level and will need support. You can offer this in lessons by planning tasks that focus on uncovering misconceptions and developing exam technique. However, it may just be that some need more one-to-one support from you. You could provide this by setting up a drop-in period or support clinic at lunchtime or after school. Alternatively, you could let students know when you have a free period – one that wouldn't be too manic – and that they can come to see you then if they need help. In these sessions, encourage students to take ownership of their learning by requesting that they bring along specific topics or exam questions that they are struggling with. This will reduce your preparation time and put the responsibility on the students. However, this does require you to have the subject knowledge to deal with anything that might come up!

You should also encourage students to support each other. Set up a platform where the class can share ideas, revision strategies and questions – Google Classroom is brilliant for this. Google Classroom works particularly well as you can be the group moderator, so any questions students cannot answer among themselves can be passed up to you.

To-do

☐ Read content up to undergraduate level to ensure your subject knowledge is strong.

☐ Thoroughly read and familiarise yourself with the exam specification; not all content is necessarily in the textbook!

☐ Include starters and plenaries just as you would for a Key Stage 3 or 4 lesson.

☐ Build flipped learning and exam practice into your SoWs.

☐ Set up a drop-in clinic to support students.

☐ Set up systems of peer support.

**To read:**

Steve Oakes and Martin Griffin, *The A Level Mindset: 40 Activities for Transforming Student Commitment, Motivation and Productivity* (Carmarthen: Crown House Publishing, 2016).

Joanne Philpott, *Captivating Your Class: Effective Teaching Skills* (London: Continuum, 2009).

# 34. Being a Form Tutor

A developing NQT will:

✓ Have an activity prepared for each tutor time.

✓ Support students pastorally and academically.

✓ Have a positive relationship with their head of year.

✓ Understand the reporting system used to monitor and support struggling students.

Being a form tutor is a privilege and a responsibility and therefore should not be seen as an 'extra' role or as secondary to teaching your subject. You have a vital role as a consistent presence in your tutees lives and you will most likely be the first teacher they speak to each day and a constant source of support and guidance. The role of the tutor extends beyond just delivering the required form sessions; it is about reliably supporting the wellbeing of the tutees, both academically and emotionally.

A thriving tutor will carefully consider what to focus on in tutor time. You may find that your school organises what you should deliver on certain days, but you will almost certainly have some scope to lead your own tutor times as well. You could assign each day of the week to a different theme – for example, you might focus on social or environmental issues, safety, numeracy, literacy or current affairs – Newsday Tuesday? – as your daily themes, among many others.

Ensure that your themes are balanced so that you cover a range of areas and topics throughout your tutor times. Also try to incorporate time within these themed days to allow your tutees to practise useful skills. For example, developing presentation skills – through show and tell, presenting a project they have completed or delivering a book review – or the ability to reflect – through peer marking or giving feedback. You might even want to set up a baking competition for your tutees or organise a tutor group charity fundraiser. This would develop the important skills of cooking, planning and working as a team, as well as building rapport and relationships with and within the group.

Developing literacy and numeracy skills in tutor time will support students across a range of academic subjects. Don't be afraid to get your tutor group to read silently, take a quick spelling test or deliver a book review to the class. Setting mental arithmetic mini-quizzes or maths problems to be solved can be a good way to develop numeracy skills. Be creative; this is your time, so use it in the best way possible for your tutees. Involve yourself as well; be part of the baking competition, help to organise the charity stall, be the one cheering loudest on sports day, be their leader, drive them to be successful and have some fun at the same time! The key is to ensure that tutor time proves useful for your tutees, whether through growing their world view or developing important life skills.

Ensure that you have consistently high expectations of your tutees. Check uniform daily, pull students up if they lack punctuality and check they have the equipment they'll need for the day. They should leave tutor time fully focused and prepared for the day of learning ahead.[41]

A thriving tutor will be proactive not only within tutor time, but also outside of it. If you notice that one of your tutees is slipping academically or that their behaviour is deteriorating, then step in straight away. Find time to have a chat with them about it and find out why this is. The outcome might involve further discussions with their subject teachers and parents, or putting them on whatever monitoring system your school employs. It is really important to take the stance of early intervention, by nipping problems in the bud and not being afraid to take action straight away. If behaviour has slipped, then put your tutee on report there and then; it will be much easier to deal with at this stage than if left for weeks or months. Likewise, if report data or feedback shows that a student's academic performance has declined, then take it upon yourself to discuss this with their subject teachers. They may be able to suggest interventions that can be put in place to best support the student or, if effort is the issue, place them on report to specifically monitor and improve this.

A thriving tutor will take their intervention further. Be sure to take a proactive stance with students who have previously struggled. Build strong relationships with your tutees' subject teachers and don't be afraid to send them an email or speak to them to check that effort or attainment levels have improved. Create a dialogue with these teachers, as well as with heads of year, about your tutor group; let them know that you are very much on top of it and that you are keen to see progress being made. If you let things slide, then positive attitudes to behaviour and learning won't become embedded and may slip again in the future, thus creating more work for you in the long run!

Being a tutor is a role in which you can make a real difference to the children you work with. You are the first point of contact with home and the interface between the child and the rest of the school. Get to

---

41  David Didau, 'The role of the form tutor – the importance of WHY', *The Learning Spy* [blog] (21 July 2012). Available at: http://www.learningspy.co.uk/featured/the-role-of-the-form-tutor-the-importance-of-why/.

know the children and parents well. Notice if the child is not doing so well in some subjects and take the time to find out why. Keep parents informed of good and bad things that happen in the life of their child at school. Make sure you have pride in your tutor group and ensure that they are smartly dressed, well equipped, punctual and well behaved around the school. They are letting you down if they aren't, so deal with it.

Lianne Allison, Deputy Head Teacher, Durrington High School

Being proactively positive is a real perk of this important role. Find the time to phone or email home regularly to celebrate the successes of your tutees, no matter how small. This might be doing something fantastic within tutor time or showing improvement in behaviour or attainment. Don't forget to celebrate the small things and not neglect those under the radar students. Phoning home to celebrate students who are consistently polite, selfless, helpful to others or who go above and beyond brings great joy to parents and will foster stronger bonds with your tutees.[42] The very best tutors are those who provide the sort of caring and supportive presence that students respond well to and are motivated by. Foster positive relationships through your kind and open approach, your warmth and your ability to intervene when necessary to make a positive difference to your tutees.

I took over my first Year 7 tutor group in the middle of the year as their previous tutor had left. There was limited structure embedded in tutor time, which left the group feeling fragmented. I quickly brought in a schedule of daily themes, and stuck to it, to bring the group together. By organising activities such as show and tell and charity ice cream sales, I found that not only did I get to know the students better, but they got to know each other a lot better too. This made them a cohesive unit, which, from then on, was much more driven to succeed during school events like sports day. If you find yourself taking on a tutor group from a previous teacher, plan to build in team working tasks to bring the group together with you as their new leader.

---

42  Zofia Niemtus, 'Six basic steps to becoming a brilliant form tutor', *The Guardian* (26 August 2015). Available at: https://www.theguardian.com/teacher-network/2015/aug/26/six-basic-steps-brilliant-form-tutor.

☐ Make a plan for your weekly tutor times and stick to it.

☐ Email or talk to the subject teachers of any students you are concerned about.

☐ Make the effort to contact different parents twice a month to celebrate their child's successes.

**To read:**

Michael Marland and Richard Rogers, *How to Be a Successful Form Tutor* (London: Continuum, 2004).

Helen Peter, *Making the Most of Tutor Time: A Practical Guide* (Abingdon: Routledge, 2013).

Molly Potter, *100 Ideas for Secondary Teachers: Tutor Time* (London: Bloomsbury Education, 2016).

Roy Watson-Davis, *The Form Tutor's Pocketbook* (Alresford: Teachers' Pocketbooks, 2005).

# 35. Character Education

A developing NQT will:

✓ Be aware of the need to uphold British values, as outlined in Part Two of the *Teachers' Standards*.

✓ Be aware of the need to develop students' resilience throughout their time at school.

✓ See the need to develop a sense of community within the school in order for students to feel part of something.

Although many enter teaching because of their passion for a subject and their desire to share this with students, we in fact hold a much deeper responsibility. It is our moral imperative to prepare students with the skills that they will need to take their place in the world. As an NQT, you should be aware of the benefits you can bring to your students through character education, both as a subject teacher and form tutor.

Values are vital in building rounded members of society and there is no better place than the school environment to teach, model and celebrate them. Hopefully by now you will have come to realise that relationships with students are key and that they not only help with behaviour and classroom management, but also have a beneficial impact on those students who may not have positive role models at home. This is why it is important that we not only teach character education but model it as well.

We already model good behaviour to our students by setting out clear routines and boundaries both inside and outside our classrooms. Yet we can extend this further and build upon skills which students need in order to be good citizens within the school, local community and beyond. Additionally, it has been found that investing time in character education can have a positive influence on students' academic achievement and behaviour.[43]

By adopting a holistic approach in your teaching you can help students to develop key attributes such as resilience, resourcefulness, interpersonal and team skills in your lessons. Many of your lessons which contain group activities, presentations, independent work or which ask students to redraft answers will already support the learning of these attributes, without you having actively thought about it. As an NQT you must be aware of the importance of building these characteristics in your students and model them. Demonstrate that it is normal to fail, explain the work and resilience required to accomplish something and show how you work well with other teachers in the school.

Theresa May has called the current mental health epidemic one of the 'greatest social challenges of our time'.[44] As teachers we are in a position from which we can positively influence students and give them guidance and support in order for them to be healthy, not only physically but also mentally. Creating an environment where students feel safe, happy and not stressed or worried is key, and all teachers have a moral imperative to create this climate within their classrooms. Always be aware of students who may be at risk of developing, or have already suffered from, mental health problems. At this stage in your career, you may not feel equipped to give students specific help and advice, but you should be able to demonstrate an understanding of mental health and help students access support when needed. By developing positive relationships with your students you can provide them with a safe space in which to express their emotions, whether this is with you personally or by directing them towards appropriate support.

---

43  Nurlaela Sari, 'The importance of teaching moral values to the students', *Journal of English and Education*, 1(1) (2013): 154–162 at 156.
44  Quoted in NatCen Social Research and the National Children's Bureau Research and Policy Team, *Supporting Mental Health in Schools and Colleges: Summary Report* (London: Department for Education, 2017), p. 3. Available at: https://www.gov.uk/government/uploads/system/uploads/attachment_data/file/634725/Supporting_Mental-Health_synthesis_report.pdf.

As an NQT this may seem a lot to take on board but it will develop within your teaching as time goes on. However, be aware of how your school promotes character education within the curriculum. Model positive relationships with other teachers and students and be an active member of your school community. By modelling yourself as a good citizen others will follow suit. By working with parents and students we can create positive relationships which promote students' wellbeing, confidence and ability to thrive in an ever-changing world.

**To-do**

☐ Be aware of the importance of character education within the school as a community and of how you convey this as an individual in your classroom.

☐ Make sure you are modelling positive morals and values to your students, both within and outside your classroom.

☐ Develop relationships with your students and their parents to promote student wellbeing.

**To read:**

Michael Hand, *A Theory of Moral Education* (Abingdon: Routledge, 2018).

Nurlaela Sari, 'The importance of teaching moral values to the students', *Journal of English and Education,* 1(1) (2013): 154–162.

# 36. Taking Advantage of Your Reduced Timetable

A developing NQT will:

✓ Spend some of their 10% extra time marking.

✓ Spend some of their 10% extra time planning.

✓ Observe other teachers or classes during this time, but only at the beginning of the year.

✓ Attend scheduled professional study sessions.

✓ Attend NQT conferences, as advised by their induction tutor.

As an NQT, you get 10% 'remission time' – basically, 10% more free periods than you can expect next year. This. Is. Amazing. Many NQTs use this time to mark and plan – both essential parts of a teacher's daily life – to observe a few classes at the start of the year and to attend obligatory CPD sessions. These are all valuable things to do, but they should be completed outside of this bonus 10% time. A thriving teacher knows they can use their 10% in a much more valuable way.

> Don't fall into the trap of using your 10% remission time for planning and marking. This is a time for you to develop as a teacher. Priorities would be observing other teachers and watching yourself back using lesson observation technology if available. Go and visit another school or another department within your school. Shadow students, TAs or senior colleagues to gain a bigger picture of the school you work in. If you have gaps in your evidence for the Teachers' Standards then use this time to fill them. Read some educational books, such as this one! Schedule this time in the most helpful way and agree your priorities with your mentor so you can make sure they are achieved.
>
> Lianne Allison, Deputy Head Teacher, Durrington High School

Observing other teachers is a really useful way to acquire new ideas or refine those you are already embedding in your practice, but there are other approaches to observation which can be of great benefit. Observing your students in other classes can give you an invaluable insight into your own teaching. What is their behaviour like with other teachers? How focused are they? Are they demonstrating a higher ability than you thought they could? How are their interactions with the teacher? How about with the rest of the class? Using these critical reflections to improve your own practice will push you to develop your ability in the classroom.

Why not shadow a student for a day? You may have done so as a trainee, as we suggested in Chapter 15: Observing Others, but doing so as an NQT will give you a different perspective, especially if you are in a new school. Perhaps choose a student who is struggling with behaviour in your lessons or one who is below target. Try to arrange this on a day when they also have a lesson with you. How does your lesson fit into their day? In which lesson are they most engaged? How will this insight influence your practice?

If there are year groups that you don't teach – especially if this is sixth form – then offer your services as a TA. If you gain experience in Year 12 or 13 lessons you will learn a lot which will allow you to hit the ground running when you get your own A level classes in future. Or assist in a subject outside of your own. This not only forms strong cross-curricular links, but you will be surprised by how many techniques you can pick up that will turn you into a thriving NQT. For example, watching a PE teacher keep the attention of thirty Year 9 students on the football field or a science teacher maintain control during an experiment can be an eye-opening experience.

If your school allows, why not visit another school for a day or an afternoon if you have a block of free periods? Have a focus in mind and choose a school that demonstrates this to an outstanding level. Look for teaching schools in your local area, or further afield, as they will often be able to not only show you excellent practice, but also tell you *why* their school is so successful.

In my NQT year I completed a 15 Minute Forum – which is a short CPD session, often run after school, to offer staff an impactful strategy or thought to develop their practice in some way – on the importance of metacognition in the classroom. A much more experienced teacher came up to me afterwards and said that she too was keen to see if we could develop these skills across our school. One of the school improvement plans for that year focused on developing our students into more independent learners, so this fitted in well. We went away and devised a short sequence of lessons to deliver to select Key Stage 3 classes to develop these skills and see how they impacted on assessment performance. Not only was this a valuable exercise for my own development and understanding, but it meant I then took on the teaching and learning responsibility to develop metacognition across the school, making the kind of impact that I sought as a thriving teacher.

You too can make this kind of impact. Keep abreast of current pedagogy and teaching strategies. If you come across something that your school isn't currently implementing, but which evidence suggests will make a tangible difference, then become a champion for it within your school. Arrange for a meeting with a member of SLT to share your passion – as well as the evidence behind the strategy which suggests the positive impact it will have – and ask if you could have some funding and/or time to implement it school-wide. If it will make a positive impact on student progress, then you will likely be supported.

After your training year, you might feel that you need a break from learning about new theories or pedagogy, yet this is one of the most important ways to thrive as an NQT. Ask your head of department to purchase a monthly magazine or journal for your subject and ensure you keep reading up-to-date articles. Engaging in this way can only improve your practice.

Twitter is also an incredibly valuable tool for finding, and sharing, thoughts and ideas about best practice. Set up an account specifically for education and begin following educators you respect and writers whose articles and books you read during your training year; you will quickly find a consistent stream of up-to-date, interesting articles, tips and advice coming your way. Ensure that you read content on social media critically, though, as there is a lot of subjective advice given in a definitive manner. As ever, look for articles or blogs which are well evidenced and then be reflective when introducing ideas into your own practice to see whether they work in your context or not.[45] Continue to attend teaching conferences and TeachMeets; search these out and sign yourself up! Being a member of an association for your subject area – for example, the Association for Science Education or the Geographical Association – will give you access to subject-specific conferences in your local area. Many are outside of school hours, but ask for the day off if an intriguing conference falls during the school day; a forward-looking head teacher will invest that time in your development without question.

Yet a thriving teacher may then take this further still. After experimenting with these strategies in your own practice and reflecting on their effectiveness – many, of course, may not work for you – you could then present your findings to the other teachers in your school. They will be incredibly grateful that you have put in the graft to trial and share these techniques. Once more, you are not just benefiting your own practice, but that of others too.

---

45 See also Ben Wright, 'Twitter can be a dangerous world. Be careful out there…', *Thrive in Teaching* [blog] (18 June 2017). Available at: https://thriveteach.wordpress.com/2017/06/18/twitter-can-be-a-dangerous-world-be-careful-out-there/.

☐ Shadow a student to gauge the school experience from their perspective.

☐ Observe teachers both within and outside of your department with a clear focus in mind.

☐ Find teachers from outside of your department to work on projects with.

☐ Visit another school for insights into outstanding practice and feed back your findings.

☐ Keep engaging with pedagogy, including on social media and through TeachMeets.

☐ Share what you learn with your department and school more widely.

**To read:**

Although there are no specific books on this topic, why not use some of your 10% time to follow up on the reading lists from any of the other chapters?

# 37. NQT-Mentor Relationships

A developing NQT will:

✓ Complete all paperwork on time.

✓ Discuss progress with their induction tutor – every school will have a designated person – regularly.

✓ Raise any issues with their mentor or tutor early in the year.

You will have had experience of working with a mentor during your training and your NQT–mentor relationship will be similar in many ways, but different in others. Your mentor is there to guide you through completing the NQT year successfully and to support you through what can be one of the hardest teaching years of your career.

You may not have a regular, designated day or time to meet with your mentor. If not, we strongly suggest keeping proactive and organised, booking in times to meet up when needed. Use your mentor meetings wisely; a thriving NQT will see this as an opportunity to consistently reflect on progress against the Teachers' Standards. Keep discussing areas of weakness and strength, thereby also developing your skills as a reflective practitioner. Make sure you keep ongoing notes or a list of CPD you have undertaken and progress you have made towards the Teachers' Standards. That way, completing any required forms will run more smoothly and nothing will be missed. The NQT–mentor relationship can develop into a collaborative working relationship. Share ideas with your mentor; they will enjoy learning new and fresh ideas from you as much as you appreciate learning from their experience!

Discuss opportunities to make the most of the extra 10% remission time in your timetable (see Chapter 36: Taking Advantage of Your Reduced Timetable). We advise you to do this early on, as a thriving teacher will want to demonstrate appropriate use of this time and will want to make the most of their mentor's advice as well.

> Just as with your PGCE year the NQT mentor will make a big differ-ence to your development and wellbeing. Expect them to be candid with you and tell you what you need to do to improve in the early days. As you evolve, they will develop a coaching relationship with you and encourage you to try new things. Remember, if you don't get along then it is still a professional relationship so you need to make it work and be pre-pared to learn from them. Be understanding if your mentor is busy, but do schedule time to meet so you both show your commitment to working together.
>
> Lianne Allison, Deputy Head Teacher, Durrington High School

Seek out your mentor when you need advice or support regarding a specific aspect of your practice, but be aware that the support you receive will be less than you became used to in your training year because you are embarking on your first year as a qualified teacher. However, having less support is a positive; use this independence to really demonstrate your strengths to your mentor. They will be grading you when completing the induction forms for the local education authority (LEA), so really take the time and effort to show what you are capable of. The grading system will be different depending on the LEA assessing you, so ask your professional tutor for full details. Remember to always listen and respond to feedback from your mentor. In order to continue to grow and develop you need to consistently strive to improve; you never stop learning and growing as a teacher, even once qualified.

Finally, observations by your mentor will take a similar format to your training year, but will most likely be only once per half term. We suggest you read over Chapter 16: Being Observed to be as well prepared for these as possible as a thriving teacher.

I have been both mentored as an NQT and been an NQT mentor myself, so feel fortunate to have gained a well-rounded understanding of this relationship. From the perspective of an NQT, I found it incredibly reassuring to still have the support of a designated member of my department who could be a first point of contact with any questions, problems or concerns I had. Having this ongoing support and professional dialogue both supported and stretched me throughout the year.

More recently, being an NQT mentor has reminded me just how challenging the NQT year is and how important the mentor role is, not only in supporting the NQT but also in providing opportunities for them. I found that the role of NQT mentor also involves giving support and advice around work–life balance and managing workload stress, things that can be a real challenge. As the year went on, I also found it important to provide opportunities for my NQT to develop, as well as thinking ahead for next year. I hope that the relationship we have formed will continue to develop in the years ahead and that my supporting role will continue long beyond the end of his NQT year. I also hope you'll have a similarly rewarding relationship with your mentors and mentees.

To-do

☐ Set up regular meetings with your mentor to discuss areas of strength, development needs and CPD opportunities.

☐ Keep note of any CPD undertaken, linked to the Teachers' Standards, to provide evidence for your induction forms.

☐ Utilise your mentor's knowledge and experience to ensure you keep improving as a teacher.

**To read:**

> Tim Potter and Rory Gallagher, 'How to make the most of your mentor', *TES* (6 June 2016). Available at: https://www.tes.com/new-teachers/how-make-most-your-mentor.

> Trevor Wright, *Guide to Mentoring: Advice for the Mentor and Mentee* (London: ATL, 2012). Available at: https://www.atl.org.uk/Images/ATL%20Guide%20to%20 mentoring%20(Nov%2012).pdf.

# 38. Working with Your Department

A developing NQT will:

✓ Follow the head of department's lead.

✓ Complete tasks which are set for them by the department.

As an NQT it can be challenging to establish yourself within your department, but it may be one of the most important things you do. Thriving within your department is an essential first step towards having a wider impact in the school and, as much as anything else, establishing professional relationships early on is important as these are the people who you will be spending most of your year with!

One of the most important things an NQT can do within the department is invest time to discuss teaching ideas and strategies with other members of staff. It is imperative that you take advantage of the wealth of experience within your department and treat asking questions not as a weakness but as a great strength. You don't know everything yet, nor are you expected to.

You will, however, be expected to show a willingness to learn, so start asking questions! Be organised and look ahead at what you will be teaching over the coming weeks, identifying areas of weakness or concern. Then find the time to discuss these with other members of your department, both to source ideas and resources and also to gain confidence before teaching these topics. Be aware that each member of your department will have their own strengths; try to identify these – either through observation or discussion with your head of department – and utilise their talents to best support your development needs.

You might need someone creative to discuss livening up a potentially dry lesson with or someone with excellent behaviour management skills to help you consider how to deal with a challenging student; the key is that you are proactive in utilising your department to help find a solution. However, a thriving teacher will also be aware that they too – even as an NQT – have areas of expertise which can be shared. If you have knowledge in a specific area, perhaps because you studied it in your training year, then find the time to share this – department meetings are good opportunities. Be especially aware that coming out of your training, your knowledge of the curriculum and exam specifications is likely to be a real strength; this could be a great thing to discuss with your department early in the year to really make your mark. Always think about what you can offer others, as well as what you can gain from them.

Even though you are an NQT, you should still take a lead in creating SoWs and assessments. Discuss with your head of department whether there are any schemes or assessments which are weaker or need updating and offer to create, improve or rewrite them. Use this not only as a way to showcase your abilities and work ethic to the department, but also to develop your planning skills. The feedback you get from more experienced teachers based on these lessons – make sure to ask for some – will then allow you to begin to tap into the virtuous cycle of planning, delivering and reflecting upon lessons that is so important for any successful teacher.

A great way to settle in and establish yourself within a department is to facilitate collaborative planning. Many departments don't do this particularly well and, if poorly organised, it can be a burden on time. However, done effectively, it is a great way to share knowledge and pick up some excellent tips. Find a teacher who is willing to plan a lesson or sequence of lessons with you; this process alone will build bonds and allow you to gain an insight into how more experienced teachers go about planning lessons. The next step is to both teach your planned lesson, observing each other if possible, and then to meet again to feed back about what was successful and what could be improved. You will then modify the lessons based upon this discussion and share with the department. Again, the combination of developing planning skills while also establishing credentials within a department is a powerful one and something you should be aiming towards.

It is important to go above and beyond when supporting your head of department, but there is also a fine line to tread. You will want to make sure you stand out from the crowd and show a real willingness to get fully involved in supporting and improving the department. Be available and willing to complete work asked of you but also be proactive in asking what other tasks may need to be completed. However, be wary of becoming a 'yes person'. While you will likely want to go above and beyond, be aware of the impact this will have on your work–life balance, as your NQT year is particularly challenging. Do your best to prioritise those tasks which are worthwhile and will have a tangible impact on your development or on the department.

A thriving NQT will demonstrate to their department that they are not just a great classroom teacher but also an all-rounder. You can do this by sharing your strengths in departmental meetings or during other collaborations. Think about what you can offer in terms of innovative resources, depth of subject knowledge, use of technology to enhance learning or expertise in literacy or numeracy.

Finally, you will find a whole range of different personalities in any department and one important skill involves being adaptable to these temperaments. Try to gauge people early on; some may be professionally guarded and not want to chat too much, others may be more open and happy to talk. Some will be morning people and others not so much. Everyone will have different individual focuses and goals that you will need to be aware of and work around. Be the member of the department who gets on well with everyone, not because your personalities necessarily fit, but because you adapt your approach to those around you. This will make your daily life that much more enjoyable, while also ensuring that you have a range of networks to utilise in the future.

A thriving NQT will take action to ensure they stand out within their department. It will take hard work, but pushing yourself beyond what's expected of a developing teacher will give you opportunities to enhance your skills both in the present and also for the future. For example, in my NQT year I worked really hard to establish myself in what was already a very strong history department. I created a Key Stage 3 SoW – including an assessment – which was successfully implemented across the department. I helped to run a history club and we raised funds to build a reflection garden, in which students could escape the hustle and bustle of school life. This was quite a radical idea, but thinking outside the box is important as a teacher. I also developed lessons on working memory and the importance of metacognition, as this was something I was particularly interested in. I taught these lessons to all of the history classes at Key Stage 4 and 5 and ended up being rewarded with the teaching and learning responsibility (TLR) to develop this more widely across the school. A TLR is a payment made to a teacher to undertake or develop a specific aspect of teaching and learning – for example, as a head of department or developing a particular idea or strategy within the school.

Through the journal club we set up (see Chapter 45: Evidence-Based Practice for further details on this), we also brought evidence-based practice into the department. This hadn't been a focus of the school before, but is an area which is still a real strength today. I really wanted to go above and beyond, both to support my department and also to improve it. I still often meet up with colleagues from that department and am proud to have a strong professional and personal relationship with them today. Look for interesting opportunities to develop yourself, your department and your school wherever you can. My advice is to be active in your approach to learning about teaching and pedagogy and proactive in how you utilise this knowledge and passion within your school.

To-do

☐ Suss out your department – identify the different personalities and how you can best work with them.

☐ Ask your head of department how you can get involved with tasks to move the department forward.

☐ Remember your own work–life balance.

**To read:**

Susan M. Kardos and Susan Moore Johnson, 'On their own and presumed expert: new teachers' experience with their colleagues', *Teachers College Record*, 109(9) (2007): 2083–2106.

Katrien Vangrieken, Filip Dochy, Elisabeth Raes and Eva Kyndt, 'Teacher collaboration: a systematic review', *Educational Research Review*, 15 (2015): 17–40.

# 39. Getting out of the Classroom

A developing NQT will:

✓ Attend any school-based CPD sessions.

✓ Attend and support school staff in the running of a club or extracurricular activity.

✓ Be an extra pair of hands on a trip.

✓ Complete all scheduled duties and tutor responsibilities as directed.

✓ Evidence whole-school impact in small ways such as creating displays.

You may notice from the above list that a developing NQT will be doing everything that is asked and expected of them outside of the classroom. Sometimes we all need a push to take a more active role around school and hopefully we'll provide you with some ideas to encourage you to do just that.

NQTs often feel that their main role in the school is to develop their own craft by learning from the advice of others. However, the desire to try new things and the reflective thinking involved can lead to some fantastic ideas that are well worth sharing. This then draws attention to you as a thriving NQT.

Reflect on your practice – what are your strengths within lessons? Are you doing anything that seems to be different to others in the school? Do students respond to a certain element of your teaching particularly well? Have you read about and trialled something that has made a difference? Are there certain students who seem to thrive in your lessons, but maybe not in others?

Any answers that you have identified to these questions are worth sharing. Present these ideas at an after-school CPD session, making sure you finish by giving colleagues tips or advice about how to trial your idea in their own practice. Once you have done that then, like us, you may even catch the bug for presenting and sharing ideas. If so, take it further by speaking outside of your own school at a local teaching event or conference, such as a TeachMeet or trainee teacher CPD event.

If you want this opportunity but there is nothing available locally, organise the event yourself (see Chapter 41: CPD for more on this). Ask your school to support you by providing a space that you can use and a keynote speaker to open the event, perhaps the head teacher? Make the most of the power of social media to advertise your event and encourage other presenters to sign up.

You can also develop your whole-school presence by leading assemblies. Delivering an assembly shows the students you are working as part of the school team, rather than just as an individual. It is an opportunity to share ideas which develop positive character traits among the students such as resilience, environmental responsibility and thoughtfulness, to name but a few. This is a great chance to talk to them about issues that matter, without having to worry about delivering a content-heavy curriculum as you do in lesson time.

If you are using slides in an assembly, make them simple, with one clear message. Be sure to check with the SLT that the message is appropriate for a school assembly and for the age of the students. If you are concerned about having to talk for the whole session, then include a video to break it up or to capture students' interest at the beginning. Including something personal, about your own life or experiences outside of teaching, can be a great way to gain students' attention and to build connections with them.

As we have mentioned, a good teacher will offer to support the running of clubs and extracurricular activities, as these all benefit the students. To make a greater impact around school – one befitting a thriving NQT – look for activities that you can support with your specific skills. Do not feel that you have to stay within your department or subject area. If you have experience with music technology then the school play may have a role for you. Or if you play for a local sports team, see if you can referee some of the school games. Whatever your particular interest, it could be something worth sharing with the students.

If there is not yet a club for your subject, such as a science club or a history club, then this is something you could start. Just as valuable are your non-curricular interests. If you enjoy a game of chess, for example, then start a chess club. This is an excellent way to build relationships with students and show them that there is more to you than being a subject teacher. It also provides a less formal space in which you can get to know more about them.

If you aren't sure about committing to setting up a club for an entire year, you could think about running a project group instead. If there is something you want to do within the school, such as entering a competition or designing a mural, then starting a dedicated project group is one way you can achieve this aim, while making an exceptional impact. Hopefully it goes without saying that if your project involves changing an area of the school permanently you will need to ask the head teacher's permission! Advertise for participants around the school and set yourself a time limit, such as a term. The group could meet every week – just like a club – and plan, organise and carry out your project. At the end of the term, reward students' efforts with a celebration. Go big with this by inviting senior staff and even the parents.

Being involved in a club offers some excellent opportunities to do something above and beyond the norm. During my NQT year the history club I was a part of decided to create a reflection and remembrance garden in the school, both as a place to commemorate victims of wars and atrocities and as a space in which our pupils could relax and find peace within their busy school lives. We got a grant from the local council – after extensive lobbying from my head of department – and, after asking around, got some very kind parents of pupils to help design and build the garden. We had it finished by the end of the year and it made a genuinely positive, long-lasting impact on the whole school community. A proud moment for us all!

To-do

- ☐ Share your strengths, successes and insights with colleagues through CPD sessions or TeachMeets.

- ☐ Take the lead in an assembly.

- ☐ Run an extracurricular club or short-term project group.

- ☐ Volunteer to take part on a trip.

### To read:

John Dabell, 'Leading great assemblies – hints, tips, and pointers', *Eteach* [blog] (15 December 2017). Available at: http://www.eteachblog.com/leading-great-assemblies-hints-tips-and-pointers/.

Susan Elkin, *100 Ideas for Secondary School Assemblies* (London: Continuum, 2007).

Ross Morrison McGill, 'Get your #AssemblyMojo working', *Teacher Toolkit* [blog] (31 May 2014). Available at: https://www.teachertoolkit.co.uk/2014/05/31/assemblymojo/.

Real World Learning Partnership, *Out-of-Classroom Learning, Practical Information and Guidance for Schools and Teachers* (Bedfordshire: RSPB, 2006). Available at: https://www.rgs.org/NR/rdonlyres/3D0B3905-8CFB-4D95-B25D-0B8818B9CA71/0/OoCLweb_pdf.pdf.

# 40. Minor Leadership

A developing NQT will:

✓ Support the school's leadership with the implementation of their policies.

✓ Take on mini-projects as suggested by their head of department, such as creating a display in a corridor.

The above is a short list, mainly because any form of responsibility that you take on during the NQT year makes you a stand-out teacher. To be clear, by minor leadership, we are not suggesting you take on a head of department role – not yet, at least! You may notice that the points on the list are more passive activities that you would be directed towards. To take the next step into minor leadership requires more initiative on your part.

Firstly, minor leadership does not have to involve titles and paid responsibilities. Dip your toe into leadership by taking responsibility for a small element of practice within your department. Have you developed and improved a particular SoW? If so, share these resources and start building a reputation as an 'expert' teacher for that topic or year group.

You can also look for gaps in the organisation of your department. For example, is there a section of the SoW that isn't completely planned or fully resourced? Normally a school will have one key stage that is less organised than the others. Take this opportunity to fill the gaps and thus present yourself as a teacher who goes above and beyond; a thriving NQT.

> During my NQT year I was given a lot of low ability groups, and spent a lot of time personalising and adapting the SoW. My classes seemed able to interact well with the tasks and used the support that I had built in to great effect. I uploaded the resources onto our school system, and other teachers started noticing and using them. In time, I was then being asked what I would do for this or that child, or how would I teach a particular lesson. It felt great and gave me a taste of responsibility within the department.

More formally, you can take on mini-responsibilities for particular groups of children or areas of your subject. One idea could be to improve G&T provision by setting up Saturday activity days, sourcing funding for additional resources or entering national competitions.

You could also find a role for yourself by promoting the career and further study opportunities within your subject, which could involve inviting guest speakers from local companies or universities.

Don't be afraid to suggest changes in your department but do be considerate about it. There will be staff who have been in the department for a long time and, as they are used to the practices and strategies currently in place, may be reluctant to change. They may have even been part of the inception of the current schemes. There will also be experienced staff in the department who have seen many changes and fads come and go. Listen to these colleagues, take into account their feedback on your ideas and involve them in the further development of your plans. If you steamroll ahead, without valuing others' opinions, you run the risk of losing the department's support.

There may also be minor leadership opportunities at a whole-school level. If these do not seem available or obvious, start by asking the head teacher or a member of the SLT for a project based around the school improvement plan. This often focuses on several areas so you could easily tailor a project to your interests.

You could focus on applying your interests or insights in a whole-school context. This could involve coming up with marking pro formas to introduce to all departments, or delivering an INSET presentation highlighting the benefits of developing metacognitive skills in lessons or tutor time. It could involve a bit of reading and research – into any topic – followed by trialling an idea in your lessons and showing the rest of the faculty your findings during a staff meeting.

Finally, just because you are an NQT does not mean that you cannot apply for any internal roles that come up throughout the year. If you have proven yourself to be reliable and organised, you are in with just as much chance as others in your department. You may also come with a fresh perspective on the school that will allow you to see areas for improvement under that role. You can draw on ideas that you have seen during your training in other schools, that you have heard about at NQT conferences and, of course, on your own research and experiences. If you are unsure whether your application would be welcome, take aside the staff member responsible for the advert – often the head of department – and ask them. Don't be afraid to put yourself forward just because you are an NQT!

☐ Use any specific areas of expertise to develop SoWs and share these with your department.

☐ Take on mini-responsibilities for areas of your subject or particular groups of students.

☐ Ask to lead a project based around the school improvement plan.

To-do

**To read:**

James Ashmore and Caroline Clay, *The New Middle Leader's Handbook* (Woodbridge: John Catt Educational Ltd, 2016).

Andy Buck, *Leadership Matters: How Leaders at All Levels Can Create Great Schools* (Woodbridge: John Catt Educational Ltd, 2017).

Gary Toward, Chris Henley and Andy Cope, *The Art of Being a Brilliant Middle Leader* (Carmarthen: Crown House Publishing, 2016).

Part Three:

# The RQT Year

Congratulations! You have made it through what will most likely be the toughest two years of your teaching career. Your RQT year lays the blueprint for how your career will progress, so deserves as much thought and attention as the previous two. However, there is a real danger of plateauing and getting stuck in safe or bad routines, especially as you are now not so closely monitored.

There are many benefits to being an RQT. You have increased freedom from observations, mentor meetings and forms – and consequently more time. You have the confidence from a successfully completed NQT year to build upon. You have the space to define yourself as a teacher and can now focus on fine-tuning and developing your abilities. You can build a thriving reputation in your school. You could even start to think about future roles and the direction you want your career to take. It is, as we said, an exciting year!

This part of the book aims to offer further support and encouragement, while reinforcing the ways you can benefit in your RQT year – and beyond – and helping you to negate and avoid the dangers. As you have survived the training and NQT years, and are well on your way to becoming a thriving teacher, the chapters in Part Three do not begin with our customary developing teacher checklist. We're confident that you now have the basics well established and can focus instead on fine-tuning and honing your already good practice!

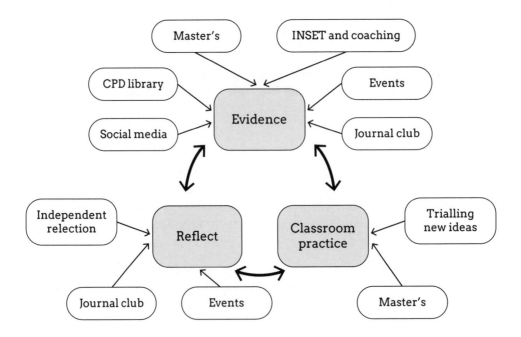

*Figure 6. The cycle of actions required to keep thriving.*

# 41. CPD

Actively engaging with CPD is an integral part of developing your classroom practice, learning new pedagogy and progressing throughout your career. After the two training years – ITT and NQT – RQTs can start to lose momentum. Don't let this happen to you! CPD is crucial in order to thrive in teaching.

## Accessing CPD

For the first time in your career, you will find that a lot of your CPD will not be organised for you. Yes, there are still INSET events and strategy briefings that you will have to attend to keep informed of new school policies and pedagogical approaches. However, there is no professional tutor or mentor to guide you this year, so it is important that you now take ownership of your personal CPD journey.

CPD should not be seen as something put in place for teachers who are struggling or have gaps in their knowledge; CPD is important for everyone and is worth making the time for, even in a busy schedule. It is critical to push your development further and stop your practice and routines becoming stagnant. Students will appreciate a teacher who continually trials new things with them and refines aspects of their practice. Be that teacher! CPD will make this easier as it provides the impetus and ideas to make changes and increase your stock of ideas and approaches.

As teachers, we wish to be seen as professionals, not merely as technicians delivering content. To this end it is vital that we each take responsibility for the teaching and learning that occurs in our own classrooms. Do not be afraid to ask for time off to attend training sessions. Union advice states that if there are more than 250 staff members in your school then you have the right to make this request.[1]

To be a thriving teacher, you should actively look for CPD opportunities. Look for courses that are particularly designed for RQTs; there are often some organised by the local authority or universities. These are great as the keynote speaker can often offer the sort of guidance and advice that a professional tutor would have during your training, as well as outlining current pedagogy appropriate for this stage of your career. Most NQTs are not directed towards leadership courses, but as an RQT these will be appropriate for you and would add additional skills and knowledge to your repertoire.

---

1   See Association of Teachers and Lecturers, 'CPD: How to access it and why it's essential' [fact sheet] (2015), p. 3. Available at: https://www.atl.org.uk/Images/worklife_campaign_cpd_factsheet.pdf.

Sign up for the email newsletters of the CPD providers that your school uses. These will alert you to any upcoming courses on offer. It is often easier to book with companies that the school has worked with before as they will have already quality-assessed their events for value for money and time. You should look at pedagogical and subject-specific courses – especially from exam boards – as these will be particularly useful to early year teachers.

Online CPD is also a growing presence, with extensive programmes available from organisations like TES and FutureLearn.[2] This is great because you don't even have to leave the house to take part! You can often work at your own pace and interact with other participants – and the course leader – through the discussion boards. Many are free but some are paid for, so pick and choose wisely. Look at who has designed the course and consider whether it will actually be valuable. Anyone can write some slides and design some tasks, so, as ever, be critical. Look for recognised names or university affiliations as indicators of quality.

If you want to undertake a paid course, ask your school for financial support. They have a CPD budget and course costs should come from that. You may have to put the case forward explaining why you want to attend, what you will get out of it and what the school will get out of it too. If the course is online, don't forget to mention the benefit of being able to complete it without needing any lessons covered, therefore not upsetting any school routines. Don't forget that the school are getting something out of CPD too in the form of improved teaching and empowered staff. Not all CPD comes in the form of courses, however; don't forget the value of observations, TeachMeets and networking with other schools.

Finally, there are lots of excellent books written by teachers for teachers that focus on specific areas of teaching and learning. Use the reference list at the back of this book as a starting point.

**To-do**

☐ Sign up to receive email newsletters from CPD providers about your subject or other areas of interest.

☐ Reflect on your career aspirations and discuss your CPD needs with more experienced members of staff.

---

2   See https://www.tes.com/institute/cpd-courses-teachers and https://www.futurelearn.com/courses/categories/teaching-courses.

# Delivering CPD

As a thriving teacher, now is the time to start delivering your own CPD to your department, school or even to teachers from other schools in your local area. Through reflective practice, you should now be aware of your strengths and areas of expertise. There is no better way of sharing this expertise than at events like whole-school or departmental meetings, INSET days and TeachMeets.

We suggest you focus on an area of your practice that has been highlighted as a strength over the last couple of years, either in lesson observations, by mentors or by members of your department. Unpick what it is you are doing that is making this particular part of your practice so successful and plan out how you would deliver this understanding to an audience. You should have attended several CPD events by this point in your career and will likely have a good idea of what sort of session you enjoyed and thus would like to deliver. The best CPD is interactive, pacey and, most importantly, full of useful ideas that can be applied in the classroom.[3] Your session could be delivered as a presentation or workshop, or you could even invite groups of attendees – for example PGCE students or NQTs – to observe your lessons.

Networking at the events you attend will build up your professional contacts and could lead to you being asked to present at one in the future. On the other hand, you may have to ask or volunteer for presentation opportunities, which is how we started out. By signing up to present at a local TeachMeet during our RQT years, this led to us gaining experience and confidence. We haven't looked back, and nor should you! We cannot emphasise enough how important it is to engage with and support local events by sharing your practice. Not only are you benefiting from receiving CPD but you are honing your pedagogical outlook and adding to your CV in the process.

If you are interested in CPD and wish to take a leading role within your school you could create a CPD library. Discuss with the member of SLT responsible for CPD whether you can arrange for a space to be made available for teachers to share books, magazines and articles. This could be in the staffroom so it is easily accessible. Advertise for colleagues to bring in any teaching books that may be sat at home gathering dust. They might have read them time and again, but for someone else they may be a goldmine of new ideas and strategies. You could also ask the SLT to look at investing in access to journal articles for members of staff. By adding any articles or books you read to your CPD library regularly, you are raising the profile of CPD within your school. Furthermore, you are ensuring that

---

3   Ross Morrison McGill, 'Training day pitfalls: what to avoid and how to put it right!', *Teacher Toolkit* [blog] (24 September 2012). Available at: https://www.teachertoolkit.co.uk/2012/10/15/badcpd/.

CPD isn't just thought about on certain INSET days or during specific training events, but is ongoing and can be accessed at any time.

The RQT year is a great time to start thinking about how you can add to whole-school development and delivering CPD is one way to start doing so. However, it is really important to note that you should not pursue this just to build your reputation. Whatever you do must add value to the school. By now, you may have already experienced new policies or strategies being rolled out by someone who is really invested in the idea. Yet you find that this has a negligible effect on student progress, while the only impact it has on your teaching practice is to add another job to your to-do list! Sometimes this can be because the idea wasn't communicated effectively, but, too often, most inefficient policies are those that someone has created just to evidence wider impact in their annual appraisal. Be sure that, regardless of the routes you use to deliver CPD and strategies in your school, the content is valuable and well planned.

We are aware that delivering CPD can take up large chunks of time, something which is very precious in teaching. However, a thriving RQT will see that the benefits of this outweigh the time spent preparing for such events. Your practice will grow, you will start to create a name for yourself and you will be directly impacting on other teachers, so get yourself out there and give it a go!

During my RQT year, I was lucky enough to attend an outstanding teachers' course at a local teaching hub school. Having completed the course, I was asked by my CPD leader to reflect on the elements of the course that could have the greatest impact in our school. Having selected challenge as our area of development, I was asked to lead an INSET day session about it. I included activities to model the ideas that I was discussing to make the session more interactive and help explain the principles. I really enjoyed the time I spent designing my presentation and looking up supporting literature – and received some good feedback. Hopefully this has helped improve the teaching and learning in our school, something which I can be really proud of.

To-do

☐ Highlight an area of expertise in your practice.

☐ Sign up to CPD events to present your area of expertise. Get yourself out there and don't forget to network!

☐ Design an engaging presentation or workshop.

# Coaching

If you have a particular strength, a great way to support your colleagues is to get involved with coaching. This is normally organised centrally so discuss your interest either with your line manager at an appraisal, so they can pass it on, or go directly to the CPD lead. Coaching is a really valuable tool that lots of schools use. It not only offers personalised and contextually relevant support to staff on specific areas of development, but also benefits the coaches themselves, who in turn learn through the reflective dialogue that occurs.

It is important to note that coaching is not mentoring. You are not training this teacher to teach. You play the role of a sounding board by offering professional dialogue and some ideas or inspiration to help *them* improve *their* practice. Often, it is a case of giving a fresh perspective rather than merely regurgitating the basics at someone, which they likely already know. Discuss the coachee's situation in detail – what's working and what isn't. Ensure they are able to reflect on their lesson – what went well and what they thought they could have improved upon.

The key to being a good coach is to remain non-judgemental. Being coached is a sign of investment in your own development, not of being a bad teacher. Your coachee is a professional and a colleague. Avoid telling them what they are doing wrong and what they should be doing in its place – this approach won't benefit anyone. Instead ask open questions, offer suggestions, build targets together, encourage reflection and help them to see the big picture.

Although this is a very brief outline of what it means to be a coach, each school will have their own system, so talk to your CPD lead. Also look at Shaun Allison and Michael

Harbour's book, *The Coaching Toolkit*, which uses detailed examples to explain how to be a great coach.[4]

---

☐ Self-evaluate your strengths and put yourself forward to coach someone who may be struggling in this area.

☐ Consider the best approaches to coaching to ensure that the impact you make is as positive as possible.

**To-do**

# Social Media

We think that social media is brilliant. For teachers, it has opened up a whole new world of possibilities to share creative, practical ideas, to discuss pedagogy in critical dialogue, to encourage reflection on our own practice and that of others and to develop networks of like-minded professionals who have the improvement of teaching practice – and therefore student outcomes – at the core of all that they do.

Pedagogical approaches are ever-changing and a thriving teacher will be aware that new ideas are being researched all the time – and are often proven to be more effective than previously held beliefs. Furthermore, teachers are creative and are always coming up with new approaches which are either more efficient or more effective so keep an eye on Twitter. Other sites are great for teachers too – for example, there are several exam board specific groups on Facebook in which you can moderate your marking through discussion with other teachers and share resources.

Blogs are, by their very nature, personal opinions which may, or may not, be accurate or rooted in evidence. This is not necessarily a bad thing, as many great teaching strategies and ideas haven't yet been put through objective research methods or analysis. Indeed, many simple classroom ideas don't warrant such detailed research. Equally, even the most thoroughly evidenced approaches do not work in every classroom. Be critical about what you read online and always think about how it will work in your context; don't feel you need to try everything you read.

---

4    Shaun Allison and Michael Harbour, *The Coaching Toolkit: A Practical Guide for Your School* (London: Sage, 2009).

Above all, be reflective of your own teaching practice. While remaining open to and trying out a range of strategies and ideas – whether this is something you've read on a blog or in a piece of research – you must also consider what is working in your classroom and for your students. If you try something out and, upon reflection, you feel it has improved the progress your students are making, then keep doing it – and keep reflecting upon it. Likewise, if, upon reflection, the impact has been small or even negative, then don't feel you have to keep following this approach. You can drop an idea or perhaps consider adapting or tweaking it. Or try it with another class. Classrooms are so diverse that what works for you may not work for someone else, and vice versa. This is what makes teaching such a stimulating and challenging profession to be in. The key is to keep reflecting upon what is or isn't working for *you*.

You may even find that, as you grow in confidence with your teaching, you feel the desire to begin posting ideas and reflections yourself. This process forces you to clarify your views on the subject. You may find that your blog posts or articles create a dialogue with other teachers. Don't feel you have to share every idea you have, but don't shy away from being an active part of the Twitter or blogging community. Even better, share your ideas with us on Twitter @thrive_teach. We would love to hear from you!

---

**To-do**

☐ Set up a Twitter account for teaching.

☐ Follow a range of educational thinkers whom you like.

☐ Take ideas and try them out in your classroom.

☐ Be a critical user of social media.

☐ Share your own ideas in an article or blog post.

---

**To read:**

Shaun Allison, *Perfect Teacher-Led CPD* (Carmarthen: Independent Thinking Press, 2014).

Jackie Beere and Terri Broughton, *The Perfect Teacher Coach* (Carmarthen: Independent Thinking Press, 2013).

Sara Bubb, *Helping Teachers Develop* (London: Sage, 2005).

Sarah Coskeran, 'Leading a CPD session', *SecEd* (8 January 2015). Available at: http://www.sec-ed.co.uk/best-practice/leading-a-cpd-session.

Edudemic, 'The teacher's guide to Twitter', *Edudemic: connecting education and technology* [blog]. Available at: http://www.edudemic.com/guides/guide-to-twitter/.

Tom Foster, '20 UK teachers to follow on Twitter', *The Educator* (17 January 2017). Available at: https://www.theeducator.com/blog/20-uk-teachers-follow-twitter/.

Ross Morrison McGill, '101 great teachers to follow on Twitter', *Teacher Toolkit* [blog] (30 November 2014). Available at: https://www.teachertoolkit.co.uk/2014/11/30/101-great-teachers-follow-twitter/.

Judith Tolhurst, *The Essential Guide to Coaching and Mentoring: Practical Skills for Teachers* (Harlow: Pearson Longman, 2010).

# 42. Trips: Residential and Non-residential

Trips are an incredibly important part of school life for a wide range of reasons. They offer opportunities that your students may not get elsewhere, whether that's travelling abroad or more locally. The benefits are not merely educational; trips offer cultural experiences and help students develop personal qualities, such as independence and confidence. Furthermore, school trips demonstrate to your students that learning doesn't only have to happen within the classroom; these excursions can often embed a lifelong love of learning that will stretch into adulthood. As a thriving teacher, participating in trips will be an important part of your development.

The main benefit of going on any trip is that you get to know the students – often those you teach – in a completely different way, seeing them in a new light. You may find that they see *you* in a new light as well! The bonds that are formed while sharing an ice cream in Rome, abseiling in Dorset or exploring a museum in London are priceless. You will find that these positive connections transcend beyond the trip and into the classroom, with the mutual respect you have forged going a long way towards improving behaviour and motivation back at school.

Trips are also a great way to get to know the teachers you work with. Going on trips is one way that this network can be strengthened, again reaping rewards upon the return to school. Finally, trips are fun! They often offer opportunities that you may not have been able to arrange yourself, thus broadening *your* horizons as well. Once you have volunteered to help out on a trip, establish close contact with whoever is leading it and ensure you are completely clear on what the itinerary is, what your role and responsibilities will be, what equipment you need to bring and which students you will be looking after – especially if they have any medical needs. Don't be afraid to hound the lead teacher to get this information – it is very important!

Many schools will have traditional yearly trips that are run by the same person each time. This does not mean, however, that there is no space for additions to the school calendar, or that these colleagues would not appreciate a fresh perspective on the school's current offerings. Once you have been on a trip or two and have got a feel for what organising a trip entails, then the next step is to organise your own! Many subject associations send out regular newsletters about trips or competitions that they are coordinating, so sign up for these.[5] Sometimes the days are even part-funded by the association. If you have been somewhere that links valuably to the curriculum, then suggest to your head of department that you would like to organise an excursion there. They should then be able to direct you regarding the next steps in your school's procedure for setting that up.

A thriving teacher will also consider what they can add to established trips, so don't be afraid to share ideas if you think it will improve the experience for the students. Perhaps start by organising a non-residential one-day trip somewhere local, to find your feet. Once you have done this, don't be afraid to organise and lead trips abroad as well; this can be a daunting experience, but is well worth the effort! You may find that your school has someone who can help you organise a trip, or you may have to do it yourself. Ensure that your excursion is valuable: primarily because it directly links to the curriculum, but also because it will enrich your students culturally and personally – you want the trip to have the maximum positive impact possible. Weigh up the value the students will get from the experience against the organisational effort and time away from the classroom when proposing any visit. Consider planning cross-curricular trips, which can show students how subjects are linked while also meaning a greater number of students would benefit from going. It also means you can share planning responsibilities with teachers from other departments. You may wish to run a trip for particular groups of students – for example, those on PP, your most able students or those putting in the most effort. Again, this can be a good way to motivate or reward students.

When planning local day trips, think about where you would like to go and then contact the place directly. Institutions like museums and galleries will probably invite you to visit beforehand, sometimes for free, so you know where everything is and what they can offer schools. Also consider transport options – usually this will be a coach, but the train or a

---

5   For more information about subject associations, see http://www.subjectassociations.org.uk/home. aspx.

minibus are also possibilities – as this will often be one of the largest expenses. Your trip must be good value for money, so consider the total cost against what the students are getting from the experience and be proactive in finding ways to reduce costs. Don't forget practical considerations like when, where and what your students will eat, and how much free time you want to allow them. From our experience, keeping the students busy – especially on residential trips when you want them to be too tired to stay up all night – and allowing only limited, and structured, free time usually results in the safest and most positive experience. Oh, and be sure to have a wet weather plan!

A thriving teacher will also be aware of the impact that their time out of school will have on the classes they miss. Be especially aware of how this will affect exam classes and consider how to negate this by setting cover work that is meaningful and focuses on consolidating and expanding knowledge of content required for the exam. You can then explore the analysis and evaluation of this content when you are back teaching your class.

Be sure to feed back to your head teacher about how the trip went. Take photos and get a student to write up a diary of their day or a report about what they learned. This could take pride of place in the school newsletter and could even be put on the school website and social media profiles. Showcase the work you have put in to organise the trip and highlight how much educational value there was, ensuring that your thriving efforts are recognised by the SLT.

I was fortunate to go on quite a few trips during my first few years as a teacher, going to Belgium in both my PGCE and NQT years, as well as to Berlin as an NQT. I learned so much about both the challenges of organising trips and also the extraordinary benefits. When I returned from the GCSE trip to Berlin I found that some of the more challenging students, with whom I had formed real connections on the trip, were suddenly much more focused back in the classroom. From then on, I have been a passionate organiser of trips, and led the Belgium visit during my RQT year. Since then I have continued to lead the annual residential to Ypres as well as organising a sixth form trip to Rome. I have also encouraged others in my department to become organisers and we now have a trip on offer for every year group.

☐ Explore the local area for new school trip ideas.

☐ Sign up to subject association newsletters.

☐ Organise a residential trip – either at home or abroad – ensuring it adds subject-specific value.

☐ Consider looking at which year groups or key groups of students – for example, those with PP or SEND – may have historically lost out on trips and tailor a visit specifically for them.

**To read:**

NUT, *School Visits: NUT Health and Safety Briefing* (March 2008). Available at: https://local.teachers.org.uk/templates/asset-relay.cfm?frmAssetFileID=651.

# 43. Reflective Practice

Reflective practice is an integral part of the training years but without continuous reflection throughout their careers, teachers risk stagnation. It is essential that you are continuously engaged in routine reflection in order to grow and improve as a teacher. In aspiring to be a thriving teacher, you sign up to embark on a journey of lifelong learning and regular reflection.

As an RQT you risk becoming bogged down in jobs that are 'more important' than reflective practice, but this should always be a priority as it acts as part of your everyday CPD. Once you have completed your training years it does not suddenly mean that you are the finished product and that your learning can stop. Even experienced teachers can, and do, fall into the trap of assuming that they know what's best for successful learning within their classroom. However, with regular reflection a teacher can identify areas where things can be even better. If you're working in a school with a culture that values evidence, then there tends to also be a culture of reflective practice.[6] This is a really good thing!

---

6    Thomas S. C. Farrell, 'Reflecting on reflective practice: (re)visiting Dewey and Schön', *TESOL Journal*, 3(1) (2012): 7–16.

It goes back to the question of plateauing. It's so easy to get stuck in a routine and go onto autopilot because something might have worked one year. But you soon stop realising that that something might not be working any more. I think being reflective allows you to question why you're doing the things that you're doing, so you know why you have made those choices. Teachers recognising what they know and questioning what they don't is absolutely key.

Teachers must then embed being reflective. It's about taking advantage of all of the opportunities that there are. So it might be mentoring, being involved in a research group within your school, doing a master's module or going along to a CPD conference. It's just about taking advantage of any opportunities that you've seen signposted. Keep talking to other teachers about what is and isn't working for them, even if they are in a different department. Keep your hand in with reading. There are so many materials and a lot of accessible books that are written by teachers, rather than academics. Twitter can expose you to lots of ideas and debates to think about. I don't think there is any reason for a teacher not to be reflective. There are so many opportunities for them to be.

Dr Simon Thompson, Head of Education, University of Sussex

All thriving teachers will evaluate what went well and what didn't at the end of a lesson. This does not have to be in quite the same detail as in the training years, nor does it need to be recorded anywhere. But you should continue to actively reflect on your lessons and use this to inform your future practice. You will no longer have a mentor to evaluate your lessons with you as a prompt, making it your responsibility to continue developing your practice. Teachers might naturally sit along a continuum of reflective practice; some will merely acknowledge that something didn't work so well, but others will *act* on that knowledge to further inform their practice.[7] Make your reflections deliberate and purposeful to ensure that this positively impacts on your teaching, aiming to move along the continuum towards maximum impact.[8]

---

7   J. John Loughran, 'Effective reflective practice: in search of meaning in learning about teaching', *Journal of Teacher Education*, 53(1) (2002): 33–43.

8   Peter Scales, *Teaching in the Lifelong Learning Sector* (Maidenhead: Open University Press, 2012).

*Figure 7. Reflective practitioner continuum.*

Start by honestly placing yourself on the continuum. Assess why you have placed yourself in that particular spot and create some targets for the year in order to move yourself further to the right. Your target could be to reflect deeply on one lesson per day, discuss strategies with another member of your department or find an educational book that focuses on an area you want to improve.

If you are struggling with 'next steps' seek ideas from colleagues and online resources as previously mentioned. But remember, not all reflections need to be occasioned by bad experiences in lessons or with classes you might be struggling with. A thriving teacher will regularly reflect on lessons that have been successful. Identifying what has been successful and why is key in order to apply this knowledge to other classes. Your success could also be another teacher's struggle, and vice versa, so share your expertise and experiences. The point is, as a teacher you should actively take time to improve your practice and hence the outcomes for your students. It is naive to think that you will ever have teaching nailed, so be sure to focus on continual improvements.

**To-do**

☐ Place yourself on the reflective practitioner continuum.

☐ Set yourself targets to increase the impact of your reflections.

**To read:**

Stephen D. Brookfield, *Becoming a Critically Reflective Teacher*, 2nd edn (San Francisco, CA: Jossey-Bass, 2017).

J. John Loughran, 'Effective reflective practice: in search of meaning in learning about teaching', *Journal of Teacher Education*, 53(1) (2002): 33–43.

Andrew Pollard, *Reflective Teaching: Evidence-Informed Professional Practice*, 3rd edn (London: Continuum, 2008).

Paula Zwozdiak-Myers, *The Teacher's Reflective Practice Handbook: Becoming an Extended Professional Through Capturing Evidence-Informed Practice* (Abingdon: Routledge, 2012).

# 44. Mentoring

How the tables have turned! Fresh out of the NQT year, having been mentored for two years yourself, you may now have the opportunity to become a mentor. We have previously discussed coaching, which is not to be confused with mentoring. Mentoring takes a lot of time, and requires you to support your mentee when they need it, rather than when it is convenient for you. They may make the same mistakes over and over again, as you may well have done yourself, but a mentor has to remain patient and supportive. Mentoring can be really rewarding, but if it doesn't play to your current strengths then spend your time on an aspect of school life to which you are better suited. You may change your mind as your confidence grows, so reassess this view at the end of the RQT year: it may be something that you want to get involved with after a few more years in the profession. At this time, you may prefer to have a student teacher take over one or two of your classes, while leaving their formal mentoring to someone else.

You may feel that, with only a few years' teaching experience behind you, you are not best placed to mentor another but you have the advantage of having experienced the system really recently. You, to a greater extent than your more experienced colleagues, will be able to recall just how overwhelming the training years can be at times. Both PGCE and NQT mentoring roles are often supported with input from the training provider or local authority, who will familiarise you with the forms and formalities and give you further advice on managing the role.

A thriving mentor is someone who is committed to trying to share their practice and their classroom with a beginning teacher, regardless of who the beginning teacher is. Meet them in September and ensure that the beginning teacher has an opportunity to observe you, with no sense of any closed doors. You need to give them the opportunity to ask questions and give you feedback. To that end, a good mentor is not someone who feels threatened by having a trainee teacher in the classroom. See this as an opportunity to learn, not as a burden. Mentoring allows you to continue being reflective as you persistently engage with someone who will challenge you to think in a different way – whether it's because they have made a mistake and you need to help them think of a way to address it or perhaps they come in with a fantastic idea that you can then try with your own class.

If you find yourself supporting a struggling trainee, the first thing you need to do is take some of the pressure off. There is a myth that we need to load trainee teachers up with so many demands and challenges to ensure that they'll survive afterwards. In actual fact, you will support them more by taking a class for them or giving them a planned lesson and asking them to just teach the first half of it to build their confidence back up. You also need to maintain that dialogue; keep talking to them about what they're doing, why they're making the choices they are and identify their emerging strengths. When discussing their next steps, be clear with the targets. Rather than simply asking them to increase differentiation, provide some strategies and ideas.

Dr Simon Thompson, Head of Education, University of Sussex

# Mentoring a Trainee

There are many benefits to mentoring a trainee teacher. As many trainees are based in a university, they will often share the up-to-date pedagogy that universities are discussing, which you can then apply to your own teaching. Trainees also spend a lot of time reflecting on and researching their lessons, which again can provide you with new ideas and approaches. Mentoring a trainee also gives you the chance to develop your observation, coaching and feedback skills. As you talk to them regularly you will develop your ability to reflect upon the impact you are making to their development, thus improving your mentoring skills as well.

The first time you meet your trainee will most likely be at the beginning of their placement, when you have already been assigned as their mentor. This does mean that you have no idea what your student is like – either personally or professionally – before you agree to take them under your wing. You need to be aware that some trainees will require more of your time than others. Some will also require more support throughout the placement if their confidence is low or if their organisational skills aren't established enough yet. Reflect upon how you felt when you first met your mentor and think about what they did that helped you – and perhaps what didn't. Use your own experiences to shape yourself as a mentor.

Before you meet your trainee, ensure that you are aware of all of the paperwork and forms that you both are expected to complete. Make a note of any deadlines somewhere very obvious so that you can use mentor meetings to help gather evidence or write reports in good time. Most universities are very clear that all mentor assessments should be carried out as a conversation with the trainee rather than as a clandestine grading from an observation. The trainee will have likely done things that you are not aware of, making these discussions valuable in ensuring that the whole spectrum of their experience is evidenced in your report.

As a mentor, you will be responsible for arranging their timetable for the duration of the placement. Make sure you know exactly when they are in school and when they have meetings such as professional studies, which normally take place in a lesson slot. Be sure to share their lesson allocation across your department. It may seem tempting to give them all of your classes – and all the marking that comes with them – but due to the feedback and lesson plan checking involved, this actually takes up a lot of time. For the trainee's sake, they need to be exposed to a variety of approaches so that they can start to develop their own teaching style. It is also nice to give others the opportunity to engage with the trainee and to see their class from a different perspective, as well as to learn from the successful tasks and resources the trainee uses.

It is important that you are aware that mentoring does take time. Aside from your scheduled mentor meetings, you should be prepared to give detailed feedback when you receive lesson plans and after lessons that you observe. Both forms of feedback are crucial for your trainee's development and shouldn't be done superficially or in a hurry. In particular, feedback on the lesson plan is helpful as it allows you to pre-empt easily avoided issues or question their reasons for doing certain things. As the class teacher, you know the students better than the trainee and therefore can help them to design an appropriate lesson in terms of content and challenge.

You should also be prepared to enter into professional dialogue with your trainee outside of your mentor meetings. For your partnership to work, not only must you give the time, you must also be approachable! Your trainee will experience a lot during the course of an individual day, and will most likely have lots of questions. Set aside time in your day to check in with them. You don't always have to offer a particular strategy or technique in answer to their queries. But you could share insights from your own experience as well as point them towards any relevant research that you are aware of. This could be as simple as suggesting some names of prolific education writers for them to go away and read. You may not be an expert on a particular area, so model the process of research to your trainee. Look online together and discuss the findings then or in your next mentor meeting. Consider the importance of these meetings from the trainee's perspective (as highlighted in Chapter 14: Mentor–Trainee Relationships).

You will no doubt remember that there are highs and lows throughout the training year. Be appreciative of this and be explicit with your trainee that this is to be expected. They will have been told this by their training provider but will feel supported when you show that you recognise it too. Support them through the bad times, offering motivation and guidance. If you observed a lesson that didn't go particularly well, then your trainee is most likely already aware of that fact. Even though you will need to discuss this with them, it is certainly not your role to make them feel worse than they already do about it, so remind them that bad lessons happen to everyone and guide them towards gradual improvements.

Instead of dwelling on any mistakes, focus on the process of improvement. Ask them what they think happened and why. At the beginning of the training year they will look to you for clear guidance and suggestions about what to do next time they see that class. It is important that you are clear and specific with focused strategies that they can implement immediately. Suggest that they note these on the lesson plan to remind them, which will also help you to check that they are responding to your advice.

As the training year progresses, your responses to queries should adjust, gradually pulling away the support. When the trainee is starting to show more confidence, let them have more freedom to try different things, but still make clear and varied suggestions. This will force them to build their repertoire of strategies. Many trainees, once they find a tactic that works, will cling to it and use it every lesson. Try to steer them away from this inclination.

Towards the end of the training year, allow your trainee to develop independence and their own teaching style, but still ask critical questions and support their decision making. Scaffold your time with them less, and start to hand ownership of the meetings and their lessons over to them. However painful it might be to watch, allow them to make mistakes in the classroom and then guide them to reflect upon the events that occurred and how they could have done things differently. Throughout the whole placement, be sure to actively praise them for the positives that you see in each lesson. Even if there are many things that need improvement, help them to focus on the big picture and highlight the bright spots as they won't necessarily do so themselves. This is really crucial in supporting their morale and confidence.

During mentor meetings, you can best support your trainee by asking them to reflect on the week as a whole and using this to drive and structure the conversation. A thriving mentor will stay up to date on pedagogy to support these conversations. Set targets that are specific and achievable in the time frame given; each target should be attainable within the deadline, which is normally the next mentor meeting. Form the targets around the language of the Teachers' Standards as this allows the trainee to better track their progress. Make sure you include ideas about *how* targets can be achieved. For instance, if the target is to stretch the most able, then suggest specific strategies – for example, including more cognitively challenging extension tasks – or places where the trainee could look for inspiration.

Use mentor meetings to help trainees structure their free time, ensuring they are getting the most out of it. It can be all too easy to spend frees chatting to fellow trainees in the staffroom! Instead, give them the names of teachers who have particular strengths – this can be from across the school, not just within your department. Observing these individuals can then feed into the trainee's targets and give them a new perspective on issues like behaviour management and questioning. Another powerful strategy is to get trainees to observe teachers who aren't as strong and then reflect on this during your mentor meetings. This will help build an awareness of both observation and reflection with regard to their own practice. Other ideas to best utilise free time include:

◼ Reading pedagogical articles and books.

◼ Writing a reflection log on their progress and challenges they have faced.

◼ Visiting another school – especially one with a different demographic – to reflect upon similarities and differences, and observe other teachers.

# Mentoring an NQT

You could also mentor an NQT, which will be a different experience as they will be further along in their professional development having already completed the ITT year. However, a lot of the advice we've given is still relevant; be supportive, guide their free time, offer detailed feedback whenever you observe and be organised with forms and deadlines! While the practicalities remain the same, your style of mentoring will need to be very different. Take on the role of professional friend and coach. Support when needed, but the impetus to schedule contact or conversation outside of arranged meetings should come from them. Most NQTs will have a formal mentor meeting once per half term. In that time, encourage them to get involved with CPD opportunities and other school events, as well as reflecting on their own progress so far.

You will be highly aware of the increased workload that comes with the NQT year, so be sure to keep an eye on how your mentee is dealing with this. Are they staying late every night? Are they working a lot at home? Are they marking inefficiently? If so, then remember it is part of your role to support them in learning to manage their workload. Remind them of the importance of downtime and of having a work–life balance, as well as offering them strategies to improve this. The NQT year was brought in to support teacher retention, so helping your mentee to develop sustainable working practices that will equip them to continue in teaching truly is one of your responsibilities.

**To-do**

☐ Speak to your head of department about mentoring opportunities.

☐ Decide if you are best suited towards mentoring a trainee or NQT.

☐ Arrange the appropriate training with the course provider.

☐ Add paperwork deadlines and mentor meetings to your teacher's planner.

## To read:

Hal Portner, *Mentoring New Teachers*, 3rd edn (Thousand Oaks, CA: Corwin, 2008).

Trevor Wright, *How to Be a Brilliant Mentor* (Abingdon: Routledge, 2010).

Trevor Wright, *Guide to Mentoring: Advice for the Mentor and Mentee* (London: ATL, 2012). Available at: https://www.atl.org.uk/Images/ATL%20Guide%20to%20 mentoring%20(Nov%202012).pdf.

# 45. Evidence-Based Practice

Using evidence to directly inform your teaching can have a positive effect on outcomes for students and ensure that policies implemented are worthwhile. We believe that teaching can learn a lot from the medical profession, which relies heavily on research to improve and implement new medicines and practices. Research continues to transform the profession and medicine thrives in a culture of evidence-based practice.[9]

As advocates for using evidence we have campaigned to move our schools towards a culture of evidence-based practice. Research provides us with a grounding of knowledge to make an informed decision about how to improve our teaching practices within our own classrooms. It is important that policies and practices are not implemented on a whim of 'this could work' or left unquestioned because 'this has always worked in the past'. By engaging with research, teachers can consider other effective strategies to build upon current knowledge and best practice and so provide better outcomes for students.

I think the benefits of evidence-based practice are that you develop a stronger understanding of what works, why it works and also what might not be working. That can give you the confidence to think, 'This is something I want to adopt in my classroom and I've seen it work elsewhere.' Equally, a policy or initiative might come into your school and you don't have any understanding of why it's been introduced or what the impact will be. Your ability to use evidence to test an intervention out is absolutely key.

There are quite a lot of opportunities to engage with evidence-based practice. Lots of universities offer free CPD opportunities and research conferences. Teaching schools are charged with developing evidence-informed practice, they've got a research agenda. Then you have research schools, which have recently been introduced and are research hubs. The other one to look out for is the Chartered College of Teaching, which you can join for a small fee. They've got a huge database of research which teachers should be taking advantage of.

---

9   See Ben Goldacre, *Building Evidence into Education* (London: Department for Education, 2013), p. 7. Available at: http://media.education.gov.uk/assets/files/pdf/b/ben%20goldacre%20paper.pdf.

Creating a culture of evidence-based practice is about working with school leaders so they recognise the value of evidence. If you can find a senior leader in the school who shares your outlook I think that is a great starting point. You can develop that culture within the school, and sometimes it's just starting with a small project, or even on a guerrilla scale where three or four teachers get together, read something and say, 'Let's try this out in the classroom.' Then other teachers get a sense of what the approach involves and think that they also want to be part of it.

Dr Simon Thompson, Head of Education, University of Sussex

If you are passionate about evidence-based practice, then speak to members of staff who are leading research within your school. There may already be a designated research lead, a member of SLT whose role is to engage teachers, and some schools now have research status. However, you may be in a school where evidence and research is still not embedded in the agenda – or even a part of the culture at all – so a thriving teacher will take the lead themselves. In order for a school to move towards a culture of evidence-based practice successfully, it is necessary to have the support of a leader or senior member of staff.[10] Seek out a willing advocate and lay out the reasons why your school should engage with evidence-based practice and the benefits it can bring, including driving up standards. In order for evidence-based practice to be actively promoted and embedded in the culture of the school, teachers need to engage with evidence routinely.

In order to get your school talking about research more, you could set up a journal club or teacher research group – the name isn't important, but what you do in it is! A journal club will allow teachers to engage with current and up-to-date teaching ideas and practices.[11] You will need access to research papers, but if you are not affiliated with a university you could become a member of the Chartered College of Teaching. For a small fee – which your school may well cover – you gain access to journals, as well as become a member of the professional body. Google Scholar is also a good source of articles and has some free-access options.

Decide on a research article or a well-evidenced blog post to share with your colleagues. This could be in a pedagogic area that you would all like to improve, a new piece of

10  Chris Brown, Alan Daly and Yi-Hwa Liou, 'Improving trust, improving schools: findings from a social network analysis of 43 primary schools in England', *Journal of Professional Capital and Community*, 1(1) (2016): 69–91.
11  Martha Boyne and Hazel Beadle, 'Journal club: a mechanism for bringing evidence based practice into school?', *Teacher Education Advancement Network Journal*, 9(2) (2017): 14–23.

research or about an approach to teaching. As a group, discuss the ideas in the article. It is important that members take away usable ideas and implement them as part of their practice – otherwise the group could just become a professional talking shop – so focus on finding usable classroom strategies. In your next meeting you can then discuss what worked, what didn't and how this will inform your practice moving forward. You can then introduce the key themes of your next discussion piece. If you're running the club it is a good idea to ask members to suggest the focus of the meetings and even to find the research pieces themselves, thus developing their interest in evidence-based practice. When conducted successfully, a journal club can be a brilliant tool for engaging colleagues and moving your school towards a culture of evidence. If you wish to read more about our experiences of setting up a journal club, there is a post on the subject on our blog.[12]

### Thriving journal club tips:

- Meet once per half term. Make this too frequent and teachers will find it hard to keep up, meaning attendance may decline.

- Choose articles carefully and check they suit the context of your school.

- Ensure articles are accessible, interesting and inspire useful ideas and strategies.

- Set questions for members to think about when they are reading.

- Ensure you have a member of SLT on board who can support and raise the profile of the journal club.

- Make sure the reading is accessible to those who cannot attend the meeting. Could you add it to your CPD library?

- Use the model below to plan out your journal club's working practice.

---

12  Martha Boyne, 'BELMAS conference: reflections on the implementation of a journal club in schools', *Thrive in Teaching* [blog] (11 July 2017). Available at: https://thriveteach.wordpress.com/2017/07/11/belmas-conference-reflections-on-the-implementation-of-a-journal-club-in-schools/.

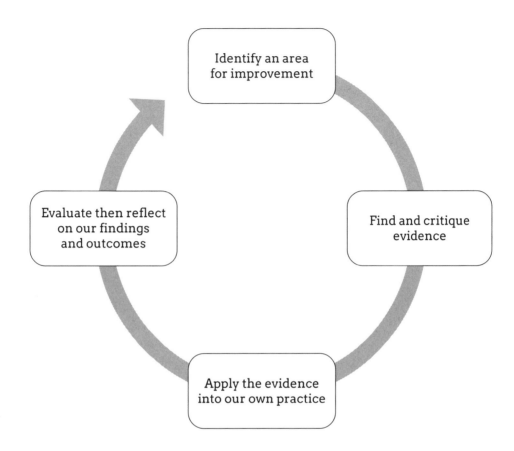

*Figure 8. Journal club evaluation model.*

Why not take this even further and set up a research hub? If you have completed – or are in the process of completing – your master's, you could be in an ideal position to do so. Equally, if there is anyone in the school who has experience of carrying out small-scale research projects, then get them involved. Small-scale research is a brilliant tool and the insights it provides can add value to ideas or practices for all teachers within the school. There are an infinite amount of research opportunities in the classroom, so pursue your interests. It is important to know how to carry out research in a robust and methodical fashion in order for your findings to be reliable and valid. There are many books on the subject, which will give you detail we don't have the space to offer you here – we could certainly write an entire book just about research methods! Regardless of the extent to which you become involved in research, always reflect on your experiences and be ready to share insights with colleagues to establish a collaborative research-informed culture.

☐ Identify colleagues who are also interested in evidence-based practice.

☐ Critically analyse research and evidence.

☐ Set up a journal club or teacher research group to encourage other members of staff to start engaging and foster a school culture of evidence-based practice.

☐ Find platforms or connections that you can use to source up-to-date research articles.

**To-do**

## To read:

Gert Biesta, 'Why "what works" won't work: evidence-based practice and the democratic deficit in educational research', *Educational Theory*, 57(1) (2007): 1–22.

Richard Churches and Eleanor Dommett, *Teacher-Led Research: Designing and Implementing Randomised Controlled Trials and Other Forms of Experimental Research* (Carmarthen: Crown House Publishing, 2016).

Robyn Foster, 'Barriers and enablers to evidence-based practices', *Kairaranga*, 15(1) (2014): 50–58.

Carl Hendrick and Robin Macpherson, *What Does This Look Like in the Classroom? Bridging the Gap Between Research and Practice* (Woodbridge: John Catt Educational Ltd, 2017).

Sandra Nutley, Alison Powell and Huw Davies, *What Counts as Good Evidence? Provocation Paper for the Alliance for Useful Evidence* (London: Alliance for Useful Evidence, 2013). Available at: https://www.alliance4usefulevidence.org/assets/What-Counts-as-Good-Evidence-WEB.pdf.

Phil Wood and Joan Smith, *Educational Research: Taking the Plunge* (Carmarthen: Crown House Publishing, 2016).

# 46. Completing a Master's Degree

We are strong advocates for completing a master's degree if you have the opportunity, whether this is a master of arts in education (MA) – which is increasingly common – or a master's of education (MEd), as it comes with huge benefits, as we'll outline shortly. It will, however, also impact upon your time and finances. You could ask your school to fund or part-fund you, and if you can sell the benefits then you may well get their support. Even if you don't get funding, if you are a passionate believer in engaging with literature and research to improve your practice then a master's programme is for you.

As a teacher it is very easy to be sucked into the daily routines of the school, but it is still important to maintain that opportunity to think critically about pedagogy. The main advantage of completing a master's of education is that it prompts you to keep questioning your choices in the classroom and gives you the space to do so.

If you go for a job interview after completing your master's, you will have a lot of material that you can talk about with real authority, specifically your project, and you can discuss how it has positively impacted your career. You should let everybody know that you have developed this expertise in a particular area and you've got this research, this evidence-informed knowledge, which you could share with other people. If the school wants to investigate something, you have developed a knowledge of research methodology, which means you could apply it to a new challenge or a new question within the school. You may then be given an opportunity to lead a small research group or project and so you get early experience of leadership.

The main challenge of completing a master's is being disciplined and ensuring you take advantage of those university sessions. For example, if something is being run as a twilight, attending after a busy day in school is probably the last thing you want to do, but you just have to prioritise it as you are investing in yourself.

Dr Simon Thompson, Head of Education, University of Sussex

The daily classroom routine can be all-encompassing and it is very easy to find yourself focused entirely on your own teaching, marking and planning. This is, of course, the bread and butter of practice, and yet a truly thriving teacher will ensure that they find time to take a step back and admire the bigger picture. Undertaking a master's forces you to think outside of your own classroom and to engage with pedagogy in a serious, critical way. Your ability to reflect upon wider reading and think critically about your own teaching is an essential skill that you will draw on throughout your career, long after the master's has been successfully completed.

The value of a master's is not only to be found in re-engaging with the bigger picture. It will also have a tangible benefit on your classroom teaching. Education is an ever-changing landscape, so keeping up to date with ideas, both new and discredited, is key in delivering the best quality teaching you can. You will also need to conduct some small-scale classroom research, again something which you could, and should, continue to do throughout your career. The ability to think critically that a master's develops will enable you to ensure that what you are doing in your classroom encompasses the very best approaches, supported by strong evidence and conducted in the most effective manner.

We are not going to talk you through how to complete your master's or write a dissertation as there are plenty of books that can do this in much more detail, but we can offer some more general advice.[13] Spend a considerable amount of time thinking about your research focus and questions. Choose an area that you are genuinely interested in and that having a greater knowledge of would improve your teaching. Don't be swayed by the wants of your school, even if they are funding you – but do ensure that you have a fair discussion with them about this – as it is *you* who will be working incredibly hard for two years to complete the research!

Don't underestimate the time impact a master's will have. A thriving teacher will be aware of this and will be organised from the very start so that the pressures of study don't negatively impact upon teaching. Work backwards from deadlines and come up with a schedule of mini-deadlines for each component. Put these deadlines in your teacher's planner and consider the time you will need to complete them alongside planning, marking, parents' evenings and the many other time pressures of school life. Try to find a balance so you can excel in both your studies and your career, and be prepared to give up some additional weekend and holiday time to complete assignments, while also being careful not to burn out! Having clear expectations about the demands involved and being organised from day one will be key.

During university sessions, which will often be on Saturdays or twilights, take advantage of the opportunity to network with like-minded teachers from other schools. This is a great way to get to know other professionals across a range of subjects and with varying levels

---

13  See, for example, Ian Menter, Dely Elliot, Moira Hulme, Jon Lewin and Kevin Lowden, *A Guide to Practitioner Research in Education* (London: Sage, 2011).

of expertise and experience. Don't be surprised to find assistant or deputy head teachers on your course. If you hear about really inspiring practice, then try to arrange a visit to that school to learn more about it. Everyone on the master's programme has demonstrated that they are aspirational, committed and forward-thinking, so enjoy the opportunity to learn from each other and build relationships outside of your school. Teaching is a small world and you may well find yourself working productively with some of your cohort in the future.

Also consider the value of the relationships you can establish with your lecturers and the links you can set up with the university, which will extend beyond the completion of your course. This may offer you opportunities to attend research conferences, TeachMeets or other CPD hosted by the university. You may even be asked to present at some or all of these, which is amazing experience for an RQT!

Completing a master's has been, for each of us, incredibly formative. It has broken down the barriers between literature and classroom practice; we now understand the ways in which these two facets are symbiotic, which has greatly improved our teaching. In a broader sense, our studies have given us the inspiration to write this book and to engage not only with teaching, but with developing and sharing new knowledge and expertise, whether through research or literature review. In short, it has been an incredible learning journey, and one we would encourage any thriving teacher to consider.

When starting my master's degree, I was very worried about being able to complete the academic work alongside my full-time teaching commitments. At the beginning of my RQT year I quickly became aware that I was managing my time better than when I was an NQT, and I got into the habit of planning assignments well in advance. Switching on and off between being a teacher and a student was difficult at first and there were weekends when I was trying to juggle writing assignments on a Sunday morning and planning on a Sunday evening, but this did get easier as time went on. I also had to be very strict about extra responsibilities I signed myself up for at work. I knew my master's was going to take up much of my spare time, and that I needed to have a work–life balance as well, so I decided not to volunteer for anything extra which could put more pressure on my time. This was difficult at first because I wanted to be involved in some of the activities taking place in school, but I knew I could not have finished the degree if I took on too much extra work. Completing my master's also opened up many other doors for me, an example of which was being given the opportunity to present at a research conference. I hope that, if you do decide to complete a master's, you too will have a positive experience and similar opportunities.

To-do

☐ Sign up to a master's programme!

☐ Use the opportunity to critically engage with literature and research, and take this understanding into your classroom practice.

☐ Be organised and adhere to strict personal deadlines. Attend university sessions, even when you may be tempted not to!

☐ Network with your cohort and the university.

**To read:**

Neil Denby, Robert Butroyd, Helen Swift, Jayne Price and Jonathan Glazzard, *Master's Level Study in Education: A Guide to Success for PGCE Students* (Maidenhead: Open University Press, 2008).

Jim McGrath and Anthony Coles, *Your Education Masters Companion: The Essential Guide to Success* (Abingdon: Routledge, 2015).

*We Are Teachers*, '5 tips for balancing a master's degree with full-time teaching' (3 August 2012). Available at: https://www.weareteachers.com/5-tips-for-balancing-a-masters-degree-with-full-time-teaching/.

# A Note for Family and Friends

When my partner told me just before she finished her degree that she wanted to become a teacher, I was excited for her. I had heard that the training requires a certain level of commitment outside of normal 'office' hours and that it can demand a lot of a person's resolve to succeed on a day-to-day level. But I knew it was a very rewarding career path to take, because ultimately you are responsible for the development of future generations.

Heading into her PGCE year, I remember her coming home in the first week with a list of deadlines for the various bits of coursework that needed to be completed throughout the year. Not too daunting. That was until she mentioned that she would also be working full-time at two different schools! Where would the time come from, I asked myself. Well, it turns out that that's what nights are for: completing assignments and lesson planning! I remember one particularly cold, dark, deadline week in winter, as there were at least four sleepless nights of frantic keyboard tapping alongside five frantic days of teaching. I remember that this was also the week of the dreaded observed lesson. Dinner seemed to have become optional and trying to be useful and find the right way to be supportive was a bit of a challenge to say the least. I did not let this deter me as I could see the struggles she was going through and often shouldered the tears. I found that a large mug of extremely strong coffee and a constant supply of dark chocolate digestives was the best help I could offer. Well, that was until I was asked to help count scores on test papers! Marking demands start in the PGCE year, continue through NQT and, to this day, are a pleasure that never seems to go away.

The PGCE and NQT years both seemed very demanding in terms of lesson planning; the threat of an observed lesson was ever-present and every lesson needed to be of the highest standard. I am pleased to say that planning demands do seem to get better after the NQT year and we have definitely lost the all-nighters.

This year my partner faced her first dreaded Ofsted inspection. I also had not been looking forward to the announcement that they would be in town, envisaging an extreme session of lesson planning and book marking with sleepless nights aplenty. Fortunately – as ever – as long as there is strong coffee and regular offerings of confectionery, you should be able to navigate your way through Ofsted week, and most others.

Although I may paint a bit of a grim picture, I know that my partner finds teaching incredibly rewarding. From my viewpoint the training years were the most challenging period, but it does get easier as time goes on. It's an incredible profession that is so often overlooked, but it also takes a certain kind of person to become a teacher. Supporting a teacher through the training years is challenging and often it can be very hard to appreciate the stress they are under to perform at work. You have to accept that your own expectations of a normal working pattern will probably be very different to those of a teacher. While you may have an appraisal once a year, a teacher's performance is constantly being monitored, assessed and commented on. It can really help to have a clear understanding of both the challenges and rewards of the profession. Teaching is a lifestyle, both for the teacher and their nearest and dearest.

# References

Aberson, Melanie and Light, Debbie (2015) *Lesson Planning Tweaks for Teachers: Small Changes That Make a Big Difference* (London: Bloomsbury).

Adams, Richard (2017) 'Demanding workload driving young teachers out of profession', *The Guardian* (15 April). Available at: https://www.theguardian.com/education/2017/apr/15/demanding-workload-driving-young-teachers-out-of-profession.

Ainsworth, Paul K. (2012) *Get That Teaching Job!* (London: Continuum).

Ali, Amjad (2016) 'Marking crib sheet', *Try This Teaching* [blog] (24 October). Available at: https://www.trythisteaching.com/2016/10/marking-crib-sheet/.

Allison, Shaun (2014) *Perfect Teacher-Led CPD* (Carmarthen: Independent Thinking Press).

Allison, Shaun (2014) 'Walking talking exams', *Class Teaching* [blog] (27 November). Available at: https://classteaching.wordpress.com/2014/11/27/walking-talking-exams/.

Allison, Shaun (2015) 'Planning to be great', *Class Teaching* [blog] (13 September). Available at: https://classteaching.wordpress.com/2015/09/13/planning-to-be-great/.

Allison, Shaun and Harbour, Michael (2009) *The Coaching Toolkit: A Practical Guide for Your School* (London: Sage).

Allison, Shaun and Tharby, Andy (2015) *Making Every Lesson Count: Six Principles to Support Great Teaching and Learning* (Carmarthen: Crown House Publishing).

Amponsah, Bianca (2017) 'How to cope with stress as a teacher', *The Education Network* (20 April). Available at: http://theeducationnetwork.co.uk/coping-with-stress/.

Andrews, John, Robinson, David and Hutchinson, Jo (2017) *Closing the Gap? Trends in Educational Attainment and Disadvantage* (London: Education Policy Institute). Available at: https://epi.org.uk/wp-content/uploads/2017/07/closing-the-gap-web.pdf.

Anstee, Peter (2011) *Differentiation Pocketbook* (Alresford: Teachers' Pocketbooks).

Armstrong, Patricia (n. d.) 'Bloom's Taxonomy', *Vanderbilt University Center for Teaching*. Available at: https://cft.vanderbilt.edu/guides-sub-pages/blooms-taxonomy/.

Ashmore, James and Clay, Caroline (2016) *The New Middle Leader's Handbook* (Woodbridge: John Catt Educational Ltd).

Association of Teachers and Lecturers (2015) 'CPD: How to access it and why it's essential' [fact sheet]. Available at: https://www.atl.org.uk/Images/worklife_campaign_cpd_factsheet.pdf.

Association of Teachers and Lecturers (2016) 'Social networking sites: how to protect yourself on the internet' [fact sheet], Ref: ADV42. Available at: https://www.atl.org.uk/advice-and-resources/publications/social-networking-sites-how-protect-yourself-internet.

Baker-Jones, Jennifer, Lord, Liz and Kuyken, Willem (2018) 'Mindfulness in schools: is it just another trend?', *Impact: Journal of the Chartered College of Teaching*, Issue 2 (February). Available at: https://impact.chartered.college/article/baker-jones-mindfulness-schools-another-trend/.

Bartlett, Jayne (2016) *Outstanding Differentiation for Learning in the Classroom* (Abingdon: Routledge).

Bartlett, Steve and Burton, Diana (2016) *Introduction to Education Studies*, 4th edn (London: Sage).

Beadle, Phil (2010) *How to Teach* (Carmarthen: Crown House Publishing).

Beere, Jackie and Broughton, Terri (2013) *The Perfect Teacher Coach* (Carmarthen: Independent Thinking Press).

Benjamin, Aaron S. and Tullis, Jonathan (2010) 'What makes distributed practice effective?', *Cognitive Psychology*, 61(3): 228–247. Available at: https://www.ncbi.nlm.nih.gov/pmc/articles/PMC2930147/.

Bennett, Tom (2010) *The Behaviour Guru: Behaviour Management Solutions for Teachers* (London: Continuum).

Berger, Ron (2012) 'Critique and feedback – the story of Austin's butterfly' [video] (8 December). Available at: https://www.youtube.com/watch?v=hqh1MRWZjms.

Best, Brin and Thomas, Will (2007) *The Creative Teaching and Learning Toolkit* (London: Continuum).

Biesta, Gert (2007) 'Why "what works" won't work: evidence-based practice and the democratic deficit in educational research', *Educational Theory*, 57(1): 1–22.

Birkett, Veronica (2003) *How to Support and Teach Children with Special Educational Needs* (Accrington: LDA).

Bjork, Robert (2012) 'Robert Bjork – spacing improves long-term retention' [video] (13 July). Available at: https://www.youtube.com/watch?v=TTo35X2rqls.

Bjork, Robert (2012) 'Robert Bjork – storage strength vs. retrieval strength' [video] (12 July). Available at: https://www.youtube.com/watch?v=1FQoGUCgb5w.

Blakey, Robert (2014) *I Hate Revision: Study Skills and Revision Techniques for GCSE, A-level and Undergraduate Exams* (lulu.com).

Blatchford, Roy (2013) 'How teachers can show student progress during lesson observations', *SecEd* (28 February). Available at: http://www.sec-ed.co.uk/best-practice/how-teachers-can-show-student-progress-during-lesson-observations/.

Blumen, Helena M. and Stern, Yaakov (2011) 'Short-term and long-term collaboration benefits of individual recall in younger and older adults', *Memory and Cognition*, 39(1) (January): 147–154. Available at: http://www.cumc.columbia.edu/dept/sergievsky/pdfs/shorttermandlongterm.pdf.

Boyne, Martha (2017) 'BELMAS conference: reflections on the implementation of a journal club in schools', *Thrive in Teaching* [blog] (11 July). Available at: https://thriveteach.wordpress.com/2017/07/11/belmas-conference-reflections-on-the-implementation-of-a-journal-club-in-schools/.

Boyne, Martha and Beadle, Hazel (2017) 'Journal club: a mechanism for bringing evidence based practice into school?', *Teacher Education Advancement Network Journal*, 9(2): 14–23.

Brookfield, Stephen D. (2017) *Becoming a Critically Reflective Teacher*, 2nd edn (San Francisco, CA: Jossey-Bass).

Brown, Chris, Daly, Alan and Liou, Yi-Hwa (2016) 'Improving trust, improving schools: findings from a social network analysis of 43 primary schools in England', *Journal of Professional Capital and Community*, 1(1): 69–91.

Brown, Peter C., Roediger, Henry L. and McDaniel, Mark A. (2014) *Make It Stick: The Science of Successful Learning* (Cambridge, MA: Harvard University Press).

Bubb, Sara (2005) *Helping Teachers Develop* (London: Sage).

Buck, Andy (2017) *Leadership Matters: How Leaders at All Levels Can Create Great Schools* (Woodbridge: John Catt Educational Ltd).

Christian, Ann Marie (2018) *A Practical Guide to Safeguarding for Schools: Advice and Strategies for Primary and Secondary Schools* (London: Jessica Kingsley Publishers).

Christodoulou, Daisy (2017) *Making Good Progress? The Future of Assessment for Learning* (Oxford: Oxford University Press).

Churches, Richard and Dommett, Eleanor (2016) *Teacher-Led Research: Designing and Implementing Randomised Controlled Trials and Other Forms of Experimental Research* (Carmarthen: Crown House Publishing).

Clark, Richard, Kirschner, Paul and Sweller, John (2012) 'Putting students on the path to learning: the case for fully guided instruction', *American Educator*, 36(1): 6–11.

Clements, Emily (2017) 'What about our language? How we can use words to give our classrooms the nudge', *Thrive in Teaching* [blog] (27 May). Available at: https://thriveteach.wordpress.com/2017/05/27/what-about-our-language-how-we-can-use-words-to-give-our-classrooms-the-nudge/.

Cornell University (n. d.) 'The Cornell note-taking system', adapted from Walter Pauk, *How to Study in College* (Belmont: Wadsworth, 2001). Available at: http://lsc.cornell.edu/study-skills/cornell-note-taking-system/.

Coskeran, Sarah (2015) 'Leading a CPD session', *SecEd* (8 January). Available at: http://www.sec-ed.co.uk/best-practice/leading-a-cpd-session.

Cowley, Sue (2013) *The Seven T's of Practical Differentiation* (Bristol: Sue Cowley Books Ltd).

Cowley, Sue (2014) *Getting the Buggers to Behave*, 5th edn (London: Bloomsbury Education).

Creasy, Mark (2014) *Unhomework: How to Get the Most out of Homework, Without Really Setting It* (Carmarthen: Independent Thinking Press).

Czerniawski, Gerry and Kidd, Warren (2013) *Homework for Learning: 300 Practical Strategies* (Maidenhead: Open University Press).

Dabell, John (2017) 'Leading great assemblies – hints, tips, and pointers', *Eteach* [blog] (15 December). Available at: http://www.eteachblog.com/leading-great-assemblies-hints-tips-and-pointers/.

Denby, Neil, Butroyd, Robert, Swift, Helen, Price, Jayne and Glazzard, Jonathan (2008) *Master's Level Study in Education: A Guide to Success for PGCE Students* (Maidenhead: Open University Press).

Department for Education (2011) *Teachers' Standards: Guidance for School Leaders, School Staff and Governing Bodies*. Ref: DFE-00066-2011 (London: Department for Education). Available at: https://www.gov.uk/government/uploads/system/uploads/attachment_data/file/665520/Teachers__Standards.pdf.

Department for Education (2016) *Keeping Children Safe in Education: Statutory Guidance for Schools and Colleges*. Ref: DfE-00140-2016 (London: Department for Education). Available at: https://www.gov.uk/government/uploads/system/uploads/attachment_data/file/550511/Keeping_children_safe_in_education.pdf.

Department for Education (2018) *Secondary Accountability Measures: Guide for Maintained Secondary Schools, Academies and Free Schools, January 2018*. Ref: DFE-00278-2017 (London: Department for Education). Available at: https://www.gov.uk/government/uploads/system/uploads/attachment_data/file/676184/Secondary_accountability_measures_January_2018.pdf.

Didau, David (2012) 'The role of the form tutor – the importance of WHY', *The Learning Spy* [blog] (21 July). Available at: http://www.learningspy.co.uk/featured/the-role-of-the-form-tutor-the-importance-of-why/.

Didau, David (2014) 'Back to school part 3: literacy', *The Learning Spy* [blog] (21 August). Available at: http://www.learningspy.co.uk/literacy/back-school-part-3-literacy/.

Didau, David (2014) *The Secret of Literacy: Making the Implicit Explicit* (Carmarthen: Independent Thinking Press).

Didau, David (2014) 'The secret of numeracy (across the curriculum)', *The Learning Spy* [blog] (10 December). Available at: http://www.learningspy.co.uk/featured/secret-numeracy/.

Didau, David (2016) 'Proof of progress – part 1', *The Learning Spy* [blog] (30 January). Available at: http://www.learningspy.co.uk/assessment/comparative-judgement-trial-part-1/.

Dix, Paul (n. d.) '10 tips for NQTs', *Pivotal Education*. Available at: https://pivotaleducation.com/classroom-behaviour-management/resource-bank/pivotal-how-to-series/10-tips-for-nqts/.

Dix, Paul (2017) *When the Adults Change, Everything Changes: Seismic Shifts in School Behaviour* (Carmarthen: Independent Thinking Press).

Doorn, Ron (2008) 'Teaching hearing impaired children', *TEACH Magazine*. Available at: http://www.teachmag.com/archives/130.

Dryden, Matt (2017) 'Radicalisation: the last taboo in safeguarding and child protection? Assessing practitioner preparedness in preventing the radicalisation of looked-after children', *Journal for Deradicalization*, 13: 101–136.

Dunlosky, John, Rawson, Katherine A., Marsh, Elizabeth J., Nathan, Mitchell J. and Willingham, Daniel T. (2013) 'Improving students' learning with effective learning techniques: promising directions from cognitive and educational psychology', *Psychological Science in the Public Interest*, 14(1): 4–58. Available at: http://elephantsdontforget.com/wp-content/uploads/2016/08/Learning-White-Paper.pdf.

Dweck, Carol (2017) *Mindset: Changing the Way You Think to Fulfil Your Potential* (London: Robinson).

Edudemic (n. d.) 'The teacher's guide to Twitter', *Edudemic: connecting education and technology* [blog]. Available at: http://www.edudemic.com/guides/guide-to-twitter/.

Elder, Linda and Paul, Richard (1998) 'The role of Socratic questioning in thinking, teaching and learning', *The Clearing House: A Journal of Educational Strategies, Issues and Ideas*, 71(5): 297–301.

Elkin, Susan (2007) *100 Ideas for Secondary School Assemblies* (London: Continuum).

Elliott, Victoria, Baird, Jo-Ann, Hopfenbeck, Therese N., Ingram, Jenni, Thompson, Ian, Usher, Natalie, Zantout, Mae, Richardson, James and Coleman, Robbie (2016) *A Marked Improvement? A Review of the Evidence on Written Marking* (London: Education Endowment Foundation). Available at: https://educationendowment-foundation.org.uk/evidence-summaries/evidence-reviews/written-marking/.

Enser, Mark (2017) 'A culture of excellence – excellent geography', *Teaching It Real* [blog] (1 July). Available at: https://teachreal.wordpress.com/2017/07/01/a-culture-of-excellence-excellent-geography/.

Fan, Weihua and Williams, Cathy (2010) 'The effects of parental involvement on students' academic self-efficacy, engagement and intrinsic motivation', *Educational Psychology*, 30(1): 53–74.

Farrell, Thomas S. C. (2012) 'Reflecting on reflective practice: (re)visiting Dewey and Schön', *TESOL Journal*, 3(1): 7–16.

Firth, Jonathan (2018) 'The application of spacing and interleaving approaches in the classroom', *Impact: Journal of the Chartered College of Teaching*, Issue 2. Available at: https://impact.chartered.college/article/firth-spacing-interleaving-classroom/.

Fletcher-Wood, Harry (2016) *Ticked Off: Checklists for Teachers, Students, School Leaders* (Carmarthen: Crown House Publishing).

Foster, David and Long, Robert (2017) *The Pupil Premium: Briefing Paper*. Number 6700 (House of Commons Library). Available at: http://www.researchbriefings.files.parliament.uk/documents/SN06700/SN06700.pdf.

Foster, Robyn (2014) 'Barriers and enablers to evidence-based practices', *Kairaranga*, 15(1): 50–58.

Foster, Tom (2017) '20 UK teachers to follow on Twitter', *The Educator* (17 January). Available at: https://www.theeducator.com/blog/20-uk-teachers-follow-twitter/.

Fulton, Kathleen (2012) 'Upside down and inside out: flip your classroom to improve student learning', *Learning and Leading with Technology*, 39(8): 12–17. Available at: http://files.eric.ed.gov/fulltext/EJ982840.pdf.

Gershon, Mike (2011) 'How to succeed with EAL students in the classroom', *The Guardian* (7 November). Available at: https://www.theguardian.com/teacher-network/2011/nov/07/eal-students-classroom-teaching-resources.

Gershon, Mike (2013) *How to Teach EAL Students in the Classroom: The Complete Guide* (CreateSpace).

Gershon, Mike (2013) *How to Use Assessment for Learning in the Classroom: The Complete Guide* (CreateSpace).

Gershon, Mike (2015) *How to Use Bloom's Taxonomy in the Classroom: The Complete Guide* (CreateSpace).

Gershon, Mike (2017) *How to Use Feedback and Marking in the Classroom: The Complete Guide* (CreateSpace).

Gershon, Mike (n.d.) 'Classroom questioning: how to ask good questions', *Mike Gershon* [blog]. Available at: https://mikegershon.com/classroom-questioning-ask-good-questions/.

Ginnis, Paul (2002) *The Teacher's Toolkit: Raising Classroom Achievement with Strategies for Every Learner* (Carmarthen: Crown House Publishing).

Goldacre, Ben (2013) *Building Evidence into Education* (London: Department for Education). Available at: http://media.education.gov.uk/assets/files/pdf/b/ben%20goldacre%20paper.pdf.

Goodall, Janet, Vorhaus, John, Carpentieri, Jon, Brooks, Greg, Akerman, Rodie and Harris, Alma (2010) *Review of Best Practice in Parental Engagement*. Research Report DFE-RR156 (London: Department for Education). Available at: https://www.gov.uk/government/uploads/system/uploads/attachment_data/file/182508/DFE-RR156.pdf.

Griffith, Andy and Burns, Mark (2014) *Outstanding Teaching: Teaching Backwards* (Carmarthen: Crown House Publishing).

Haigh, Gerald (2015) *Good Ideas for Good Teachers Who Want Good Jobs* (Carmarthen: Crown House Publishing).

Hand, Michael (2018) *A Theory of Moral Education* (Abingdon: Routledge).

Harris, Richard J. (2005) 'Does differentiation have to mean different?', *Teaching History*, 118: 5–12.

Hattie, John and Timperley, Helen (2007) 'The power of feedback', *Review of Educational Research*, 77(1): 81–112.

Hays, Matthew, Kornell, Nate and Bjork, Robert (2013) 'When and why a failed test potentiates the effectiveness of subsequent study', *Journal of Experimental Psychology*, 39(1): 290–296.

Hendrick, Carl and Macpherson, Robin (2017) *What Does This Look Like in the Classroom? Bridging the Gap Between Research and Practice* (Woodbridge: John Catt Educational Ltd).

Henley, Martin (2009) *Classroom Management: A Proactive Approach* (London: Pearson).

Hensley, Pat (n. d.) '22 tips for teaching students with autism spectrum disorders', *Teaching Community*. Available at: http://teaching.monster.com/benefits/articles/8761-22-tips-for-teaching-students-with-autism-spectrum-disorders.

Herbert, Sarah (2011) *The Inclusion Toolkit* (London: Sage).

Higgins, Steve (2011) 'What works in raising attainment and closing the gap: research evidence from the UK and abroad', Presentation for the Education Endowment Foundation (Durham University). Available at: https://v1.educationendowmentfoundation.org.uk/uploads/pdf/What_works_in_raising_attainment_and_closing_the_gap.pdf.

Huat See, Beng and Gorard, Stephen (2013) *What Do Rigorous Evaluations Tell Us About the Most Promising Parental Involvement Interventions? A Critical Review of What Works for Disadvantaged Children in Different Age Groups* (London: Nuffield Foundation). Available at: https://www.nuffieldfoundation.org/sites/default/files/files/What_do_rigorous_evaluations_tell_us_about_the_most_promising_parental_involvement_interventions.pdf.

Imrie, David (2013) 'Supporting students with dyslexia: tips, tricks and tech for teachers', *The Guardian* (9 September). Available at: https://www.theguardian.com/teacher-network/teacher-blog/2013/sep/09/supporting-students-with-dyslexia-teachers-tips-pupils.

Jeynes, William H. (2007) 'The relationship between parental involvement and urban secondary school student academic achievement: a meta-analysis', *Urban Education*, 42(1): 82–110.

Kang, Sean (2017) 'The benefits of interleaved practice for learning'. In Jared Cooney Horvath, Jason Lodge and John Hattie (eds), *From the Laboratory to the Classroom: Translating Science of Learning for Teachers* (Abingdon: Routledge), pp. 79–93.

Kardos, Susan M. and Moore Johnson, Susan (2007) 'On their own and presumed expert: new teachers' experience with their colleagues', *Teachers College Record*, 109(9): 2083–2106.

Kerry, Trevor (2001) *Working with Support Staff: Their Roles and Effective Management in Schools* (London: Pearson Education).

Lawrence, Tracey (2017) 'Five ways to ensure a successful ITT year', *UCAS* [blog] (11 August). Available at: https://www.ucas.com/connect/blogs/five-ways-ensure-successful-itt-year-tracey-lawrence.

Lemov, Doug (2015) *Teach Like a Champion 2.0: 62 Techniques That Put Students on the Path to College* (San Francisco, CA: Jossey-Bass).

Lemov, Doug (2017) 'Engaged cerebral classroom culture: Aidan Thomas' master class on wait time', *Teach Like a Champion* [blog] (4 January). Available at: http://teachlikeachampion.com/blog/engaged-cerebral-classroom-culture-aidan-thomas-master-class-wait-time/.

Lessing, Ansie and Wulfsohn, Renee (2015) 'The potential of behaviour management strategies to support learners with Attention Deficit Hyperactivity Disorder in the classroom', *Education as Change*, 19(1): 54–77.

Liverpool John Moores University (n.d.) *The LJMU Guide to Observing Teaching and Learning for Postgraduate Secondary Initial Teacher Education*. Available at: http://www.itt-placement.com/downloads/section-e/secondary/LJMU_GuideToLessonObservingTeachingAndLearning.pdf.

Lindon, Jennie and Webb, Janet (2016) *Safeguarding and Child Protection: Linking Theory and Practice*, 5th edn (London: Hodder Education).

Loughran, J. John (2002) 'Effective reflective practice: in search of meaning in learning about teaching', *Journal of Teacher Education*, 53(1): 33–43.

Macleod, Shona, Sharp, Caroline, Bernardinelli, Daniele, Skipp, Amy and Higgins, Steve (2015) *Supporting the Attainment of Disadvantaged Pupils: Articulating Success and Good Practice*. Research report, Ref: DFE-RR411 (National Foundation for Educational Research, Ask Research and Durham University).

Mccrea, Peps (2015) *Lean Lesson Planning: A Practical Approach to Doing Less and Achieving More in the Classroom* (CreateSpace).

Mccrea, Peps (2015) 'The 7 habits of highly effective lesson plans', *Medium* (22 June). Available at: https://medium.com/@pepsmccrea/the-7-habits-of-highly-effective-lesson-plans-f785f1f8974e.

McGrath, Jim and Coles, Anthony (2015) *Your Education Masters Companion: The Essential Guide to Success* (Abingdon: Routledge).

Marchant, Gregory, Paulson, Sharon and Rothlisberg, Barbara (2001) 'Relations of middle school students' perception of family and school contexts with academic achievement', *Psychology in the Schools*, 38(6): 505–519.

Marland, Michael and Rogers, Richard (2004) *How to Be a Successful Form Tutor* (London: Continuum).

Mayer, Richard E. and Anderson, Richard B. (1992) 'The instructive animation: helping students build connections between words and pictures in multimedia learning', *Journal of Educational Psychology*, 84(4): 444–452.

Menter, Ian, Elliot, Dely, Hulme, Moira, Lewin, Jon and Lowden, Kevin (2011) *A Guide to Practitioner Research in Education* (London: Sage).

Moore, Alex (2012) *Teaching and Learning: Pedagogy, Curriculum and Culture*, 2nd edn (Abingdon: Routledge).

Morrison McGill, Ross (2012) 'Training day pitfalls: what to avoid and how to put it right!', *Teacher Toolkit* [blog] (24 September). Available at: https://www.teachertoolkit.co.uk/2012/10/15/badcpd/.

Morrison McGill, Ross (2014) '#TakeAwayHmk', *Teacher Toolkit* [blog] (28 January). Available at: https://www.teachertoolkit.co.uk/2014/01/28/takeawayhmk/.

Morrison McGill, Ross (2014) '101 great teachers to follow on Twitter', *Teacher Toolkit* [blog] (30 November). Available at: https://www.teachertoolkit.co.uk/2014/11/30/101-great-teachers-follow-twitter/.

Morrison McGill, Ross (2014) 'Get your #AssemblyMojo working', *Teacher Toolkit* [blog] (31 May). Available at: https://www.teachertoolkit.co.uk/2014/05/31/assemblymojo/.

Morrison McGill, Ross (2016) *Mark. Plan. Teach.: Save Time. Reduce Workload. Impact Learning.* (London: Bloomsbury Education).

Morrison McGill, Ross and Allison, Shaun (2013) 'The #5MinReview by @TeacherToolkit and @shaun_allison', *Class Teaching* [blog] (29 September). Available at: https://classteaching.wordpress.com/2013/09/29/the-5minreview-by-teachertoolkit-and-shaun_allison/.

NatCen Social Research and the National Children's Bureau Research and Policy Team (2017) *Supporting Mental Health in Schools and Colleges: Summary Report* (London: Department for Education). Available at: https://www.gov.uk/government/uploads/system/uploads/attachment_data/file/634725/Supporting_Mental-Health_synthesis_report.pdf.

Niemtus, Zofia (2015) 'Six basic steps to becoming a brilliant form tutor', *The Guardian* (26 August). Available at: https://www.theguardian.com/teacher-network/2015/aug/26/six-basic-steps-brilliant-form-tutor.

NUT (2008) *School Visits: NUT Health and Safety Briefing* (March). Available at: https://local.teachers.org.uk/templates/asset-relay.cfm?frmAssetFileID=651.

NUT (2017) *NUT NQT Guide: Workload*. Available at: https://neu.org.uk/help-and-advice/publications-and-resources.

Nutley, Sandra, Powell, Alison and Davies, Huw (2013) *What Counts as Good Evidence? Provocation Paper for the Alliance for Useful Evidence* (London: Alliance for Useful Evidence). Available at: https://www.alliance4usefulevidence.org/assets/What-Counts-as-Good-Evidence-WEB.pdf.

Oakes, Steve and Griffin, Martin (2017) *The GCSE Mindset: 40 Activities for Transforming Student Commitment, Motivation and Productivity* (Carmarthen: Crown House Publishing).

Oakes, Steve and Griffin, Martin (2016) *The A Level Mindset: 40 Activities for Transforming Student Commitment, Motivation and Productivity* (Carmarthen: Crown House Publishing).

Ofsted (2012) *The Pupil Premium: How Schools Are Using the Pupil Premium Funding to Raise Achievement for Disadvantaged Pupils*. Ref: 120197 (September). Available at: https://www.gov.uk/government/uploads/system/uploads/attachment_data/file/413222/The_Pupil_Premium.pdf.

Ofsted (2015) *Key Stage 3: The Wasted Years?* Ref: 150106 (September). Available at: https://www.gov.uk/government/publications/key-stage-3-the-wasted-years.

O'Leary, Matt (2014) *Classroom Observation: A Guide to the Effective Observation of Teaching and Learning* (Abingdon: Routledge).

Packer, Natalie (2017) *The Teacher's Guide to SEN* (Carmarthen: Crown House Publishing).

Parents24 (2016) 'How to study flashcards using the Leitner system' [video] (24 August). Available at: https://www.youtube.com/watch?v=C20EvKtdJwQ.

Payne, Ruth (2015) 'Using rewards and sanctions in the classroom: pupils' perceptions of their own responses to current behaviour management strategies', *Educational Review*, 67(4): 483–504.

Payne, Torsten (2017) *Stretch and Challenge for All: Practical Resources for Getting the Best Out of Every Student* (Carmarthen: Crown House Publishing).

Peter, Helen (2013) *Making the Most of Tutor Time: A Practical Guide* (Abingdon: Routledge).

Philpott, Joanne (2009) *Captivating Your Class: Effective Teaching Skills* (London: Continuum).

Pim, Chris and Driver, Catharine (2018) *100 Ideas for Secondary Teachers: Supporting EAL Learners* (London: Bloomsbury Education).

Plevin, Rob (2016) *Take Control of the Noisy Class: From Chaos to Calm in 15 Seconds* (Carmarthen: Crown House Publishing).

Pollard, Andrew (2008) *Reflective Teaching: Evidence-Informed Professional Practice*, 3rd edn (London: Continuum).

Pollard, Andrew (ed) (2014) *Readings for Reflective Teaching in Schools* (London: Bloomsbury Academic).

Portner, Hal (2008) *Mentoring New Teachers*, 3rd edn (Thousand Oaks, CA: Corwin).

Potter, Molly (2016) *100 Ideas for Secondary Teachers: Tutor Time* (London: Bloomsbury Education).

Potter, Tim and Gallagher, Rory (2016) 'How to make the most of your mentor', *TES* (6 June). Available at: https://www.tes.com/new-teachers/how-make-most-your-mentor.

Powley, Ruth (2015) 'Meaningful manageable differentiation', *Love Learning Ideas* [blog] (31 January). Available at: http://www.lovelearningideas.com/blog-archive/2015/1/31/meaningful-manageable-differentiation.

Quigley, Alex (2012) 'Questioning – top ten strategies', *The Confident Teacher* [blog] (10 November). Available at: https://www.theconfidentteacher.com/2012/11/questioning-top-ten-strategies/.

Quigley, Alex (2013) 'Effective revision strategies', *The Confident Teacher* [blog] (7 April). Available at: https://www.theconfidentteacher.com/2013/04/effective-revision-strategies/.

Ratcliffe, Rebecca (2014) 'Top 10 questions teachers are asked at job interviews', *The Guardian* (29 January). Available at: https://www.theguardian.com/teacher-network/teacher-blog/2014/jan/29/teacher-job-interview-questions-top-ten.

Real World Learning Partnership (2006) *Out-of-Classroom Learning, Practical Information and Guidance for Schools and Teachers* (Bedfordshire: RSPB). Available at: https://www.rgs.org/NR/rdonlyres/3D0B3905-8CFB-4D95-B25D-0B8818B9CA71/0/OoCLweb_pdf.pdf.

Roediger, Henry L. and Karpicke, Jeffrey D. (2006) 'Test-enhanced learning: taking memory tests improves long-term retention', *Psychological Science,* 17(3): 249–255.

Roediger, Henry L., Putnam, Adam L. and Smith, Megan A. (2011) 'Ten benefits of testing and their applications to educational practice'. In Jose P. Mestre and Brian H. Ross (eds), *The Psychology of Learning and Motivation: Cognition in Education,* 55 (Oxford: Elsevier), pp. 1–36.

Rogers, Bill (2012) 'Ensuring a settled and focused class' [video] (26 September). Available at: https://www.youtube.com/watch?v=PLFcaovsriA&t=0s&list=PLF1FBp_bi4gbXAvyDu1oO5o_LaJ6PufZm&index=6.

Rogers, Bill (2012) 'Establishing trust to enable classroom co-operation' [video] (21 September). Available at: https://www.youtube.com/watch?v=r351z1MqL10.

Rogers, Bill (2015) *Classroom Behaviour: A Practical Guide to Effective Teaching, Behaviour Management and Colleague Support* (London: Sage).

Rogers, Bill (2017) 'Bill Rogers on behaviour' [video] (27 January). Available at: https://www.youtube.com/watch?v=KTxGXiuLgb4.

Sadler, Philip M., Sonnert, Gerhard, Coyle, Harold P., Cook-Smith, Nancy and Miller, Jaimie L. (2013) 'The influence of teachers' knowledge on student learning in middle school physical science classrooms', *American Educational Research Journal,* 50(5): 1020–1049.

Sari, Nurlaela (2013) 'The importance of teaching moral values to the students', *Journal of English and Education,* 1(1): 154–162.

Scales, Peter (2012) *Teaching in the Lifelong Learning Sector* (Maidenhead: Open University Press).

Senior, John (2014) *100 Ideas for Secondary Teachers: Gifted and Talented* (London: Bloomsbury Education).

Shaw, Ryan (2017) 'I can hardly wait to see what I am going to do today: lesson planning perspectives of experienced band teachers', *Contributions to Music Education,* 42: 129–151.

Sherrington, Tom (2016) 'Rethinking marking and feedback. It's all about the response', *teacherhead* [blog] (9 October). Available at: https://teacherhead.com/2016/10/09/rethinking-marking-and-feedback-its-all-about-the-response/.

Shoreham Academy (2014) 'Maths walking talking mock calculator paper part 1' [video] (7 February). Available at: https://www.youtube.com/watch?v=ATK76UyFYY0&feature=youtu.be.

Simmons, Betty Jo (1996) 'Teachers should dress for success', *The Clearing House: A Journal of Educational Strategies, Issues and Ideas,* 69(5): 297–298.

Smith, Jim (2017) *The Lazy Teacher's Handbook: How Your Students Learn More When You Teach Less* (Carmarthen: Independent Thinking Press).

Smith, Megan (2016) 'Five benefits of quizzing according to cognitive science', *TES* (25 May). Available at: https://www.tes.com/us/news/breaking-views/five-benefits-quizzing-according-cognitive-science.

Spooner, Wendy (2011) *The SEN Handbook for Trainee Teachers, NQTs and Teaching Assistants* (Abingdon: Routledge).

Stern, Julian (2009) *Getting the Buggers to Do their Homework* (London: Continuum).

Strong, Julia (2013) *Talk for Writing in Secondary Schools: How to Achieve Effective Reading, Writing and Communication across the Curriculum* (Maidenhead: Open University Press).

*Teach Thought* (n. d.) '101 Twitter tips for teachers'. Available at: https://www.teachthought.com/technology/100-twitter-tips-for-teachers/.

*Teach Thought* (n. d.) '101 Ways For Teachers To Be More Creative'. Available at: https://www.teachthought.com/pedagogy/101-ways-for-teachers-to-be-more-creative/.

Tharby, Andy (2013) 'Strategic marking for the DIRTy-minded teacher', *Reflecting English* [blog] (13 December). Available at: https://reflectingenglish.wordpress.com/2013/12/13/strategic-marking-for-the-dirty-minded-teacher/.

Tharby, Andy (2014) 'The dangers of differentiation … and what to do about them', *Reflecting English* [blog] (5 October). Available at: https://reflectingenglish.wordpress.com/2014/10/05/the-dangers-of-differentiation-and-what-to-do-about-them/.

Tobin, Kenneth (1987) 'The role of wait time in higher cognitive level learning', *Review of Educational Research*, 57(1): 69–95.

Tolhurst, Judith (2010) *The Essential Guide to Coaching and Mentoring: Practical Skills for Teachers* (Harlow: Pearson Longman).

Toward, Gary, Henley, Chris and Cope, Andy (2016) *The Art of Being a Brilliant Middle Leader* (Carmarthen: Crown House Publishing).

Vangrieken, Katrien, Dochy, Filip, Raes, Elisabeth and Kyndt, Eva (2015) 'Teacher collaboration: a systematic review', *Educational Research Review*, 15: 17–40.

Wang, Tianchong (2017) 'Overcoming barriers to "flip": building teacher's capacity for the adoption of flipped classroom in Hong Kong secondary schools', *Research and Practice in Technology Enhanced Learning*, 12(6): 1–11.

Waring, Michael and Evans, Carol (2014) *Understanding Pedagogy: Developing a Critical Approach to Teaching and Learning* (Abingdon: Routledge).

Watson-Davis, Roy (2005) *The Form Tutor's Pocketbook* (Alresford: Teachers' Pocketbooks).

Watson-Davis, Roy (2010) *Creative Teaching Pocketbook*, 2nd edn (Alresford: Teachers' Pocketbooks).

Weade, Ginger and Evertson, Carolyn (1991) 'On what can be learned by observing teaching', *Theory into Practice*, 30(1): 37–45.

*We Are Teachers* (2012) '5 tips for balancing a master's degree with full-time teaching' (3 August). Available at: https://www.weareteachers.com/5-tips-for-balancing-a-masters-degree-with-full-time-teaching/.

Wiliam, Dylan (2011) *Embedded Formative Assessment* (Bloomington, IN: Solution Tree Press).

Wiliam, Dylan (2014) 'The right questions, the right way', *Educational Leadership*, 71(6) (March): 16–19. Available at: http://www.ascd.org/publications/educational-leadership/mar14/vol71/num06/The-Right-Questions,-The-Right-Way.aspx.

Wiliam, Dylan (2015) 'Designing great hinge questions', *Educational Leadership*, 73(1): 40–44.

Williams, Mark and Penman, Danny (2011) *Mindfulness: A Practical Guide to Finding Peace in a Frantic World* (London: Piatkus).

Willingham, Daniel T. (2010) *Why Don't Students Like School? A Cognitive Scientist Answers Questions About How the Mind Works and What It Means for the Classroom* (San Francisco, CA: Jossey-Bass).

Wood, Phil and Smith, Joan (2016) *Educational Research: Taking the Plunge* (Carmarthen: Crown House Publishing).

Wright, Ben (2017) 'Twitter can be a dangerous world. Be careful out there…', *Thrive in Teaching* [blog] (18 June). Available at: https://thriveteach.wordpress.com/2017/06/18/twitter-can-be-a-dangerous-world-be-careful-out-there/.

Wright, Trevor (2010) *How to Be a Brilliant Mentor* (Abingdon: Routledge).

Wright, Trevor (2012) *Guide to Mentoring: Advice for the Mentor and Mentee* (London: ATL). Available at: https://www.atl.org.uk/Images/ATL%20Guide%20to%20mentoring%20(Nov%2012).pdf.

Zwozdiak-Myers, Paula (2012) *The Teacher's Reflective Practice Handbook: Becoming an Extended Professional Through Capturing Evidence-Informed Practice* (Abingdon: Routledge).

# Of Teaching, Learning and Sherbet Lemons

## A compendium of careful advice for teachers

**Nina Jackson**

**ISBN: 978-178135134-5**

---

Teachers always want to be the best they can be for their students and Nina reignites our passion for teaching so we can continue to change people's lives through education.

Dr Barbara Van der Eecken, Associate Director for Quality, BMET College

---

Nina Jackson's mission in *Of Teaching, Learning and Sherbet Lemons* is to put the fizz back into classrooms by solving some of the toughest dilemmas facing teachers.

You know the child in the class who never asks that burning question because they worry it might make them look silly, even if everyone else is thinking the same thing? Sometimes teachers can be like that child. And they don't know where to turn to get the answers. Which is where Nina comes in. The teachers' questions in *Of Teaching, Learning and Sherbet Lemons* have been anonymised, but Nina's answers will resonate with teachers everywhere, offering them support and practical advice.

# The Lazy Teacher's Handbook – New Edition

## How your students learn more when you teach less

**Jim Smith**

**ISBN: 978-178135268-7**

The book has a great title, but in truth *The Lazy Teacher's Handbook* isn't for the lazy amongst us. It's for those most committed to immersing students in the messy business of actual learning, guided by a teacher with the confidence to know when to step back and watch that learning happen.

Geoff Barton, General Secretary, ASCL

This new edition is packed full of even more easy-to-apply, highly effective strategies, all with the seal of approval from real students in real classrooms. Next time someone tells you to get a life, you will be able to – thanks to this book.

Every chapter has been revised and some have been significantly expanded, particularly those on planning, conducting and reviewing lazy lessons. If you want your students to learn more and you to work less, then this book provides you with all the arguments and evidence you need.

Previously published as *The Lazy Teacher's Handbook*, ISBN 978-184590289-6.